Sam¹ Williams's
Book

Sam¹ Williams

THE METHODIST DISCIPLINE
OF 1798

Including the Annotations of
Thomas Coke and Francis Asbury

Facsimile Edition

Edited by Frederick A. Norwood

Published under the Sponsorship of
The Institute for the Study of Methodism
and Related Movements
Garrett-Evangelical Theological Seminary
Evanston, Illinois

Academy Books

Rutland
1979

ISBN 0-914960-17-2
Library of Congress Card No. 78-74848
Printed in the United States of America

Printed and bound by
Sharp Offset Printing Inc.
P. O. Box 757
Rutland, VT 05701

INTRODUCTION

A very rare printing of the Discipline is the tenth, dated 1798 and entitled *The Doctrines and Discipline of the Methodist Episcopal Church, in America. With Explanatory Notes, by Thomas Coke and Francis Asbury.* It is not only rare but unique in carrying the extensive annotations prepared by the two bishops at the request of the General Conference of 1796.

One of the most valuable sources on the development of American Methodism is the series of volumes usually called simply the Discipline. Under whatever title and in whatever form it appeared, it accurately although legalistically reflects the issues which brought change in structure. These issues are not always self-evident in the legislation. The impact of the controversy over slavery is obvious, but all the motives involved are not at all explicit. Sometimes struggles which ran lively, like Asbury's early plan for a "Council," find no direct expression. Nevertheless, the establishment of a General Conference in 1792 is a direct result of the failure of the Council.

In like manner, the notes prepared by Coke and Asbury are explained by forces outside the direct legislative view of the Discipline. Outwardly the bishops responded to the request of the General Conference. They diligently gathered two types of material: (1) biblical texts which defined Methodist polity on scriptural grounds, and (2) explanations of the importance or significance of particular standards and regulations. There is nothing in the Discipline to explain *why* all this was requested and performed.

The factors were, as usual in history, complex. Uncertainty continued over the actions taken in

1784 by John Wesley, especially his ordinations and his setting apart Thomas Coke as "super-intendent." Confessional churches of the Continental Reformation, Lutheran and Reformed, as well as English and Scottish Calvinist denominations, Congregationalist and Presbyterian, were very critical of this new-fangled sect which seemed to them to be, ecclesiastically speaking, neither fish nor fowl. Anglican leaders, until their own church fell on hard times in the American Revolution, with a few notable exceptions had either rejected or ignored the Wesleyan movement. There were critics aplenty to be answered.

But the central cause can be singled out: James O'Kelly. This assertive Methodist preacher lived and worked mostly in Virginia, where he served long as presiding elder (early term for district superintendent). Upon several occasions he had come into conflict with Bishop Asbury, whom he regarded as a power-hungry dictator. William McKendree, who as a young man had come under O'Kelly's spell, shared these views until personal encounter with Asbury completely changed his mind.

O'Kelly was not that easily swayed. As time went on he became more rigid and more bitter. When his famous motion at the General Conference of 1792 for an appeal of ministerial appointment from the bishop to Annual Conference failed after extended debate, he angrily walked out and subsequently founded the Republican Methodist Church, which had an unhappy history. During the 1790s he carried on a public controversy with the episcopal leadership of the Methodist Episcopal Church, with Methodist polity in general, and with Francis Asbury in particular. In some of his writings, affecting the linguistic style of the

King James Version, he attacked "Francis" for his tyrannical domination of the church. From this he went on to deny scriptural validity of the whole connectional system of Methodism and ultimately of all historic forms of Christianity which departed from his own view of the plain scriptural norm. Although the first big gun in a continuing literary war was fired by O'Kelly only in 1798, the conflict had been raging openly ever since 1792, and internally some years before that.

Hence the conclusion is clear that the O'Kelly rumpus was a direct cause of concern of General Conference in 1796 and of the episcopal annotations in 1798. The issue of authority versus democracy in the life of the church underlies much of the notes. In a letter to George Roberts, 11 February 1797, Asbury explicitly noted that, since O'Kelly had claimed the Bible as his standard, "we have abounded in scripture."[1] Likewise, in directions to Ezekiel Cooper in October of that year he laid out the arrangement of materials, and then went on: "I am sure I am right in my desire of promoting the notes on the discipline. You in your annual distant station can hardly conceive the mischief and abuse we meet with from unchristian and illiberal minds."[2]

The bishops, however, undertook more than answering O'Kelly. They wished to show first of all that the Methodist system was firmly

---

[1] J. Manning Potts, *et al.*, eds., *The Journal and Letters of Francis Asbury* (Nashville: Abingdon Press, 1958, 3 vols.), III, 159.

[2] *Ibid.*, III, 165. This letter, which is incomplete in the printed form, is dated 24 October 1797. The quotation is from the unprinted portions located in the library of Garrett-Evangelical Theological Seminary. Pertinent references in the *Journal* are: 20 Jan. 1795 (II, 41); 19, 23, 26 Jan. 1797 (II, 117); 26 Feb. 1797 (II, 121) 13; Oct. 1797 (II, 135).

grounded in Scripture, as well as in the practice of the primitive church. Wesley had called himself a "scriptural *episcopos*." Coke and Asbury sought justification in the Bible for this understanding, and all it meant for the subsequent organization of the Methodist Episcopal Church. A large part of the notes consists of proof texts from the Bible. A very interesting topic of research would be analysis of the use of Scripture and the hermeneutical principles which governed.

Beyond this, the notes offer a running commentary on those features of Methodism which were regarded as noteworthy or distinctive. Occasionally the bishops' silence also speaks loudly. In the history of the Discipline this edition of 1798, the only one to contain the annotations, is unique. Extracts from the notes are in the appendix to another rare book, David Sherman, *History of the Revisions of the Discipline of the Methodist Episcopal Church* (3rd ed., New York: Hunt & Eaton, 1890), pp. 401-59.

Modern historical notes have been prepared by the editor and will be found following the text of the Discipline. They refer to pages of the Discipline on which particular passages are starred.

THE
DOCTRINES
AND
DISCIPLINE

OF THE

Methodist Episcopal Church,

IN

AMERICA.

WITH

EXPLANATORY NOTES,

BY

THOMAS COKE AND FRANCIS ASBURY.

———◆———

THE TENTH EDITION.

———◆———

PHILADELPHIA:

PRINTED BY HENRY TUCKNISS,

Sold by John Dickins, No. 41, Market-street, between
Front and Second-streets, and by the Methodist
Ministers and Preachers throughout
the United States.

1798.

DEARLY BELOVED BRETHREN,

WE think it expedient to give you a brief account of the rise of Methodism, both in Europe and America. " In 1729, two young men, in " England, reading the Bible, saw they could not be " saved without holiness, followed after it, and incited " others so to do. In 1737, they saw likewise, that " men are justified before they are sanctified : But still " holiness was their object. God then thrust them " out, to raise a holy people."*

In the year 1766, Philip Embury, a local preacher of our society, from Ireland, began to preach in the city of New-York, and formed a society of his own countrymen and the citizens : and the same year, Thomas Webb preached in a hired room, near the barracks. About the same time, Robert Strawbridge, a local preacher from Ireland, settled in Frederic county, in the state of Maryland, and preaching there, formed some societies. The first Methodist church in New-York was built in 1768 or 1769 ; and in 1769, Richard Boardman and Joseph Pilmoor came to New-York ; who were the first regular Methodist preachers on the continent. In the latter end of the year 1771, Francis Asbury and Richard Wright, of the same order, came over.

We humbly believe that God's design in raising up the preachers called Methodists, in America, was to reform the continent, and spread scripture-holiness over these lands. As a proof hereof, we have seen, since that time, a great and glorious work of God, from New-York through the Jersies, Pennsylvania, Delaware, Maryland, Virginia, North and South Carolina, and Georgia ; as also, of late, to the extremities of the western and eastern states.

We esteem it our duty and privilege most earnestly to recommend to *you* as members of our church, our FORM OF DISCIPLINE, which has been founded on the experi-

---

* These are the words of the Messrs. Wesleys themselves.

ence of a long feries of years; as alfo on the obfervations and remarks we have made on ancient and modern churches.

We wifh to fee this little publication in the houfe of every Methodift, and the more fo as it contains our plan of Chriftian education, and the articles of religion maintained, more or lefs, in part or in the whole, by

* every reformed church in the world. We would like-wife declare our real fentiments on the fcripture doctrine of election and reprobation; on the infallible, unconditional perfeverance of all who ever have believed, or ever fhall; and on the doctrine of Chriftian perfection.

Far from wifhing you to be ignorant of any of our doctrines, or any part of our difcipline, we defire you to read, mark, learn, and inwardly digeft the whole. We know you are not in general able to purchafe many books: But you ought, next to the word of God, to procure the Articles and Canons of the church to which you belong. This prefent edition is fmall and cheap, and we can affure you that the profits of the fale of it fhall be applied to charitable purpofes.

We remain your very affectionate brethren and paftors, who labour night and day, both in public and private, for your good,

THOMAS COKE,
FRANCIS ASBURY.

Baltimore,
Nov. 16. 1792.

——-‹‹‹‹€›››-›-——

Advertifement to the Reader.

☞ *THE laft General Conference defired the Bifhops to draw up Annotations on the Form of Difcipline, and to publifh them with the prefent edition: —The Bifhops have accordingly complied, and have proved or illuftrated every thing by quotations from the Word of God, agreeably, alfo, to the advice of the Conference; and they fincerely pray that their labour of love may be made a bleffing to many.*

1797.

CHAP. I.

SECTION I.

Of the Origin of the Methodist Episcopal Church.

THE preachers and members of our society in general, being convinced that there was a great deficiency of vital religion in the church of England in America, and being in many places destitute of the christian sacraments, as several of the clergy had forsaken their churches, requested the late Rev. *John Wesley* to take such measures, in his wisdom and prudence, as would afford them suitable relief in their distress.

In consequence of this, our venerable friend, who, under God, had been the father of the great revival of religion now extending over the earth, by the means of the Methodists, determined to ordain ministers for America ; and for this purpose, in the year 1784, sent over three regularly ordained clergy ; but preferring the episcopal mode of church-government to any other, he solemnly set apart, by the imposition of his hands, and prayer, one of them, viz. *Thomas Coke*, Doctor of Civil Law, late of Jesus-college in the university of Oxford, and a presbyter of the church of England, for the episcopal office ; and having delivered to him letters of episcopal orders, commissioned and directed him to set apart *Francis Asbury*, then general assistant of the Methodist society in America, for the same episcopal office, he the said *Francis Asbury* being first ordained deacon and elder. In consequence of which, the said *Francis Asbury* was solemnly set apart for the said episcopal office, by prayer and the imposition of the hands of the said *Thomas Coke*, other regularly ordained ministers assisting in the sacred ceremony. At which time the general conference held at Baltimore, did unanimoufly receive the faid *Thomas Coke* and *Francis Afbury* as their bifhops, being fully fatisfied of the validity of their epifcopal ordination.

N O T E S

    It cannot be needful in this country, to vindicate the right of every chriftian fociety, to poffefs, within itfelf, all the privileges neceffary or expedient for the comfort, inftruction, or good government of the members thereof. The two facraments of baptifm and the Lord's fupper have been allowed to be effential to the formation of a chriftian church, by every party and denomination in every age and country of chriftendom, with the exception only of a fingle-modern fociety: and ordination by the impofition of hands has been allowed to be highly expedient, and has been practifed as univerfally as the former. And thefe two points as above defcribed, might, if need were, be confirmed by the Scriptures, and by the unanimous teftimony of all the primitive fathers of the church for the three firft centuries; and, indeed, by all the able divines who have written on the fubject in the different languages of the world down to the prefent times.

    The only point which can be difputed by any fenfible perfon, is the *epifcopal* form which we have adopted; and this can be contefted by *candid* men, only from their want of acquaintance with the hiftory of the church. The moft bigotted devotees to religious eftablifhments (the clergy of the church of Rome excepted) are now afhamed to fupport the doctrine of *the apoftolic, uninterrupted fucceffion of bifhops*. Dr. Hoadley, bifhop of Winchefter, who was, we believe, the greateft advocate for epifcopacy, whom the proteftant churches ever produced, has been fo completely overcome by Dr. Calamy, in refpect to the uninterrupted fucceffion, that the point has been entirely given up. Nor do we recollect that any writer of the proteftant churches has fince attempted to defend what all the learned world at prefent know to be utterly indefenfible.

    And yet nothing but *an apoftolic, uninterrupted fucceffion* can poffibly confine the right of epifcopacy to any particular church. The idea, that the fupreme magiftrate or legiflature of a country, ought to be the head of the church in that nation, is a pofition, which, we think, no one *here* will prefume to affert. It follows, therefore, indubitably, that every church has a right to choofe, if it pleafe, the *epifcopal* plan.

    The late reverend John Wefley recommended the *epifcopal* form to his focieties in America; and the general conference, which is the chief fynod of our church, unanimoufly accepted of it. Mr. Wefley did more. He firft confecrated one for the office of a bifhop, that our epifcopacy might defcend from himfelf. The general conference unanimoufly accepted of the perfon fo confecrated, as well as of Francis Afbury, who had for many years before exercifed every branch of the epifcopal office, excepting that of ordination. Now, the idea of an apoftolic fucceffion being exploded, it follows, that the Methodift church has every thing which is fcriptural and effential to juftify its epifcopacy. Is the unanimous approbation of the chief fynod of a church neceffary? This it has had. Is the ready compliance of the members of the church with its decifion, in this refpect, neceffary? This it has had, and continues to have. Is it highly expedient, that the fountain of the epifcopacy fhould be refpectable? This has been the cafe. The moft refpectable divine fince the primitive ages, if not fince the time of the apoftles, was Mr. Wefley. His knowledge of the fciences was very extenfive. He was a general fcholar: and for any to call his learning in queftion, would be to call their own. On his death the literati of England bore teftimony to his great character. And where has been the individual fo ufeful in the fpread of religion? But in this we can appeal only to the lovers of *vital* godlinefs. By his long and inceffant labours he raifed a multitude of focieties, who looked up to him for direction: and certainly his directions in things lawful, with the full approbation of the people, were fufficient to give authenticity to what was accordingly done. He was peculiarly attached to the laws and cuftoms of the church in the primitive times of chriftianity. He knew, that the primitive churches univerfally followed the epifcopal plan: and indeed bifhop Hoadley has demonftrated that the epifcopal plan was univerfal till the time of the reformation. Mr. Wefley therefore preferred the *epifcopal* form of church government; and God has (glory be to his name!) wonderfully bleffed it amongft us.

To the obfervations above made, we would add, that it muft be evident to every difcerning reader of the epiftles of St. Paul to Timothy and Titus, that *Timothy*, who was appointed by St. Paul, bifhop of the Ephefians, and *Titus*, who was appointed by the fame apoftle, bifhop of the Cretians, were bifhops in the proper *epifcopal* fenfe, and that they were *travelling* bifhops. The *epifcopal office in all its parts* was invefted in them. *Timothy* is charged (1) to be attentive to *the teachers*, refpecting the purity of their doctrine, and to regulate every thing with due authority: " I befought thee to abide ftill at Ephefus,—that thou mighteft charge fome, that *they teach* no other doctrine, &c." 1 Tim. i. 3, &c. " thefe things *command* and teach." iv. 11. (2) To *fuperintend* the *elders* of the church: " Rebuke not an *elder*, but intreat him as a father," v. 1. " let the *elders* that rule well, be counted

worthy of double honour, especially they who labour in the word
and doctrine," ver. 17. "against an *elder* receive not an accusati-
on, but before two or three witnesses. Them that sin, rebuke
before all, that others may fear," &c. ver. 19. 21. (3) To lay
on hands for the ministry: "Lay hands suddenly on no man,"
ver. 22   (4) To choose men for the preaching of the gospel:
"The things that thou hast heard of me among many witnesses,
the same commit thou to faithful men, *who shall be able to teach
others also*," 2 Tim. ii. 2.   And throughout these two epistles, *St.
Paul* addresses himself to *Timothy* as one who had the chief super-
intendance over the private members of his church, and in all
the affairs thereof. He also authorizes *Titus* to *ordain elders* (a
peculiar part of the *episcopal office*) and to regulate every thing:
"For this cause left I thee in Crete, that thou shouldest set in order *the things that are wanting*, and *ordain elders in every city*, as I
had appointed thee," Titus i. 5.

Nor is it less evident, that the seven angels of the seven churches
of Asia Minor (the seven stars held in the right hand of Christ)
mentioned in the 2d and 3d chapters of the Revelation, possessed
all the parts and requisites of the *episcopal* office. For our Lord
would never have addressed those epistles, which so deeply concerned the interests of those churches, to *single individuals*, if those
single individuals had not been, by the superior offices with which
they were invested, proper representatives of those churches respectively. We must also observe, that each of those churches
belonged to a great metropolitan* city, to which many other cities, towns, and villages, were considered as adjoined: so that as
Titus, bishop of Crete, was required to "ordain elders and to set
in order the things that were wanting, *in every city*" in the Isle of
Crete, so the other bishops (as soon as possible) had each an extensive diocese, through which they travelled, and over which
they superintended.

Nor must we omit to observe, that each diocese had a college
of elders or presbyters, in which the bishop presided. So that
the bishop by no means superintended his diocese in a despotic
manner, but was rather the chief executor of those regulations,
which were made in the college of presbyters, which answered
to the convocations, synods, or conferences of all the well-organ-
ized churches in modern times.

But in all we have observed on this subject, we by no means
intend to speak disrespectfully of the presbyterian church, or of
any other: we only desire to defend our own from the unjust ca-
lumnies of its opponents.

---

* *The chief city of a nation.*

SECTION II.

Articles of Religion. *

I. *Of Faith in the Holy Trinity.*

THERE is but one living and true God, everlasting, without body or parts, of infinite power, wifdom, and goodnefs; the maker and preferver of all things, both vifible and invifible. And in unity of this God-head, there are three perfons of one fubftance, power, and eternity;—the Father, the Son, and the Holy Ghoft.

NOTES.

This article is proved from the following fcriptures, viz. (1) John iv. 24. God is a fpirit. Ephef. iii. 9. God, who created all things by Jefus Chrift. (2) John i. 14. We beheld his glory, the glory as of the only *begotten* of *the Father.* viii. 54. Jefus anfwered—it is *my Father* that honoureth me. x. 29. *My Father,* which gave them me, is greater than all. (3) John i. 1. The *Word* was God. Ifai. 9. 6. Unto us *a child* is born, unto us *a fon* is given, and his name fhall be called *The mighty God.* John xx. 28. Thomas faid unto him [Chrift] my Lord and *my God.* Acts xx. 28. Feed the church *of God,* which he hath purchafed *with his own blood.* Rom. ix. 5. Chrift, who is over all, *God* bleffed for ever. Phil. ii. 6. Who [Chrift Jefus] being in *the form of God,* thought it not robbery to be *equal with God.* Tit. ii. 13. The glorious appearing of *the great God* and our Saviour, *Jefus Chrift.* Heb. i. 8. Unto *the Son* he faith, Thy throne, *O God,* is for ever and ever. 1 John v. 20. His Son *Jefus Chrift:* This is *the true God,* and eternal life. (4) John xiv. 26. *The Comforter,* which is *the Holy Ghoft,*—fhall teach you all things, and bring all things to your remembrance, whatfoever I have faid unto you. xv. 26. When *the Comforter* is come, whom I will fend unto you from the Father;—he fhall teftify of me. xvi. 8. When he [the Comforter] is come, he will reprove the world of fin, and of righteoufnefs, and of judgment. (5) 1 John v. 7. There are *three* that bear record in heaven, *the Father, the Word,* and *the Holy Ghoft:* and *thefe three are one.* Matt. xxviii. 19. Go ye, therefore, and teach all nations, baptizing them in the name of *the Father,* and of *the Son,* and of *the Holy Ghoft.*

Luke 3. 22. The *Holy Ghost* descended in a bodily shape, like a dove, upon *him* [Christ] and a *voice* came from heaven, which said, Thou art *my beloved Son*; in thee I am well pleased. 2 Cor. xiii. 14. The grace *of our Lord Jesus Christ*, and the love *of God*, and the communion *of the Holy Ghost*, be with you all. Amen.

II. *Of the Word, or Son of God, who was made very Man.*

THE Son, who is the Word of the Father, the very and eternal God, of one substance with the Father, took man's nature in the womb of the blessed Virgin; so that two whole and perfect natures, that is to say, the God-head and manhood, were joined together in one person, never to be divided, whereof is one Christ, very God and very man, who truly suffered, was crucified, dead and buried, to reconcile his Father to us, and to be a sacrifice, not only for original guilt, but also for actual sins of men.

N O T E S.

This article is proved by many of the above-quoted as well as by the following scriptures, viz. (1) John i. 14. And *the Word* [who was God, *ver.* 1.] was made *flesh*. Phil. ii. 7, 8. Christ Jesus, [who thought it not robbery to be equal with God, *ver.* 5, 6.] was made *in the likeness of men*; and being found in fashion *as a man*, he humbled himself, and became obedient unto death, even the death of the cross. 1 Tim. iii. 16. Without controversy, great is the mystery of godliness, *God* was manifest *in the flesh*. (2) Col. i. 14. In whom [God's dear Son] we have *redemption* through his blood, even *the forgiveness of sins*. Ephes. ii. 13, 16. Now, *in Christ Jesus*, ye who sometimes were far off, are *made nigh by the blood of Christ*. For he is *our peace*,—that he might *reconcile* both [Jews and Gentiles] *unto God* in one body by *the cross*, having slain the enmity thereby. 1 Tim. ii. 6. Who [Christ Jesus] gave himself *a ransom for all*.

III. *Of the Resurrection of Christ.*

CHRIST did truly rise again from the dead, and took again his body, with all things appertaining to the perfection of man's nature, wherewith he ascended into heaven, and there sitteth until he return to judge all men at the laft day.

N O T E S.

Matt. xxviii. 6. He [Jefus] is not here; for he is *rifen*, as he faid. Luke xxiv. 39. Behold my hands and my feet, that it is I myfelf. Handle me, and fee: for a fpirit hath not flefh and bones, as ye fee me have. Mark xvi. 19. After the Lord had fpoken unto them, he was received up into heaven, and fat on the right hand of God.

IV. *Of the Holy Ghoft.*

THE Holy Ghoft, proceeding from the Father and the Son, is of one fubftance, majefty, and glory with the Father and the Son, very and eternal God.

N O T E S.

(1) John xiv. 16, 17. I will pray *the Father*, and he fhall give you *another Comforter*, that he may abide with you for ever, even *the Spirit* of truth. John xiv. 26. *The Comforter*, which is *the Holy Ghoft*, whom *the Father* will fend in my name, &c. (2) Rom. viii. 9. Ye are not in the flefh, but in the Spirit, if fo be that *the Spirit of God* dwell in you: now if any man have not *the Spirit of Chrift*, he is none of his. Gal. iv. 6. Becaufe ye are fons, God hath fent forth *the Spirit of his Son* into your hearts. (3) 2 Cor. iii. 3. *The Spirit of the living God.* 2 Cor. iii. 17. Now *the Lord is that Spirit;* and where *the Spirit of the Lord* is, there is liberty. 1 Pet. iv. 14. *The Spirit of glory* and *of God* refteth upon you.

V. *The Sufficiency of the Holy Scriptures for Salvation.*

HOLY Scripture containeth all things neceffary to falvation: fo that whatfoever is not read therein, or may be proved thereby, is not to be required of any man, that it fhould be believed as an article of faith, or be thought requifite or neceffary to falvation. In name of the Holy Scripture, we do underftand canonical books of the Old and New Testament, of whose authority was never any doubt in the church.

The Names of the Canonical Books.

GENESIS,
Exodus,
Leviticus,
Numbers,
Deuteronomy,
Joshua,
Judges,
Ruth,
The First Book of Samuel,
The Second Book of Samuel,
The First Book of Kings,
The Second Book of Kings,
The First Book of Chronicles,
The Second Book of Chronicles,
The Book of Ezra,
The Book of Nehemiah,
The Book of Esther,
The Book of Job,
The Psalms,
The Proverbs,
Ecclesiastes, or the Preacher,
Cantica, or Songs of Solomon,
Four Prophets the greater,
Twelve Prophets the less :

All the Books of the New Testament, as they are commonly received, we do receive and account canonical.

NOTES.

2 Tim. iii. 16, 17. All scripture is given by inspiration of God, and is profitable for doctrine, for reproof, for correction, for instruction in righteousness; that the man of God may be perfect, thoroughly furnished unto all good works. 2 Pet. i. 19, 20, 21. We have also a more sure word of prophecy, whereunto ye do well that ye take heed, as unto a light that shineth in a dark place, until the day dawn, and the Day-star arise in your hearts

knowing this firſt, that no prophecy of the Scripture is of any private interpretation; for the prophecy came not in old time by the will of man, but holy men of God ſpake as they were moved by the Holy Ghoſt. Iſai. viii. 20. To the law and to the teſtimony: if they ſpeak not according to *this word*, it is becauſe there is *no light* in them. 1 Pet. iv. 11. If any man ſpeak, let him ſpeak *as the oracles of God*. Pſalm cxix. 72. The law of thy mouth is better unto me than thouſands of gold and ſilver. Ver. 97. O how love I thy law! It is my meditation all the day. Pſalm cxxxviii. 2. Thou haſt magnified *thy word above all thy name*.

By the word *canonical* is meant *whatever* reſpects, or is confirmed by, the laws of the church; and here it particularly refers to the deciſions of the councils in the *firſt* and *pureſt* ages of chriſtianity concerning the holy ſcriptures; in which times the inſpired writings were collected into one volume. The ſcriptures of the *Old* Teſtament had indeed been publiſhed in one volume long before by the Jews; but the ſcriptures of the *New* were then added to them.

We could enter minutely into the proofs of the divine authority of each book, both of the Old and New Teſtament, and into an account of the times in which they were written, and the perſons by whom: but it would require a treatiſe of itſelf, to do juſtice to ſo extenſive a ſubject.

VI. *Of the Old Teſtament.*

THE Old Teſtament is not contrary to the New: for both in the Old and New Teſtament, everlaſting life is offered to mankind by Chriſt, who is the only Mediator between God and man, being both God and man. Wherefore, they are not to be heard, who feign that the old Fathers did look only for tranſitory promiſes. Although the law given from God by Moſes, as touching ceremonies and rites, doth not bind chriſtians, nor ought the civil precepts thereof of neceſſity to be received in any commonwealth; yet, notwithſtanding, no chriſtian whatſoever is free from the obedience of the commandments, which are called moral.

N O T E S.

(1) Luke xxiv. 27. And beginning at Moſes and all the prophets, he [Chriſt] expounded unto them, *in all the ſcriptures*, the

things concerning himself. John v. 39. *Search the scriptures* [of the Old Testament, which alone were then in being] for in them ye think ye have eternal life; and they are they, *which testify of me.* (2) Job xix. 25—27. I know that my Redeemer liveth, and that he shall stand at the latter day upon the earth; and though, after my skin, worms destroy this body, yet in my flesh shall I see God; whom I shall see for myself, and mine eyes shall behold, and not another. Psalm xvii. 15. As for me, I will behold thy face in righteousness. I shall be satisfied when I awake with thy likeness. (3) Matt. xxii. 40. On these two commandments [the love of God, and love of man] hang *all the law and the prophets.* Matt. vii. 12. All things, whatsoever ye would that men should do to you, do ye even so to them; for this is *the law and the prophets.*

VII. *Of Original or Birth Sin.*

ORIGINAL sin standeth not in the following of Adam (as the Pelagians do vainly talk) but it is the corruption of the nature of every man, that naturally is engendered of the offspring of Adam, whereby man is very far gone from original righteousness, and of his own nature inclined to evil, and that continually.

N O T E S.

Gen. vi. 5. God saw that the wickedness of man was great in the earth; and that every imagination of the thoughts of his heart was only evil continually. Jer. xvii. 9. The heart is deceitful above all things, and desperately wicked: who can know it? Psalm xiv. 3. They are all gone aside; they are altogether become filthy; there is none that doeth good, no, not one. Psalm liii. 3. Every one of them is gone back; they are altogether become filthy; there is none that doeth good, no, not one. Rom. iii. 10. As it is written, There is none righteous, no, not one. Psalm li. 5. Behold, I was *shapen* in iniquity, and in sin did my mother *conceive* me. Eph. ii. 1—3. And you hath he quickened, who were *dead in trespasses and sins:* wherein in times past ye walked according to the course of this world, according to the prince of the power of the air, the spirit that now worketh in the children of disobedience; among whom also we all had our conversation, in times past, in the lusts of our flesh, fulfilling the desires of the flesh and of the mind; and were, *by nature, the children of wrath,* even as others. Mark vii. 21—23.

From within, out of *the heart* of men, proceed evil thoughts, adulteries, fornications, murders, thefts, covetoufnefs, wickednefs, deceit, lafcivioufnefs, an evil eye, blafphemy, pride, foolifhnefs: all thefe evil things come from within, and defile the man.

VIII. *Of Free-Will.*

THE condition of man after the fall of Adam is fuch, that he cannot turn and prepare himfelf by his own natural ftrength and works to faith, and calling upon God: Wherefore, we have no power to do good works, pleafant and acceptable to God, without the grace of God by Chrift preventing us, that we may have a good will, and working with us, when we have that good will.

NOTES.

(1) 2 Cor. iii. 5. Not that we are fufficient of ourfelves, to think any thing as of ourfelves, but our fufficiency is of God. Eph. ii. 5. Even when we were dead in fins [God] hath quickened us together with Chrift (by grace are ye faved.) Ver. 8, 9. By grace are ye faved through faith; and that not of yourfelves, it is the gift of God: not of works, left any man fhould boaft. (2) John xv. 5. Without me [Chrift] ye can do nothing. Phil. ii. 12, 13. Work out your own falvation with fear and trembling; for it is God which worketh in you both to will and to do, of his good pleafure.

IX. *Of the Juftification of Man.*

WE are accounted righteous before God, only for the merit of our Lord and Saviour Jefus Chrift by faith, and not for our own works or defervings:—Wherefore, that we are juftified by faith only, is a moft wholefome doctrine, and very full of comfort.

NOTES.

(1) Rom. iii. 24—26. Being juftified freely by his grace, through the redemption that is in Chrift Jefus; whom God hath fet forth to be a propitiation through faith in his blood, to de-

clare his righteoufnefs for the remiffion of fins that are paft, through the forbearance of God: to declare, I fay, at this time, his righteoufnefs, that he might be juft, and the juftifier of him which believeth in Jefus. Rom. v. 18. Therefore as by the offence of one, judgment came upon all men to condemnation ; even fo, by the righteoufnefs of one, the free gift came upon all men unto juftification of life. Rom. x. 4. For Chrift is the end of the law for righteoufnefs to every one that believeth. Gal. ii. 16. Knowing that a man is not juftified by the works of the law, but by the faith of Jefus Chrift; even we have believed in Jefus Chrift, that we might be juftified by the faith of Chrift, and not by the works of the law ; for by the works of the law fhall no flefh be juftified. (2) Pfalm xxxii. 1. Bleffed is he whofe tranfgreffion is forgiven, whofe fin is covered. Rom. v. 1. Being juftified by faith, we have peace with God, through our Lord Jefus Chrift.

X. *Of Good-Works.*

ALTHOUGH good works, which are the fruits of faith, and follow after juftification, cannot put away our fins, and endure the feverity of God's judgment ; yet are they pleafing and acceptable to God in Chrift, and fpring out of a true and lively faith, infomuch that by them a lively faith may be as evidently known, as a tree difcerned by its fruit.

NOTES

(1) Gal. v. 6. In Jefus Chrift neither circumcifion availeth any thing, nor uncircumcifion, but faith which *worketh* by love. James ii. 22. Seeft thou how faith wrought with his [Abraham's] *works ;* and by *works* was faith made perfect. Ver. 26. As the body without the fpirit is dead, fo faith without *works* is dead alfo. (2) Heb. xiii. 16. To do good and to communicate, forget not ; for with fuch facrifices God is well pleafed. James i. 27. Pure religion and undefiled before God and the Father, is this, To vifit the fatherlefs and widows, in their affliction; and to keep himfelf unfpotted from the world. Tit. iii. 8. This is a faithful faying, and thefe things I will that thou *affirm conftantly,* that they which have believed in God, might be careful to maintain *good works.*

XI. *Of Works of Supererogation.*

VOLUNTARY works, besides over and above God's commandments, which they call works of supererogation, cannot be taught without arrogancy and impiety. For by them men do declare, That they do not only render unto God as much as they are bound to do, but that they do more for his sake than of bounden duty is required: Whereas Christ saith plainly, When ye have done all that is commanded you, say, We are unprofitable servants.

N O T E S.

Job xxii. 2, 3. Can a man be profitable unto God, as he that is wife may be profitable unto himself? Is it any pleasure to the Almighty that thou art righteous? Or is it gain to him that thou makeft thy ways perfect? 1 Cor. iv. 7. Who maketh thee to differ from another? And what haft thou, which thou didft not receive? Now, if thou didft receive it, why doft thou glory as if thou hadft not received it? Tit. iii. 5. *Not by works of righteoufnefs*, which we have done, but according to his mercy he faved us, by the wafhing of regeneration, and renewing of the Holy Ghoft.

XII. *Of Sin after Juftification.*

NOT every fin willingly committed after juftification, is the fin againft the Holy Ghoft, and unpardonable. Wherefore the grant of repentance is not to be denied to fuch as fall into fin after juftification: After we have received the Holy Ghoft, we may depart from grace given, and fall into fin, and, by the grace of God, rife again, and amend our lives. And therefore they are to be condemned, who fay they can no more fin as long as they live here, or deny the place of forgivenefs to fuch as truly repent.

N O T E S.

(1) 2 Sam. xii. 13. David said unto Nathan, I have sinned against the Lord. And Nathan said unto David, The Lord also hath put away thy sin; thou shalt not die. Matt. xxvi. 75. Peter remembered the words of Jesus, which said unto him, Before the cock crow, thou shalt deny me thrice. And he went out, and wept bitterly [and Peter certainly was pardoned.] (2) Jer. iii. 22. Return, ye backsliding children, and I will heal your backslidings. Hosea xiv. 4. I will heal their backsliding, I will love them freely. 1 John ii. 1. My little children, these things write I unto you, that ye sin not: and if *any man* sin, we have an Advocate with the Father, Jesus Christ the righteous.

XIII. *Of the Church.*

THE visible Church of Christ is a congregation of faithful men, in which the pure word of God is preached, and the sacraments duly administered according to Christ's ordinance, in all those things that of necessity are requisite to the same.

N O T E S.

Matt. xviii. 20. Where *two or three* are gathered together in my name, there am I in the midst of them. Rom. xvi. 5. Greet *the church*, which is *in their house*. 1 Cor. xvi. 19. *The churches of Asia* salute you. 1 Cor. xi. 18. When *ye* come together *in the church*, &c.

XIV. *Of Purgatory.*

THE Romish doctrine concerning purgatory, pardon, worshipping, and adoration, as well of images as of reliques, and also invocation of saints, is a fond thing vainly invented, and grounded upon no warrant of scripture, but repugnant to the word of God.

N O T E S.

(1) Exod. xx. 4, 5. Thou shalt not make unto thee any graven image, or any likeness of any thing that is in heaven above, or that is in the earth beneath, or that is in the water under the

earth: *thou shalt not bow down* thyself to them, &c. Matt. iv. 10. Jesus said unto him,—It is written, Thou shalt worship the Lord thy God, and him *only* shalt thou serve. Col. ii. 18. Let no man beguile you of your reward, in a voluntary humility, and *worshipping* of angels, &c. 1 Tim. ii. 5. There is one God, and *one* Mediator between God and men, the man Christ Jesus. Rev. xix. 10. I [John] fell at his feet to *worship* him; and he said unto me, See *thou do it not;* I am thy fellow-servant, and of thy brethren that have the testimony of Jesus. *Worship God.* Rev. xxii. 8, 9. I fell down to *worship* before the feet of the angel which shewed me these things. Then saith he unto me, *See thou do it not,* for I am thy fellow-servant, and of thy brethren, the prophets, and of them which keep the sayings of this book. *Worship God.* (2) Luke xvi. 26. Besides all this, between us and you there is a great gulph fixed, *so that they which would pass from hence to you, cannot: neither can they pass to us, that would come from thence.* John viii. 21. Then said Jesus again unto them, I go my way, and ye shall seek me, and shall die in your sins. Whither I go, ye *cannot* come. (3) Mark. ii. 5, &c. When Jesus saw their faith, he said unto the sick of the palsy, Son, thy sins be forgiven thee. But there were certain of the scribes sitting there, and reasoning in their hearts, Why doth this man thus speak blasphemies? *who can forgive sins but God only?* And immediately, when Jesus perceived in his spirit, that they so reasoned within themselves [he did not deny the justness of their reasoning, in ascribing to God *only* the power of forgiving sins, but] he said unto them, Why reason ye these things in your hearts? Whether is it easier to say to the sick of the palsy, Thy sins be forgiven thee; or to say, Arise, and take up thy bed, and walk? But that ye may know that *the Son of man* [he does not add, *and the pope and his priests*] hath power on earth to forgive sins, He saith to the sick of the palsy, I say unto thee, arise and take up thy bed, and go thy way into thine house. And immediately he arose, &c. See also Matt. ix. 2, &c. and Luke v. 18, &c.

XV. *Of speaking in the Congregation in such a Tongue as the People understand.*

IT is a thing plainly repugnant to the word of God, and the custom of the primitive church, to have public prayer in the church, or to minister the sacraments, in a tongue not understood by the people.

N O T E S.

1 Cor. xiv. 11. If I know not the meaning of the voice, I shall be unto him that speaketh, a barbarian; and he that speaketh shall be a barbarian unto me. Ver. 14. *If I pray* in an *unknown tongue*, my spirit prayeth, but my understanding is unfruitful. Ver. 16. When thou shalt bless with the spirit, how shall he that occupieth the room of the unlearned, say Amen at *the giving of thanks*, seeing *he understandeth not* what thou sayest. Ver. 19. In the church I had rather speak five words with my understanding, that by my voice I might teach others also, than ten thousand words in an unknown tongue. See the whole chapter.

XVI. *Of the Sacraments.*

SACRAMENTS ordained of Christ, are not only badges or tokens of christian men's profession: but rather they are certain signs of grace, and God's good will towards us, by the which he doth work invisibly in us, and doth not only quicken, but also strengthen and confirm our faith in him.

There are two Sacraments ordained of Christ our Lord, in the Gospel; that is to say, Baptism and the Supper of the Lord.

Those five commonly called Sacraments; that is to say, Confirmation, Penance, Orders, Matrimony, and extreme Unction, are not to be counted for Sacraments of the Gospel, being such as have partly grown out of the *corrupt* following of the Apostles; and partly are states of life allowed in the Scriptures, but yet have not the like nature of Baptism and the Lord's Supper, because they have not any visible sign or ceremony ordained of God.

The Sacraments were not ordained of Christ to be gazed upon, or to be carried about; but that we should duly use them. And in such only as worthily receive the same, they have a wholesome effect or operation: but they that receive them unworthily, purchase to themselves condemnation, as St. Paul saith.

NOTES

(1) Matt. xxviii. 19. Mark xvi. 16. He that believeth and *is baptized*, shall be saved. Acts ii. 38. Peter said unto them, Repent, and *be baptized*, every one of you, in the name of Jesus Christ, for the remission of sins. viii. 12. When they believed Philip preaching,——they were *baptized*, both men and women. Ver. 16. As yet he [the Holy Ghost] was fallen on none of them, only they were *baptized* in the name of the Lord Jesus. xvi. 15. When she [Lydia] was *baptized*, and *her household*, &c. xix. 5. They were *baptized* in the Name of the Lord Jesus. xxii. 16. And now why tarriest thou ? Arise, and *be baptized*, &c. Rom. vi. 3, 4. Know ye not that so many of us as were *baptized into Jesus Christ, were baptized* into his death ? Therefore we are buried with him *by baptism* into death : that like as Christ was raised up from the dead by the glory of the Father, even so we also should walk in newness of life. 1 Cor. i. 16. I *baptized* also *the household* of Stephanus. 1 Pet. iii. 21. The like *figure* whereunto even *baptism* doth also now save us ; not the putting away of the filth of the flesh, but the answer of a good conscience towards God, by the resurrection of Jesus Christ. (2) Luke xxii. 19. He [Jesus] took bread and gave thanks, and brake it, and gave unto them, saying, This is my body which is given for you : *this do in remembrance of me.* 1 Cor. xi. 24—26. When he had given thanks, he brake it, and said, Take, eat; this is my body which is broken for you : *this do in remembrance of me.* After the same manner also he took the cup, when he had supped, saying, This cup is the new testament in my blood ; *this do ye, as oft as ye drink it, in remembrance of me.* For *as often* as ye eat *this bread*, and drink *this cup*, ye do shew the Lord's death, *till he come.* Chap. x. 16. The cup of blessing, which we bless, is it not *the communion* of the blood of Christ ; the bread which we break, is it not *the communion* of the body of Christ ? (3) chap. xi. 27. Whosoever shall eat this bread, and drink this cup of the Lord unworthily, shall be guilty of the body and blood of the Lord. See also the 29th verse.

In respect to the five additional *sacraments*, which the church of Rome has been pleased to adopt, there is not the least imaginable authority from the word of God to consider them *as such.* They want the *essential* requisites of a sacrament ; and have been *imposed* on a considerable part of mankind by a most corrupt priesthood, whose only aim was to enrich and aggrandize themselves.

And from the same corrupt fountain sprung the gaudy, superstitious custom of carrying about the Host, that the poor blinded multitude might gaze at it, and worship it, to the degradation of human nature, as well as the dishonor of God.

XVII. *Of Baptifm.*

BAPTISM is not only a fign of profeffion, and mark of difference, whereby chriftians are diftinguifhed from others that are not baptized ; but it is alfo a fign of regeneration, or the new birth. The baptifm of young children is to be retained in the church.

N O T E S.

Matt. iii. 11. I [John the Baptift] indeed baptize you with water unto repentance ; but he that cometh after me,—*fhall baptize you with the Holy Ghoft, and with fire.* John iii. 5. Jefus anfwered, Verily, verily, I fay unto thee, except a man be born of water and *of the Spirit*, he cannot enter into the kingdom of God. Mark x. 13—16. They brought young children to him [Chrift] that he fhould touch them, and his difciples rebuked thofe that brought them ; but when Jefus faw it, he was much difpleafed, and faid unto them, Suffer the little children to come unto me, and forbid them not; for of fuch is the kingdom of God.—And he took them up in his arms, put his hands upon them, and bleffed them.

The preceding fcripture evidently demonftrates, that the *little children* were entitled to all the privileges of *the kingdom of glory*, and, of neceffary confequence, to all the privileges of *the kingdom of grace.* They muft, therefore, be entitled to the benefit of *that ordinance*, which initiates the members of Chrift's kingdom into his church below. See alfo the texts, concerning baptifm, on the preceding article, particularly thofe which refpect the baptizing of whole houfeholds or families.

XVIII. *Of the Lord's Supper.*

THE Supper of the Lord is not only a fign of the love that chriftians ought to have among themfelves one to another, but rather is a facrament of our redemption by Chrift's death : infomuch, that to fuch as rightly, worthily, and with faith receive the fame, the bread which we break is a partaking of the body of Chrift ; and likewife the cup of bleffing is a partaking of the blood of Chrift.

Tranfubftantiation, or the change of the fubftance of bread and wine in the Supper of our Lord, cannot be proved by Holy Writ; but is repugnant to the plain words of Scripture, overthroweth the nature of a facrament, and hath given occafion to many fuperftitions.

The body of Chrift is given, taken, and eaten in the Supper, only after a heavenly and fpiritual manner. And the mean whereby the body of Chrift is received and eaten in the Supper, is faith.

The Sacrament of the Lord's Supper was not by Chrift's ordinance referved, carried about, lifted up, or worfhipped.

N O T E S.

Matt. xxvi. 28. This is *my blood* of the New Teftament, which *is fhed* for many, for the remiffion of fins. Mark xiv. 24. This is *my blood* of the New Teftament, which *is fhed* for many. Luke xxii. 19. This is *my body*, which *is given* for you. 1 Cor. xi. 24. This is *my body*, which *is broken* for you. v. 7. For even *Chrift, our paffover, is facrificed for us.* See the texts on the 16th article.

In refpect to the doctrine of tranfubftantiation, or the change of the bread and wine in the Lord's fupper into the *real* body and blood of Chrift, fo that the divinity as well as humanity of Chrift is contained in the tranfubftantiated elements, we have little hopes of convincing thofe of their error, who can hold fo abfurd a notion. If they can credit the affertion, that a man can put his God into his mouth and fwallow him down his throat, or thát he can even fwallow the whole humanity of the bleffed Jefus, " whom the heavens muft receive until the times of reftitution of all things,"* they muft indeed be prepared to receive any error, which a corrupt and interrefted clergy may think proper to impofe upon them, however abfurd or monftrous it may be. Nor do we know of any opinion of the heathen mythologifts, concerning their Jupiters, Junos, and Venuses, fo aftonifhingly monftrous as the doctrine of tranfubftantiation.

At the fame time, we are well affured that the true believer does, in a *fpiritual* manner, feed upon the body and blood of Jefus Chrift . and in this *fpiritual* fenfe we take thofe words of our Lord, John vi. 51—58. " I am the living bread which came down from heaven : if any man eat of this bread, he fhall live for ever : and the bread that I will give, is my flefh, which I

---

* *Acts* iii. 21.

will give for the life of the world.——Verily, verily, I fay unto you, Except ye eat the flefh of the Son of man, and drink his blood, ye have no life in you. Whofo eateth my flefh, and drinketh my blood, hath eternal life, and I will raife him up at the laft day. For my flefh is meat indeed, and my blood is drink indeed. He that eateth my flefh, and drinketh my blood, dwelleth in me, and I in him:" and faith is the grand inftrument, whereby we thus *fpiritually* difcern the Lord's body, and *fpiritually* eat his flefh, and drink his blood.

XIX. *Of both Kinds.*

THE cup of the Lord is not to be denied to the lay-people: for both the parts of the Lord's Supper, by Chrift's ordinance and commandment ought to be adminiftered to all chriftians alike.

N O T E S.

It is indubitable, from the 11th chapter of St. Paul's 1ft Epiftle to the Corinthians, that the Lord's fupper was adminiftered in *both* kinds to all the communicants in the apoftolic age. The apoftle, addreffing himfelf to *the Corinthians*, obferves in the 20th, 21ft, and 22d verfes, " When *ye* come together, therefore, into one place, this it not to eat the Lord's fupper. For in eating, every one taketh before other his own fupper: and one is hungry, and *another is drunken.* What! have ye not houfes to eat and to *drink in?*" Here St. Paul does not complain of their *drinking the wine* at the Lord's fupper, which he certainly would, if the cup was to be confined to the minifters; but of their both *eating* and *drinking* moft intemperately. He adds, in the 26th verfe, &c. " As often as *ye* [*Corinthians*] eat this bread, and *drink this cup, ye* do fhew the Lord's death, till he come. Wherefore, *whofoever* fhall eat this bread, and *drink this cup* of the Lord unworthily, fhall be guilty of the body and blood of the Lord. But let a man [any chriftian, not a prieft only, for neither prieft nor minifter is here mentioned] examine himfelf, and fo let him eat of that bread, and *drink of that cup,*" &c. The whole paffage removes all poffibility of difpute, where the fcripture is the rule of judgment. And indeed the refufal of the cup to the people is, even in the church of Rome, of very late date: however, it fhews much of that wifdom which is from beneath; for it requires much more faith to believe in the tranfubftantiation of *the wine* after confecration, than of *the wafer* which has little or no tafte.

XX. *Of the one Oblation of Chrift, finifh-ed upon the Crofs.*

THE offering of Chrift once made, is that perfect redemption, propitiation, and fatisfaction for all the fins of the whole world, both original and actual; and there is none other fatisfaction for fin but that alone. Wherefore the facrifice of maffes, in the which it is commonly faid that the prieft doth offer Chrift for the quick and the dead, to have remiffion of pain or guilt, is a blafphemous fable, and dangerous deceit.

N O T E S.

Heb. vii. 26, 27. Such an high prieft became us,—who *needeth not daily* as thofe high priefts [of the tribe of Levi] to offer up facrifice, firft for his own fins, and then for the people's: *for this he did once,* when he offered up himfelf. Heb. x. 11—14. Every prieft ftandeth *daily* miniftering and offering *oftentimes the fame facrifices,* which can never take away fins: But this man [Chrift] after he had offered *one* facrifice for fins, for ever fat down on the right hand of God.—For by *one* offering he hath perfected for ever them that are fanctified. John xix. 30. He [Jefus] faid, *It is finifhed;* and he bowed his head, and gave up the ghoft.

The facrifice of maffes, in which Chrift is fuppofed to be offered again, is wholly grounded on the doctrine of tranfubftantiation: and it muft be granted, that if the wafer after confecration, be the *real* body of Chrift, the prieft may offer it, or crucify it, or do what he pleafe with it.

XXI. *Of the Marriage of Minifters.*

THE minifters of Chrift are not commanded by God's law either to vow the eftate of fingle life, or to abftain from marriage; therefore it is lawful for them, as for all other chriftians, to marry at their own difcretion, as they fhall judge the fame to ferve beft to godlinefs.

N O T E S.

1 Tim. iv. 1—3. Now, *the Spirit fpeaketh exprefsly,* that in the latter times fome fhall depart from the faith, giving heed to fe-

ducing fpirits, and *doctrines of devils ;——forbidding to marry*, &c. 1 Cor. ix. 5. Have *we* not power to lead about *a fifter, a wife*, as well as *other apoftles,* and as *the brethren of the Lord*, and *Cephas?* Heb. xiii. 4. Marriage is *honourable in all.*

XXII. *Of the Rites and Ceremonies of Churches.*

IT is not neceffary that rites and ceremonies fhould in all places be the fame, or exactly alike, for they have been always different, and may be changed according to the diverfity of countries, times, and men's manners, fo that nothing be ordained againft God's word.——Whofoever, through his private judgment, willingly and purpofely doth openly break the rites and ceremonies of the church to which he belongs, which are not repugnant to the word of God, and are ordained and approved by common authority, ought to be rebuked openly, that others may fear to do the like, as one that offendeth againft the common order of the church, and woundeth the confciences of weak brethren.

Every particular church may ordain, change, or abolifh rites and ceremonies, fo that all things may be done to edification.

N O T E S.

(1) Heb. xiii. 17. Obey them that have the rule over you, and fubmit yourfelves: for they watch for your fouls, as they that muft give account, that they may do it with joy, and not with grief. 1 Cor. xi. 16. But if any man feem to be contentious, we have no fuch cuftom, neither the churches of God. (2) Rom. ii. 8. Unto them that are *contentious*, indignation and wrath. xvi. 17, 18. Now, I befeech you, brethren, *mark* them which *caufe divifions and offences*, contrary to the doctrine which ye have learned, and *avoid them*. For they that are fuch ferve not our Lord Jefus Chrift, but their own belly; and *by good words and fair fpeeches* deceive the hearts of the fimple. 1 Cor. i. 10. Now *I befeech you, brethren, by the name of our Lord Jefus Chrift*, that ye all fpeak the fame thing, and *that there be no divifions* among you; but that ye be perfectly joined together in the fame mind, and in

the fame judgment. iii. 3. *Ye are yet carnal:* for whereas there is among you envying, and ftrife, and divifions, *are ye not carnal,* and walk as men? Tit. iii. 9. Avoid—*contentions.* (3) 1 Cor. xiv. 33. God is not the author of *confufion,* but of *peace,* as in all churches of the faints. Ver. 40. Let all things be done decently, and *in order.* Col. ii. 5. Though I be abfent in the flefh, yet am I with you in the fpirit, joying and *beholding your order.*

From thefe texts, we may obferve,

1. That the word of God requires, that the members of a church fhould fhew obedience and fubmiffion to thofe who have the paftoral care and fuperintendence over them. In *effential* points they fhould make no facrifice to the judgment of others: but in *uneffential* matters (as all rites and ceremonies are, which are not repugnant to the word of God) *they are required to obey, and fubmit to, their chief paftors.* And if the contentious are determined to cenfure this doctrine, they muft lay the blame at the proper door, and criminate the fcriptures themfelves.

2. The texts which are produced, to fhew the great fin and dreadful confequences of ftrife, contention, and divifion, fhould place every good man on his guard againft a practice fo injurious to the work of God. Well is Satan reprefented as the fpirit of divifion! It is the great work of Chrift to unite God to man, and man to man; and the great work of the devil to divide man from God, and man from man. And, alas! this great enemy of mankind has been but too fuccefsful!—fo fuccefsful, that we doubt whether greater injury has not been done, in the different ages of the world, to the caufe of religion, by this grand engine of the evil one, than by all the grofs vices committed by mankind! The unregenerate are under the wrath of God, whether they be formalifts or open finners: but *the fpirit of divifion* enters within the vail—enters into the fanctuary, and eats up the very vitals of religion: it changes the peace and concord and union of religious focieties, into jealoufy, evil furmifings, malice, and envy: and too often concludes with every evil word and work.

3. And how is it poffible to bring the difcipline of a church to any degree of perfection, or even to preferve that order in it, which is effentially neceffary for its peace and profperity, if every member has a right to oppofe or defpife its laws, and to fet up his judgment or fancy againft the united wifdom of thofe, who, by common confent, have exercifed the government thereof? It is this miferable fpirit which has broken the moft lively chriftian focieties into parties, and given their enemies fuch plaufible grounds to defpife and ridicule the great truths of experimental religion. O that the Prince of peace and concord may preferve *us* from this fchifmatic fpirit!

XXIII. *Of the Rulers of the United States of America.*

THE prefident, the congrefs, the general affemblies, the governors, and the councils of ftate, *as the delegates of the people,* are the rulers of the United States of America, according to the divifion of power made to them by the general act of confederation, and by the conftitutions of their refpective ftates. And the faid ftates ought not to be fubject to any foreign jurifdiction.

N O T E S.

Rom. xiii. 1—7. Let every foul be fubject unto the higher powers; for there is no power but of God: the powers that be are ordained of God. Whofoever, therefore, refifteth the power, refifteth the ordinance of God; and they that refift fhall receive to themfelves damnation; for rulers are not a terror to good works, but to the evil. Wilt thou then not be afraid of the power? Do that which is good, and thou fhalt have praife of the fame: for he is the minifter of God to thee for good. But if thou do that which is evil, be afraid; for he beareth not the fword in vain: for he is the minifter of God, a revenger to execute wrath upon him that doeth evil. Wherefore, ye muft needs be fubject, not only for wrath, but alfo for confcience' fake. For, for this caufe pay ye tribute alfo: for they are God's minifters, attending continually upon this very thing. Render, therefore, to all, their dues: tribute, to whom tribute is due; cuftom, to whom cuftom; fear, to whom fear; honour, to whom honour. Tit. iii. 1, Put them in mind to be fubject to principalities and powers, to obey magiftrates. 2 Pet. ii. 9—11. The Lord knoweth how—to referve the unjuft unto the day of judgment to be punifhed: but *chiefly them* that walk after the flefh in the luft of uncleannefs, and *defpife government.* Prefumptious are they, felf-willed, *they are not afraid to fpeak evil of dignities:* whereas angels, which are greater in power and might, bring not railing accufation againft them before the Lord. Jude 8. Likewife, alfo, thefe filthy dreamers defile the flefh, *defpife dominion,* and *fpeak evil of dignities.* 1 Tim. ii. 1, 2. I exhort, therefore, that, firft of all, fupplications, prayers, interceffions, and giving of thanks, be made for all men,——and *for all that are in authority.*

XXIV. *Of Christian Men's Goods.*

THE riches and goods of christians are not common as touching the right, title, and poffeffion of the fame, as fome do falfely boaft. Notwithftanding, every man ought, of fuch things as he poffeffeth, liberally to give alms to the poor, according to his ability.

N O T E S.

* (1) Acts v. 3, 4. Peter faid, Ananias, why hath Satan filled thine heart to lye to the Holy Ghoft, and to keep back part of the price of the land? Whiles it remained, *was it not thine own?* and after it was fold, *was it not in thine own power?* 1 Cor. xvi. 2. Upon the firft day of the week, let every one of you lay by him in ftore, as God hath profpered him, that there be no gatherings when I come. 1 Tim. vi. 17, 18. Charge them that are rich in this world [not, that they throw their property into a common ftock with the other members of the church, to which they belong, but] that they do good, that they be *rich in good works*, ready to diftribute, willing to communicate. (2) Matt. xxv. 34—40. Then fhall the king fay unto them on his right hand, come, ye bleffed of my Father, inherit the kingdom prepared for you from the foundation of the world: for I was an hungered, and ye gave me meat: I was thirfty, and ye gave me drink: I was a ftranger, and ye took me in: naked, and ye clothed me: I was fick, and ye vifited me: I was in prifon, and ye came unto me.——Verily, I fay unto you, Inafmuch as ye have done it unto one of the leaft of thefe my brethren, ye have done it unto me.

XXV. *Of a Christian Man's Oath.*

AS we confefs that vain and rafh fwearing is forbidden chriftian men by our Lord Jefus Chrift, and James his apoftle; fo we judge that the chriftian religion doth not prohibit, but that a man may fwear when the magiftrate requireth, in a caufe of faith and charity, fo it be done according to the prophet's teaching, in juftice, judgment, and truth.

N O T E S.

(1) Matt. **v.** 34—37. I fay unto you, Swear not at all:——— But let your *communication* be yea, yea; nay, nay: for whatfoever is more than thefe, cometh of evil. Jam. v. 12. Above all things, my brethren, fwear not; neither by heaven, neither by the earth, neither by any other oath: but let *your yea be yea;* and *your nay, nay;* left ye fall into condemnation. (2) Matt. xxvi. 63, 64. The high prieft anfwered, and faid unto him, *I adjure thee by the living God,* that thou tell us whether thou be the Chrift, the Son of God. Jefus faith unto him, Thou haft faid: [or, as St. Mark expreffes it ch. xiv. 62.] Jefus faid, I am. [Jefus anfwered the high prieft on being folemnly adjured or *fworn* by him *in the name of the living God;* though he would not anfwer him, when queftioned without an oath: and we may alfo obferve, that the Jews always confidered themfelves *upon oath*, when thus adjured by the high prieft. Why then fhould our Saviour give fanction to an oath by anfwering the adjuration, if no perfon ought to fwear or take an oath before a magiftrate?] 2 Cor. i. 18. *As God is true*, our word toward you was not yea and nay. Ver. 23. Moreover, *I call God for a record upon my foul,* that to fpare you I came not as yet unto Corinth. Gal. i. 20. Now, the things which I write unto you, behold, *before God*, I lye not. [St. Paul, in each of thefe inftances, calls *God to witnefs* the truth which he afferted, which has in it the nature and properties of *a folemn oath*.] Heb. vi. 13. When God made promife to Abraham, *becaufe he could fwear by no greater, he fware by himfelf.* Ver. 16, 17. For men verily fwear by the greater: and *an oath for confirmation is to them an end of all ftrife.* Wherein God, willing more abundantly to fhew unto the heirs of promife the immutability of his counfel, confirmed it by an oath.

When we candidly compare together the texts quoted above, we do not fee the poffibility of reconciling them, but by allowing, on the one hand, that it is finful (it " cometh of evil") to ufe any affeveration in common difcourfe, ftronger than the fimple *yes* and *no;* and, on the other hand, that it is *perfectly lawful* to *make oath*, before the magiftrate, on all important occafions.

Neverthelefs, we do not object to any of our brethren, who ftill have doubts on this fubject, and demand, where it can be obtained, an affirmation inftead of an oath.

SECTION III.

Of the General and Yearly Conferences.

IT is defired that all things be confidered on thefe occafions, as in the immediate prefence of God: That every perfon fpeak freely whatever is in his heart.

Queſt. 1. How may we beſt improve our time at the conferences?

Anſw. 1. While we are converſing, let us have an eſpecial care to ſet God always before us.

2. In the intermediate hours, let us redeem all the time we can for private exerciſes.

3. Therein let us give ourſelves to prayer for one another, and for a bleſſing on our labour.

Queſt. 2. Who ſhall compoſe the general conference?

Anſw. All the travelling preachers who ſhall be in full connection at the time of holding the conference.

Queſt. 3. Who ſhall attend the yearly conferences?

Anſw. All the travelling preachers who are in full connection, and thoſe who are to be received into full connection.

Queſt. 4. Who ſhall appoint the times of holding the yearly conferences?

Anſw. The biſhops.

Queſt. 5. What is the method wherein we uſually proceed in the yearly conferences?

Anſw. We inquire,

1. What preachers are admitted on trial?
2. Who remain on trial?
3. Who are admitted into full connection?
4. Who are the deacons?
5. Who are the elders?
6. Who have been elected by the unanimous ſuffrages of the general conference to exerciſe the epiſcopal office, and ſuperintend the Methodiſt epiſcopal church in America?
7. Who are under a location, through weakneſs of body, or family concerns?
8. Who are the ſupernumeraries? *
9. Who have died this year?

---

* A ſupernumerary preacher is one ſo worn out in the itinerant ſervice, as to be rendered incapable of preaching conſtantly: but, at the ſame time, is willing to do any work in the miniſtry, which the conference may direct, and his ſtrength enable him to perform.

10. Are all the preachers blamelefs in life and converfation?
11. Who are expelled from the connection?
12. Where are the preachers ftationed this year?
13. What numbers are in fociety?
14. What has been collected for the contingent expences?
15. How has this been expended?
16. What is contributed towards the fund for the fuperannuated preachers, and the widows and orphans of the preachers?
17. What demands are there upon it?
18 Where and when fhall our next conference be held?

Queft. 6. Is there any other bufinefs to be done in
the yearly conferences?

Anfw. The electing and ordaining of elders and
deacons.

Queft. 7. Are there any other directions to be giv-
en concerning the yearly conferences?

* *Anfw.* There fhall be fix conferences in the year,
as follows, viz.

1ft, The New-England conference,—under the di-
rection of which fhall be the affairs of our church in
New-England, and in that part of the ftate of New-
York, which lies on the eaft fide of Hudfon's river:
Provided, That if the bifhops fee it neceffary, a con-
ference may be held in the Province of Maine.

2. The Philadelphia conference, for the direction
of our concerns in the remainder of the ftate of New-
York, in New-Jerfey, in all that part of Pennfylvania
which lies on the eaft fide of the Sufquehannah river,
the ftate of Delaware, and all the reft of the peninfula.

3. The Baltimore conference, for the remainder of
Pennfylvania, the remainder of Maryland, and the
Northern neck of Virginia.

4. The Virginia conference, for all that part of Virginia which lies on the fouth fide of the Rappahan-
nock river, and for all that part of North-Carolina
which lies on the north fide of Cape-Fear river, includ-

ing alfo the circuits which are fituated on the branches of the Yadkin.

5. The South-Carolina conference, for South-Carolina, Georgia, and the remainder of North-Carolina.

* 6. The weftern conference, for the ftates of Kentucky and Tenneffee; *Provided*, That the bifhops fhall have authority to appoint other yearly conferences in the interval of the general conference, if a fufficiency of new circuits be any where formed for that purpofe.

Queft. 8. How are the diftricts to be formed?

Anfw. According to the judgment of the bifhop.

N. B. In cafe that there be no bifhop to travel. through the diftricts, and exercife the epifcopal office, on account of death, the diftricts fhall be regulated in every refpect by the yearly conferences and the prefiding elders, till the enfuing general conference, (ordinations only excepted).

N O T E S.

It is indifpenfably neceffary for every great body of people, whether united by civil or religious bonds, to have among them a.felect number, invefted with the authority of making regulations, for the government of the fociety. It is of fmall importance by what name this felect body is diftinguifhed. The name which our venerable father in the gofpel, the late Mr. Wefley, preferred, in refpect to our fociety, was that of *Conference*, and we have, therefore, continued to ufe it. Indeed *the name* is perfectly fcriptural. In the Acts of the Apoftles we are informed, that Paul and Barnabas went up to Jerufalem to confult the apoftles and elders, in refpect to the difpute concerning circumcifion. But after they had delivered their meffage, " and declared all things that God had done with them,——there rofe up certain of the fect of the Pharifees, which believed, faying, that it was needful to circumcife them [the gentiles] and to command them to keep the law of Mofes." See the 15th chapter of the Acts. This very meeting is called, by St Paul, Gal. ii. 1—10. a *confer ence.* " For they who feemed to be fomewhat *in conference* added nothing to me." It is impoffible for any difcerning perfon who attentively compares the two chapters together, not to fee that *the conference* here fpoken of refpected the meeting of the apoftles and elders with Paul and Barnabas, on the above occafion : and

St. Paul feems to ufe the word as if it was well known, and frequently applied to fuch meetings.

*   Our focieties are fcattered over a vaft country, extending about fourteen hundred miles from north to fouth, and from five to eight hundred from eaft to weft. We could not, therefore, in juftice to the work of God, nor from the ftate of our finances, hold our general conferences oftener than once in four years. If they were more frequent, the long abfence of fo many minifters from their refpective circuits and diftricts, would be an irreparable lofs to the focieties and congregations. Nor do we think, that the nature of a religious conftitution renders it neceffary to revife more frequently the regulations by which it is governed. But there are various particulars, which do not come under the name of laws, which require more frequent affemblies or conferences for their confideration. The admiffion of preachers on trial and into full connection, the ordination of elders and deacons, the examination of the characters of the minifters and preachers, and the ftationing of them all, as well as the management of the fund for the fuperannuated preachers, &c. are points of the firft moment, and call for frequent meetings. On this account, the *general* conference has appointed *yearly* conferences, divided in the beft manner they were able; to be compofed, as far as poffible, of at leaft one bifhop—the prefident elder of each diftrict within the controul of thofe conferences, refpectively—the elders, deacons, and the preachers in full connection. Thefe men, who have been travelling the preceding year among all the focieties in thofe diftricts and circuits, refpectively, can give the fulleft, the completeft information on all the fubjects which come under the cognizance of the yearly conferences.

But it may be afked, Why are not *delegates* fent to thefe conferences from each of the circuits? We anfwer, It would utterly deftroy our *itinerant plan*. *They* would be concerned chiefly, if not only, for the interefts of their own conftituents. They could not be expected, from *the nature of things*, to make the neceffary facrifices, and to enter impartially into *the good of the whole*. They would neceffarily endeavour to obtain the moft able and lively preachers for their refpective circuits, without entering, perhaps at all, into that enlarged, apoftolic fpirit, which would endeavour, whatever might be the facrifice, to make all things *tally*. The difference of gifts in the minifters, and the oppofing interefts of the delegates, would produce conflicts, of a pernicious tendency; and, in many inftances, improper means would be ufed for obtaining the defired point. Frequently the delegates, if unfuccefsful in their application for their favourite preacher, would probably make him fecret offers to fettle among them; and if unfuccefsful in every point, and the preacher appointed for them and their conftituents, was not agreeable to their wifhes, they might grow indignant, and, through refentment, and by their unfavourable reports, on their return, might caufe a feparation from the general body. And thofe who imagine this to be a mere chimera, fhew, we think, but little knowledge of human nature : they do not confider how eafily and powerfully the heated paffions would plead in favour of a fettled miniftry— how eafily difappointment and jealoufy would prefent the pureft and moft difinterefted conduct in the moft unfavourable light: to fay nothing of the labour and expence of fuch a plan. Whilft; on the other hand, the prefent members who compofe our con- ferences, who know not, when they meet, what may be their next fphere of action, and are willing to run any where on the errands of their Lord, are not nearly as much expofed to the temptations mentioned above.*

The following portions of the Word of God are pointed in fup- port of the itinerant plan for the propagation of the gofpel; which plan renders moft of the regulations contained in this fec- tion, effential to the exiftence of our united fociety : Matt. x. 5 —11. " Thefe twelve [apoftles] Jefus fent forth, and command- ed them, faying, Go—to the loft fheep of the houfe of Ifrael. And *as ye go, preach,* faying, The kingdom of heaven is at hand. And into *whatfoever city or town* ye fhall enter, inquire," &c. xxii. 8—10. " Then faith he to his fervants, The wedding is rea- dy, but they which were bidden were not worthy. Go ye, therefore, into *the high-ways, and as many as ye fhall find,* bid to the marriage. So thofe fervants went out into *the highways,*" &c. xxviii. 19. " Go ye, therefore, and *teach all nations,*" be as extenfively ufeful as poffible. Mark vi. 7—12. " And he call- eth unto him the twelve, and began to fend them forth by two and two, —— and commanded them that they fhould take no- thing for their journey, *fave a ftaff only.*——And he faid unto them, *In what place foever* ye enter into an houfe, there abide, till ye *depart* from that place.——And *they went out,* and preached

---

* *We are very far from making thefe remarks out of any difrefpect to our* located *brethren. On the contrary, we are very confcious that many of them equal any of us, and perhaps much exceed us in grace and wifdom. We have made thefe obfervations only on account of their* located *fituation, well knowing that our people would on no occafion choofe any for their delegates who were not wife and good men. But fuch is the nature of man, and perhaps fuch is the duty of man, that he will always prefer the people for whom he acts, and to whom he is refponfible, before all others. We fhould, probably, act in the fame manner ourfelves, if we were delegates for a fingle circuit or diftrict.*

that men should repent." Luke x. 1—9. " After these things, the Lord appointed other seventy also, and sent them two and two before his face *into every city and place*, whither he himself would come.——And into *whatsoever house* ye enter," says our Lord to them, " first say, Peace be to this house.——And into *whatsoever city* ye enter, and they receive you,—say unto them, The kingdom of God is come nigh unto you." xiv. 23. " And the Lord said unto the servant, *Go out into the high-ways and hedges*, and compel them to come in, that my house may be filled." Acts. viii. 4. " They that were scattered abroad *went every where* preaching the word." Ver. 40 " Philip—preached *in all the cities*, till he came to Cesarea." xvi 36. " Paul said unto Barnabas, Let us go *again* and visit our brethren *in every city* where we have preached the word of the Lord," &c.

We have already shewn, that *Timothy* and *Titus* were *travelling bishops*. In short, every candid person, who is thoroughly acquainted with the New Testament, must allow, that whatever excellencies other plans may have, *this* is the primitive and *apostolic plan*. But we would by no means speak with disrespect of the faithful *located* ministers of any church. We doubt not, but, from the nature and circumstances of things, there must have been many located ministers in the primitive churches : and we must acknowledge, with gratitude to God, that the *located* brethren in our church are truly useful and of considerable consequence, in their respective stations. But, on the other hand, we are so conscious of the vast importance of the *travelling plan*, that we are determined, through the grace of God, to support it to the utmost of our power: nor will any plea which can possibly be urged, however plausible it may appear, or under whatever name proposed, induce us to make the least sacrifice in this respect, or, by the introduction of any novelty, to run the least hazard of wounding *that plan*, which God has so wonderfully owned, and which is so perfectly consistent with the apostolic and primitive practice.

We will now humbly beg leave to drop a few *hints* (for laws or regulations we have no authority to make) *as explanatory* of those words in the introduction to this section, " It is desired, that every person speak freely whatever is in his heart :" and we propose them the more readily, as they are extracted from the minutes drawn up by our elder brethren, the members of the British conference :

1. Be tender of the character of every brother ; but keep at the utmost distance from countenancing sin.

2. Say nothing in the conference but what is strictly necessary, and to the point.

3. If accused by any one, remember recrimination is no acquittance ; therefore avoid it.

4. Beware of impatience of contradiction; be firm; but be open to conviction. The caufe is God's, and he needs not the hands of an Uzzah to fupport his ark. The being too tenacious of a point, becaufe you brought it forward, may be only feeding felf. Be quite eafy, if a majority decide againft you.

5. Ufe no craft or guile to gain any point. Genuine fimplicity will always fupport itfelf. But there is no need always to fay all you know or think.

6. Beware of too much confidence in your own abilities; and never defpife an opponent.

7. Avoid all lightnefs of fpirit, even what would be innocent any where elfe.————Thou, God, feeft me.

The appointment of *the times* for holding the *yearly* conferences muft neceffarily be invefted in the bifhops, otherwife they cannot poffibly form their plans for travelling through the continent, fo that they may be enabled to attend each of the conferences. But the right of fixing *the places* refts with the conferences.

We cannot omit noticing, before we conclude this fection, the ftrict examination which the characters of the preachers pafs through, in the yearly conferences. When that eminent faint of God, and great writer, John Fletcher, was once prefent, in the Britifh conference, at the examination of the characters, he feemed aftonifhed, and expreffed his furprize and approbation in very ftrong terms. The examination is equally ftrict in all the conferences throughout the connection. And we know of no church where the purity of the morals, the orthodoxy of the doctrines, and the ufefulnefs of the lives and labours of the minifters (for all thefe are included in the examination) are more ftrictly attended to than in ours.

In refpect to the divifion of the continent, for the purpofe of holding the yearly conferences, we may obferve, that for feveral years the annual conferences were very fmall, confifting only of the preachers of a fingle dictrict, or of two or three very fmall ones. This was attended with many inconveniences.————1. There were but few of the fenior preachers, whofe years and experience had matured their judgments, who could be prefent at any one conference. 2. The conferences wanted that dignity which every religious fynod fhould poffefs, and which always accompanies a *large* affembly of Gofpel minifters. 3. The itinerant plan was exceedingly cramped, from the difficulty of removing preachers from one diftrict to another. All thefe inconveniences will we truft, be removed on the prefent plan; and at the fame time the conferences are fo arranged, tha tall the members, refpectively, may attend with little difficulty.

To all which may be added, that the active, zealous, unmarried preachers, may move on a larger fcale, and preach the ever-bleffed gofpel far more extenfively through the fixteen ftates, and other parts of the continent; whilft the married preachers, whofe circumftances require them, in many inftances, to be more located than the fingle men, will have a confiderable field of action opened to them; and alfo the bifhops will be able to attend the conferences with greater eafe, and without injury to their health.

The regulation concerning thofe who are to attend the conferences, is made, that our focieties and congregations may be fupplied with preaching during the conferences. We would, therefore, wifh to have a few of the travelling preachers among our dear flocks at thofe times. But as we defire to make the conferences as refpectable and weighty as poffible, we can fpare none at thofe important feafons, except the preachers upon trial. They, alfo, will be abfent from the yearly conferences only for one year, as they muft be prefent on the fecond to be admitted into full connection.

SECTION IV.

Of the Election and Confecration of Bifhops, and of their Duty.

Queft. 1. HOW is a bifhop to be conftituted in future?

Anfw. By the election of the general conference, and the laying on of the hands of three bifhops, or at leaft of one bifhop and two elders.

Queft 2. If by death, expulfion, or otherwife, there * be no bifhop remaining in our church, what fhall we do?

Anfw. The general conference fhall elect a bifhop; and the elders, or any three of them, who fhall be appointed by the general conference for that purpofe, fhall ordain him according to our office of ordination.

Queft. 3. What is the bifhop's duty?

Anfw. 1. To prefide in our conferences.

2. To fix the appointments of the preachers for the feveral circuits.

3. In the intervals of the conferences, to change, receive, or fufpend preachers, as neceffity may require.

4. To travel through the connection at large.

5. To overfee the fpiritual and temporal bufinefs of the focieties.

6. To ordain bifhops, elders, and deacons.

Queft. 4. To whom is the bifhop amenable for his conduct?

Anfw. To the general conference, who have power to expel him for improper conduct, if they fee it neceffary.

Queft. 5. What provifion fhall be made for the trial of an immoral bifhop, in the interval of the general conference?

Anfw. If a bifhop be guilty of immorality, three travelling elders fhall call upon him, and examine him on the fubject; and if the three elders verily believe that the bifhop is guilty of the crime, they fhall call to their aid two prefiding elders from two diftricts in the neighbourhood of that were the crime was committed, each of which prefiding elders fhall bring with him two elders, or an elder and a deacon. The above mentioned nine perfons fhall form a conference, to examine into the charge brought againft the bifhop: and if two thirds of them verily believe him to be guilty of the crime laid to his charge, they fhall have authority to fufpend the bifhop till the enfuing general conference, and the diftricts fhall be regulated in the mean time as is provided in the cafe of the death of a bifhop.

Queft. 6. If the bifhop ceafe from travelling at large among the people, fhall he ftill exercife his office among us in any degree?

Anfw. If he ceafe from travelling without the confent of the general conference, he fhall not hereafter exercife any minifterial function whatfoever in our church.

N. B. The bifhops have obtained liberty, by the fuffrages of the conference, to ordain local preachers to the office of deacons, provided they obtain a teftimonial from the fociety to which they belong, and from the ftewards of the circuit, figned alfo by three elders, three deacons, and three travelling preachers.

N O T E S.

In confidering the prefent fubject, we muft obferve, that nothing has been introduced into Methodifm by the prefent epifcopal form of government, which was not before fully exercifed by Mr. Wefley. He prefided in the conferences; fixed the appointments of the preachers for their feveral circuits; changed, received, or fufpended preachers, wherever he judged that neceffity required it; travelled through the European connection at large; fuperintended the fpiritual and temporal bufinefs; and confecrated two bifhops, Thomas Coke and Alexander Mather, one before the prefent epifcopal plan took place in America, and the other afterwards, befides ordaining elders and deacons. But the authority of Mr. Wefley and that of the bifhops in America differ in the following important points:

1. Mr. Wefley was the patron of all the Methodift pulpits in Great Britain and Ireland *for life*, the fole right of nomination being invefted in him by all the deeds of fettlement, which gave him exceeding great power. But the bifhops in America poffefs no fuch power: The property of the preaching-houfes is invefted in the truftees; and the right of nomination to the pulpits, in the general conference—and in fuch as the general conference fhall, from time to time, appoint. This divifion of power in favour of the general conference was abfolutely neceffary. Without it the itinerant plan could not exift for any long continuance. The truftees would probably, in many inftances, from their *located* fituation, infift upon having their favourite preachers ftationed in their circuits, or endeavour to prevail on the preachers themfelves to *locate* among them, or choofe fome other fettled minifter for their chapels. In other cafes, the truftees of preaching-houfes *in different circuits* would probably infift upon having the *fame* popular or favourite preachers.* Here, then,

---

* *We muft repeat nearly the fame obfervations concerning truftees, which we have in our notes on the laft fection, concerning the fending of delegates to our conferences. We have a great refpect for our truftees. We confider them as men, to whom the connection is greatly obliged. They fill up an important province in our church, and have a claim to a high rank among us. Humanly fpeaking, the work could not be carried on without them to any extent in the cities and towns. Their refponfibility for the debts of our buildings, and the difinterestednefs which muft neceffarily influence them when they make themfelves refponfible, lay our focieties under very great obligations. We both love and honour them. But ftill they are located men. They cannot be expected to act impartially for the whole. They will think it their duty, and perhaps it is their duty, to prefer the interefts of their own congregations to any other. We fhould probably act in the fame manner in their fituation.*

lies the grand difference between Mr. Wesley's authority, in the present instance, and that of our American bishops. The former, as (under God) the father of the connection, was allowed to have the *sole, legal, independent* nomination of preachers to all the chapels: the latter are *entirely dependent* on the general conference.

* But why, may it be asked, does the general conference lodge the power of stationing the preachers in the episcopacy? We answer, On account of their entire confidence in it. If ever, through improper conduct, it loses that confidence in any considerable degree, the general conference will, upon evidence given, in a proportionable degree, take from it this branch of its authority. But if ever it evidently betrays a spirit of tyranny or partiality, and *this* can be proved before the general conference, the whole will be taken from it: and we pray God, that in such case the power may be invested in other hands! And alas! who would envy any one the power? There is no situation in which a bishop can be placed, no branch of duty he can possibly exercise, so delicate, or which so exposes him to the jealousies not only of false but of true brethren, as this. The removal of preachers from district to district and from circuit to circuit, very nearly concerns them, and touches their tenderest feelings: and it requires no small portion of grace for a preacher to be *perfectly* contented with his appointment, when he is stationed in a circuit, where the societies are small, the rides long, and the fare coarse. Any one, therefore, may easily see, from the nature of man, that though the bishop has to deal with some of the best of men, he will sometimes raise himself opposers, who, by rather over-rating their own abilities, may judge him to be partial in respect to their appointments: and these circumstances would weigh down his mind to such a degree, as those who are not well acquainted with the difficulties which necessarily accompany public and important stations among mankind, can hardly conceive.

May we not add a few observations concerning the high expediency, if not necessity, of the present plan. How could an itinerant ministry be preserved through this extensive continent, if the yearly conferences were to station the preachers? They would, of course, be taken up with the *sole* consideration of the spiritual and temporal interests of *that part* of the connection, the direction of which was intrusted to them. The necessary consequence of this mode of proceeding would probably, in less than an age, be *the division of the body* and *the independence* of each yearly conference. The conferences would be more and more estranged from each other for want of a mutual exchange of preachers: and *that grand spring, the union of the body at large,* by which, under divine grace, the work is more and more extended through this vaſt country, would be gradually weakened, till at laſt it might be entirely deſtroyed. The connection would no more be enabled to ſend miſſionaries to the weſtern ſtates and territories, in proportion to their rapid population. The grand circulation of miniſters would be at an end, and a mortal ſtab given to the itinerant plan. The ſurplus of preachers in one conference could not be drawn out to ſupply the deficiencies of others, through declenſions, locations, deaths, &c. and the revivals in one part of the continent could not be rendered beneficial to the others. *Our grand plan,* in all its parts, leads to an *itinerant* miniſtry. Our biſhops are *travelling* biſhops. All the different orders which compoſe our conferences are employed in the *travelling line;* and our local preachers are, *in ſome degree,* travelling preachers. Every thing is kept moving as far as poſſible; and we will be bold to ſay, that, next to the grace of God, there is nothing *like this* for keeping the whole body alive from the centre to the circumference, and for the continual extenſion of that circumference on every hand. And we verily believe, that, if our epiſcopacy ſhould, at any time, through tyrannical or immoral conduct, come under the ſevere cenſure of the general conference, the members thereof would ſee it highly for the glory of God to preſerve the preſent form, and *only* to change the men.

2. Mr. Weſley, as the venerable founder (under God) of the whole Methodiſt ſociety, governed without any reſponſibility whatever; and the univerſal reſpect and veneration of both the preachers and people for him, made them cheerfully ſubmit to this: nor was there ever, perhaps, a mere human being who uſed ſo much power better, or with a purer eye to the Redeemer's glory, than that bleſſed man of God. But the American biſhops are as reſponſible as any of the preachers. They are *perfectly ſubject* to the general conference. They are indeed conſcious that the conference would neither degrade nor cenſure them, unleſs they deſerved it. They have, on the one hand, the fulleſt confidence in their brethren; and, on the other, eſteem the confidence which their brethren place in them, as the higheſt earthly honour they can receive.

But this is not all. They are ſubject to be tried by ſeven elders and two deacons, as preſcribed above, for any immorality, or ſuppoſed immorality; and may be ſuſpended by two-thirds of theſe, not only from all public offices, but even from being private members of the ſociety, till the enſuing general conference. This mode ſubjects the biſhops to a trial before a court of judicature, conſiderably inferior to that of a yearly conference. For there is not one of the yearly conferences which will not, proba bly, be attended by more presiding elders, elders, and deacons, than the conference which is authorized to try a bishop, the yearly conferences consisting of from thirty to sixty members. And we can, without scruple, assert, that there are no bishops of any other episcopal church upon earth, who are subject to so strict a trial as the bishops of the Methodist episcopal church in America. We trust, they will never *need* to be influenced by motives drawn from the fear of temporal or ecclesiastical punishments, in order to keep *from vice:* But if they do, may the rod which hangs over them have its due effect; or may they be expelled the church, as " salt which hath lost its favour, and is thenceforth good for nothing but to be cast out, and trodden under foot of men !"

3. Mr. Wesley had the entire management of all the conference-funds and the produce of the books. It is true, he expended all upon the work of God, and for charitable purposes; and rather than appropriate the least of it to his own use, refused, even when he was about seventy years of age, to travel in a carriage, till his friends in London and Bristol entered into a private subscription for the extraordinary expense. That great man of God might have heaped up thousands upon thousands, if he had been so inclined; and yet he died worth nothing but a little pocket money, the horses and the carriage in which he travelled, and the clothes he wore. But our American bishops have no probability of being rich. For not a cent of the public money is at their disposal: the conferences have the entire direction of the whole. Their salary is sixty-four dollars a year; and their travelling expenses are also defrayed. And with this salary they are to travel about six thousand miles a year, " in much patience," and sometimes " in afflictions, in necessities, in distresses, in labours, in watchings, in fastings," through " honour and dishonour, evil report and good report: as deceivers, and yet true; as unknown, and yet well known; as dying, and, behold," they " live; as chastened, and not killed; as sorrowful, yet alway rejoicing; as poor, yet making many rich; as having nothing, and yet possessing all things;" and, we trust, they can each of them through grace say, in their small measure, with the great apostle, that " they are determined not to know any thing, save Jesus Christ, and him crucified; yea, doubtless, and count all things but loss for the excellency of the knowledge of Christ Jesus their Lord: for whom they have suffered the loss of all things, and do count them but dung, that they may win Christ."

We have drawn this comparison between our venerable father and the American bishops, to shew to the world that they possess not, and, we may add, they aim not to possess, that power which he exercised and had a right to exercise, as the father of the connection: that, on the contrary, they are perfectly de pendent; that their power, their ufefulnefs, themfelves, are entirely at the mercy of the general conference, and, on the charge of immorality, at the mercy of two-thirds of the little conference of nine.

To thefe obfervations we may add, 1. That a branch of the epifcopal office, which, in every epifcopal church upon earth, fince the firft introduction of chriftianity, has been confidered as effential to it, namely, *the power of ordination*, is *fingularly* limited in our bifhops. For they not only have no power to ordain *a perfon for the epifcopal office* till he be firft elected by the *general* conference, but they poffefs no authority to ordain *an elder or a travelling deacon*, till he be firft elected by a *yearly* conference; or a local deacon, till he obtain a teftimonial, fignifying the approbation of the fociety to which he belongs, counterfigned by the general ftewards of the circuit, three elders, three deacons, and three travelling preachers. They are, therefore, not under the temptation of ordaining through intereft, affection, or any other improper motive; becaufe it is not in their power fo to do. They have, indeed, authority to fufpend the ordination of an elected perfon, becaufe they are anfwerable *to God* for the abufe of their office, and the command of the apoftle, " Lay hands fuddenly on no man," is abfolute: and, we truft, where confcience was really concerned, and they had *fufficient reafon* to exercife their power of fufpenfion, they would do it, even to the lofs of the efteem of their brethren, which is more dear to them than life; yea, even to the lofs of their ufefulnefs in the church, which is more precious to them than all things here below. But every one muft be immediately fenfible, how cautious they will neceffarily be, as men of wifdom, in the exercife of this fufpending power. For unlefs they had fuch weighty reafons for the exercife of it, as would give fome degree of fatisfaction to the conference which had made the election, they would throw themfelves into difficulties, out of which they would not be able to extricate themfelves, but by the meekeft and wifeft conduct, and by reparation to the injured perfon.

2. The bifhops are obliged to travel, till the general conference pronounces them worn-out or fuperannuated: for that certainly is the meaning of the anfwer to the 6th queftion of this fection. What a reftriction! Where is the like in any other epifcopal church? It would be a difgrace to our epifcopacy, to have bifhops fettled on their plantations here and there, evidencing to all the world, that inftead of breathing the fpirit of their office, they could, without remorfe, *lay down their crown*, and bury the moft important talents God has given to men! We would rather choofe that our epifcopacy fhould be blotted out from the face of the earth, than be fpotted with fuch difgraceful conduct! All the epifcopal churches in the world are confcious of the dig-

ﺎity of the epifcopal office. The greateſt part of them endeavour to preſerve this dignity by large ſalaries, ſplendid dreſſes,
and other appendages of pomp and ſplendour. But if an epiſcopacy has neither the dignity which ariſes from theſe worldly trap-
pings, nor that infinitely ſuperior dignity which is the attendant
of labour, of ſuffering and enduring hardſhip for the cauſe of
Chriſt, and of a venerable old age, the concluding ſcene of a
life, devoted to the ſervice of God, it inſtantly becomes the diſgrace of a church and the juſt ridicule of the world !

Some may think, that the mode of travelling, which the biſhops are obliged to purſue, is attended with little difficulty, and
much pleaſure. Much pleaſure they certainly do experience,
becauſe they know that they move in the will of God, and that
the-Lord is pleaſed to own their feeble labours. But if to travel
through the heat and the cold, the rain and the ſnow, the ſwamps
and the rivers, over the mountains and through the wilderneſs,
lying for nights together on the bare ground and in log-houſes,
open to the wind on every ſide, fulfilling their appointments,
as far as poſſible, whatever be the hinderance,——if theſe be little
difficulties, then our biſhops have but little to endure.

We have already quoted ſo many texts of Scripture in defence
of epiſcopacy and the itinerant plan, that we need only refer
our reader to the notes on the 1ſt and 3d ſections. The whole
tenor of St. Paul's epiſtles to Timothy and Titus clearly evi-
dences, that *they* were inveſted, on the whole, with abundantly
more power than our biſhops : nor does it appear that *they* were
reſponſible to any but God and the apoſtle. The texts quoted in
the notes on the 3d ſection, in defence of the itinerant plan, we
would particularly recommend to the reader's attention ; as we
muſt inſiſt upon it, that *the general itinerancy* would not probably
exiſt for any length of time on this extenſive continent, if the
biſhops were not inveſted with that authority which they now
poſſeſs. They alone travel through the whole connection, and,
therefore, have ſuch a view of the whole, as no yearly conference
can poſſibly have.

One biſhop, with the elders preſent, may conſecrate a biſhop
who has been previouſly elected by the general conference. This
is agreeable to the Scriptures. We read, 2 Tim. i. 6. " I put
thee in remembrance, that thou ſtir up *the gift* of God *which is in
thee,* by the putting on of *my* hands :" here we have the impoſition of the hands of the apoſtle. Again, we read, 1 Tim. iv.
14. " Neglect not *the gift that is in thee,* which was given thee by
prophecy, with the laying on of the hands of *the preſbytery :*"
here we have the laying on of the hands of *the elders.* And by
comparing both paſſages, it is evident that the impoſition of
hands was, both in reſpect to the apoſtle and the elders, *for the
ſame gift.* Nor is the idea, that three biſhops are neceſſary to

consecrate a bishop, grounded on any authority whatever, drawn from the Scriptures, or the practice of the apostolic age.

The authority given to, or rather declared to exist in, the general conference, that in case there shall be no bishop remaining in the church, they shall elect a bishop, and authorize the elders to consecrate him, will not admit of an objection, except on the supposition that the fable of an uninterrupted apostolic succession be allowed to be true. St. Jerome, who was as strong an advocate for episcopacy as perhaps any in the primitive church, informs us, that in the church of Alexandria (which was, in ancient times, one of the most respectable of the churches) the college of presbyters not only elected a bishop, on the decease of the former, but consecrated him by the imposition of their own hands *solely*, from the time of St. Mark, their first bishop, to the time of Dionysius, which was a space of about two hundred years: and the college of presbyters in ancient times answered to our general conference.

SECTION V.

Of the Presiding Elders, and of their Duty.

Quest. 1. BY whom are the presiding elders to be chosen?

Answ. By the bishop.

Quest. 2. What are the duties of a presiding elder?

Answ. 1. To travel through his appointed district.

2. In the absence of a bishop, to take charge of all the elders, deacons, travelling and local preachers, and exhorters in his district.

3. To change, receive, or suspend preachers in his district during the intervals of the conferences, and in the absence of the bishop.

4. In the absence of a bishop, to preside in the conference.

5. To be present, as far as practicable, at all the quarterly meetings: and to call together at each quarterly meeting all the travelling and local preachers, exhorters, stewards, and leaders of the circuit, to hear complaints, and to receive appeals.

6. To oversee the spiritual and temporal business of the societies in his district.

7. To take care that every part of our difcipline be enforced in his diftrict.

8. To attend the bifhop when prefent in his diftrict; and to give him when abfent all neceffary information, by letter, of the ftate of his diftrict.

Queft. 3. By whom are the prefiding elders to be ftationed and changed?

Anfw. By the bifhop.

Queft. 4. How long may the bifhop allow an elder to prefide in the fame diftrict?

Anfw. For any term not exceeding four years fucceffively.

Queft. 5. How fhall the prefiding elders be fupported?

Anfw. If there be a furplus of the public money, in one or more circuits in his diftrict, he fhall receive fuch furplus, provided he do not receive more than his annual falary. In cafe of a deficiency in his falary, after fuch furplus is paid him, or if there be no furplus, he fhall fhare with the preachers of his diftrict, in proportion with what they have refpectively received, fo that he receive no more than the amount of his falary upon the whole.

N O T E S.

We have already fhewn by Scripture and argument, in our annotations on the twenty-fecond article of religion, that every church muft neceffarily be invefted with the authority of ordaining rites and ceremonies in refpect to all *uneffential* matters, that is, refpecting every thing which is not contrary to the Word of God. The fame arguments will hold with exactly equal force, in refpect to the powers which any church may think proper to inveft in its public officers. The New Teftament is almoft entirely filent about all fuch things, as they depend fo much on the circumftances of the churches, and the cuftoms and manners of different nations.

However, there are fome fundamental principles and general data* afforded us in the New Teftament (to which alone we can have recourfe on this fubject) on which we may build ac-

---

* *Points which are granted, and perfectly evident.*

cording to the circumstances in which we are placed. In the present instance, we have texts which indubitably prove that there were *presiding*, *superintending*, or *ruling* elders (the words bear the same meaning) in the church in the apostolic age, and that this office is fully warranted by the Word of God. Thus we read in Acts xx. 17—28. " From Miletus he [Paul] sent to Ephesus, and called the *elders* of the church. And, when they were come to him, he said unto them,——Take heed—unto yourselves, and to all the flock over the which the Holy Ghost hath made you OVERSEERS," &c. The word *overseers* in this place signifies, as it does every where, persons who had a considerable degree of superintendency over the work in which they were employed. Again, in 1 Tim. v. 17, we read, " Let the elders that *rule well* be counted worthy of double honour," &c. Every person who understands the original or even our own language, well knows that there is no difference at all in the sense between the words *presiding* and *ruling*, and that one might be substituted for the other. Once more, St. Peter, in his 1st Epistle, v. 1—3, observes " The *elders* which are among you, I exhort,——Feed the flock of God which is among you, taking the *oversight* thereof, not by constraint, but willingly; not for filthy lucre, but of a ready mind, neither as being *lords* over God's heritage, but being ensamples to the flock." Here we also see, that there were *elders*, who had the *oversight* or *superintendence* (for so the word signifies) of *the flock of God:* nor could St. Peter have cautioned these against *lording it* over God's heritage, if they had not had some authority in the church, which they might abuse. And we must desire our readers to remember, that we are not speaking here or in our observations concerning the episcopacy, of the powers which the apostles themselves exercised, but of those with which they invested others, or which the churches conferred upon their ministers respectively.

On the principles or data above-mentioned, all the episcopal churches in the world have, in some measure, formed their church-government. And we believe we can venture to assert, that there never has been an episcopal church of any great extent, which has not had *ruling* or *presiding* elders, either expressly *by name* as in the apostolic churches, or otherwise *in effect*. On this account it is, that all the modern episcopal churches have had their *presiding* or *ruling* elders under the names of grand vicars, archdeacons, rural deans, &c. The Moravians have presiding elders, who are invested with very considerable authority, though we believe they are simply termed elders. And we beg leave to repeat, that we are confident, we could, if need were, shew that all the episcopal churches ancient and modern, *of any great extent*, have had an order or set of ministers corresponding, more or lefs, to our prefiding or ruling elders, all of whom were, more or lefs, invefted with the fuperintendence of other mi-nifters.

Mr. Wefley informs us in his works, that the whole plan of Methodifm was introduced, ftep by ftep, by the interference and openings of divine Providence. This was the cafe in the prefent inftance. When Mr. Wefley drew up a plan of government for our church in America, he defired that no more elders fhould be ordained in the firft inftance than were abfolutely neceffary, and that the work on the continent fhould be divided between them, in refpect to the duties of their office. The general conference accordingly elected twelve elders for the above purpofes. Bifhop Afbury and the diftrict conferences afterwards found that this order of men was fo neceffary, that they agreed to enlarge the number, and give them *the name* by which they are at prefent called, and which is perfectly fcriptural, though not *the word* ufed in our tranflation: and this proceeding afterwards received the approbation of Mr. Wefley.

In 1792 the general conference, equally confcious of the ne-ceffity of having fuch an office among us, not only confirmed every thing that bifhop Afbury and the diftrict conferences had done, but alfo drew up or agreed to the prefent fection for the explanation of the nature and duties of the office. The confer-ence clearly faw that the bifhops wanted affiftants; that it was impoffible for one or two bifhops fo to fuperintend the vaft work on this continent as to keep every thing in order in the intervals of the conference, without other official men to act under them and affift them : and as thefe would be only the agents of the bifhops in every refpect, the authority of appointing them, and of changing them, ought, from the nature of things, to be in the epifcopacy. If the prefiding or ruling elders were not men in whom the bifhops could fully confide, or on the lofs of confi-dence, could exchange for others, the utmoft confufion would enfue. This alfo renders the authority invefted in the bifhops of fixing the extent of each diftrict, highly expedient. They muft be fuppofed to be the beft judges of the abilities of the prefiding elders whom they themfelves choofe : and it is a grand part of their duty, to make the diftricts and the talents of the prefiding elders who act for them, fuit and agree with each other, as far as poffible : for it cannot be expected, that a fufficient number of them can at any time be found, *of equal talents*, and, there-fore, the extent of their field of action muft be proportioned to their gifts.

From all that has been advanced, and from thofe other ideas which will prefent themfelves to the reader's mind on this fub-

* ject, it will appear that the presiding elders must, of course, be appointed, directed, and changed by the episcopacy. And yet their power is so considerable, that it would by no means be sufficient for them to be responsible to the bishops *only* for their conduct in their office. They are as responsible in this respect, and in every other, to the *yearly* conference to which they belong, as any other preacher; and may be censured, suspended, or expelled from the connection, if the conference see it proper: nor have the bishops any authority to over-rule, suspend, or meliorate in any degree, the censures, suspensions, or expulsions of the conference.

Many and great are the advantages arising from this institution. 1. It is a great help and blessing to the quarterly meetings respectively, through the connection, to have a man at their head, who is experienced not only in the ways of God, but in men and manners, and in all things appertaining to the order of our church. Appeals may be brought before the quarterly meeting from the judgment of the preacher who has the oversight of the circuit, who certainly would not be, in such cases, so proper to preside as the ruling elder. Nor would any local preacher, leader, or steward be a suitable president of the meeting, as his parent, his child, his brother, sister, or friend, might be more or less interested in the appeals which came before him: besides, his *local* situation would lead him almost unavoidably to *prejudge* the case, and, perhaps, to enter warmly into the interests of one or other of the parties, previously to the appeal. It is, therefore, indisputably evident, that the *ruling elder* is most likely to be impartial, and, consequently, the most proper person to *preside*.

2. Another advantage of this office arises from the necessity of changing preachers from circuit to circuit in the intervals of the yearly conferences. Many of the preachers are young in years and gifts; and this must always be the case, more or less, or a fresh supply of travelling preachers in proportion to the necessities of the work could not be procured. These young men, in general, are exceedingly zealous. Their grand *forte* is to awaken souls; and in this view they are highly necessary for the spreading of the gospel. But for some time their gifts cannot be expected to be *various;* and, therefore, half a year at a time, or sometimes even a quarter, may be sufficient for them to labour in one circuit: to change them, therefore, from circuit to circuit, in the intervals of the yearly conferences, is highly necessary in many instances. Again, the preachers themselves, for family-reasons or on other accounts, may desire, and have reason to expect, a change. But who can make it in the absence of the bishops, unless there be a presiding elder appointed for the district? A recent instance proves the justice of this remark. A large district was lately without a presiding elder for a year.

Many of the preachers, sensible of the necessity of a change in the course of the year, met together, and settled every preliminary for the purpose. Accordingly, when the time fixed upon for the change arrived, several of them came to their new appointments according to agreement, but, behold, the others had changed their minds, and the former were obliged to return to their old circuits, feeling not a little disgrace on account of their treatment. And this would be continually the case, and all would be confusion, *if there were no persons invested with the powers of ruling elders, by whatever name they might be called;* as it would be impossible for the bishops to be present every where, and enter *into the details* of all the circuits.

3. Who is able properly to supply the vacancies in circuits on *the deaths* of preachers, or on *their withdrawing* from the travelling connection? Who can have a thorough knowledge of the state of the district, and of its resources for the filling up such vacancies, except the presiding elder who travels through the whole district? And shall circuits be often neglected for months together, and the flocks, during those times, be, more or less, without shepherds, and many of them, perhaps, perish for want of food, merely that one of the most scriptural and useful offices among us may be abolished? Shall we not rather support it, notwithstanding every thing which may be subtilly urged by our enemies under the cry of tyranny, which is the common cry of restless spirits even against the best governments, in order that they may throw every thing into confusion, and then ride in the whirlwind and direct the storm.

4. When a bishop visits a district, he ought to have one to accompany him, in whom he can fully confide; one, who can inform him of the whole work in a complete and comprehensive view; and, therefore, one who has travelled *through the whole,* and, by being present at all the quarterly meetings, can give all the information, concerning every circuit in particular, and the district in general, which the bishop can desire. Nor is the advantage small that the bishops, when at the greatest distance, may receive from the presiding elders a full account of their respective districts, and may thereby be continually in possession of a more comprehensive knowledge of the whole work, than they could possibly procure by any other means.

5. The only branch of the presiding elder's office, the importance and usefulness of which is not so obvious to some persons, but which is, at the same time, perhaps the most expedient of all, is *the suspending power,* for the preservation of *the purity* of our ministry, and that our people may never be burdened with preachers of *insufficient* gifts. Here we must not forget, that the presiding elder acts as agent to the bishops; and that the bishops are, the greatest part of their time, at a vast distance from him

he muft, therefore, exercife epifcopal authority (ordination excepted) or he cannot act as their agent. All power may be abufed. The only way which can be devifed to prevent the abufe of it, if we will have a good and effective government, is to make the executive governors completely refponfible, and their refponfibility within the reach of the aggrieved. And, in the prefent inftance, not only the general conference may expel the prefiding elder—not only the epifcopacy may fufpend him from the exercife of his office—but the yearly conference may alfo impeach him, try him, and expel him: and fuch a threefold guard muft be allowed, by every candid mind, to be as full a check to the abufe of his power, as, perhaps, human wifdom can devife.

But is it not ftrange, that any of *the people* fhould complain either of *this* or of the *epifcopal* office? *Thefe offices* in the church are peculiarly defigned to meliorate the feverity of chriftian difcipline, as far as they refpect *the people*. In them the people have a refuge, an afylum to which they may fly upon all occafions. To them they may appeal, and before them they may lay all their complaints and grievances. The perfons who bear thefe offices are their fathers in the gofpel, ever open of accefs, ever ready to relieve them under every oppreffion. And we believe we can venture to affert, that the people have never had even a *plaufible* pretence to complain of the authority either of the bifhops or the prefiding elders.

6. We may add, as was juft hinted above, that the bifhops ought not to enter into *fmall details*. It is not their calling. To felect the proper men who are to act as their agents—to preferve in order and in motion the wheels of the vaft machine—to keep a conftant and watchful eye upon the whole—and to *think deeply* for the general good——form their peculiar and important avocation. All of which fhews the neceffity of the office now under confideration.

The objection brought by fome, that many of the moft ufeful preachers are taken out of the circuits for this purpofe, whofe preaching-talents are thereby loft to the connection, will by no means bear examination. Even if this was the cafe, the vaft advantage arifing from a complete and effective fuperintendence of the work would, we believe, far over-balance this confideration. But the objection is deftitute of weight. Their preaching abilities are, we believe, abundantly more ufeful. Though all the preachers of matured talents and experience cannot be employed as prefiding elders, yet thofe who are employed as fuch, generally anfwer this character. They are qualified to build up believers on their moft holy faith, and to remove fcruples and anfwer cafes of confcience, more than the younger preachers in general. In many circuits, fome parts of the fociety might fuffer much in refpect to the divine life, for want of thofe gifts peculiarly neceffary for *them*, were it not for this additional help; whilſt the junction of the talents of the preſiding elder with thoſe of the circuit-preachers will, in general, make the whole complete. And as the preſiding elder is, or ought to be, always preſent at the quarterly meetings, he will have opportunities of delivering his whole mind to a very conſiderable part of the people : nor is there any reaſonable ground to fear that he will ever wear out his talents, if we conſider the extent of a diſtrict, and the obligation the epiſcopacy is under to remove him, at fartheſt, on the expiration of four years.

To theſe obſervations we may add, that the calling of diſtrict-conferences, on the immorality of travelling preachers, on their deaths, the neceſſity of removals, &c. would be attended with the moſt pernicious conſequences to the circuits on this vaſt continent, where the diſtricts are ſo large, and the abſence of the preachers would be neceſſarily ſo long upon every ſuch occaſion. And we will venture to aſſert, that if any effective government ought to exiſt at all in the connection, during the intervals of the yearly and general conferences, there is *no alternative* between the authority of the biſhops and their agents, the preſiding elders, on the one hand, and the holding of diſtrict conferences on the other hand.

We will conclude our notes on this ſection with obſerving, that there is no ground to believe that the work of God has been injured, or the numbers of the ſociety diminiſhed, by the inſtitution of this order, but juſt the contrary. In the year 1784, when the preſiding elderſhip did, *in fact*, though not in *name*, commence, there were about 14000 in ſociety on this continent; and *now* the numbers amount to upwards of 56000 : ſo that the ſociety is, at preſent, four times as large as it was twelve or thirteen years ago. We do not believe that the office now under conſideration was *the principal cauſe* of this great revival, but the Spirit and grace of God, and the conſequent zeal of the preachers in general. Yet we have no doubt, but the full organization of our body, and giving to the whole a complete and effective executive government, of which the preſiding elderſhip makes a very capital branch, has, under God, been a grand means of preſerving the peace and union of our connection and the purity of our miniſtry, and, therefore, *in its conſequences*, has been *a chief inſtrument*, under the grace of God, of this great revival.

SECTION VI.

Of the Election and Ordination of Travelling Elders, and of their Duty.

Queſt. 1. HOW is an *Elder* conſtituted?
 Anſw. By the election of a majority of the yearly conference, and by the laying on of the hands of a biſhop, and of the elders that are preſent.

Queſt. 2. What is the duty of a travelling elder?

Anſw. 1. To adminiſter baptiſm and the Lord's ſupper, and to perform the office of matrimony, and all parts of divine worſhip.

2. To do all the duties of a travelling preacher.

N. B. No elder that ceaſes to travel, without the conſent of the yearly conference, certified under the hand of the preſident of the conference, ſhall on any account exerciſe the peculiar functions of his office amongſt us.

N O T E S.

Acts xiv. 23. When they [Paul and Barnabas] had *ordained* them *elders* in every church,——they commended them to the Lord. Titus i. 5. For this cauſe left I thee in Crete, that thou ſhouldeſt—*ordain elders* in every city. See alſo Acts xv. 2, 4, 6, 22, 23. xvi. 4. 1 Tim. v. 1, 17, 19. Jam. v. 14.

We need not enlarge upon the neceſſity of an office, which every organized chriſtian church in the world, in all ages, has adopted. We would only remark, that the reſtriction reſpecting the elders' withdrawing themſelves from the travelling line, without the conſent of the yearly conference, ſhews the confirmed regard our church has for *the itinerant plan*, and its determination to ſupport it by every method in its power, confiſtent with juſtice and truth. And no elder has a right to complain, as he cannot but be previouſly acquainted with the conditions on which he accepts of ordination.

SECTION VII.

Of the Election and Ordination of Travelling Deacons, and of their Duty.

Queſt. 1. HOW is a *travelling* deacon conſtituted? *Anſw.* By the election of the majority of the yearly conference, and the laying on of the hands of a biſhop.

Queſt. 2. What is the duty of a *travelling deacon?*

Anſw. 1. To baptize, and perform the office of matrimony, in the abſence of the elder.

2. To aſſiſt the elder in adminiſtering the Lord's ſupper.

3. To do all the duties of a travelling preacher.

Queſt. 3. What ſhall be the time of probation of a travelling deacon for the office of an elder.

Anſw. Every travelling deacon ſhall exerciſe that office for two years, before he be eligible to the office of an elder; except in the caſe of miſſions, when the yearly conferences ſhall have authority to elect for the elders office ſooner, if they judge it expedient.

N. B. No deacon who ceaſes to travel without the conſent of the yearly conference, certified under the hand of the preſident of the conference, ſhall on any account exerciſe the peculiar functions of his office.

N O T E S.

Acts vi. 1—6. " In thoſe days, when the number of the diſciples was multiplied, there aroſe a murmuring of the Grecians againſt the Hebrews, becauſe their widows were neglected in the daily miniſtration. Then *the twelve* called the multitude of the diſciples unto them, and ſaid, It is not reaſon that *we* ſhould leave the word of God and ſerve tables. Wherefore, brethren, look ye out among you ſeven men of honeſt report, full of the Holy Ghoſt and wiſdom, whom we may appoint over this buſineſs. But *we* will give ourſelves continually to prayer, and to the miniſtry of the word. And the ſaying pleaſed the whole multitude : and they choſe Stephen, a man full of faith and of the

Holy Ghoſt, and Philip, and Prochorus, and Nicanor, and Timon, and Parmenas, and Nicolas a proſelyte of Antioch, whom they ſet before the Apoſtles: and, when they had prayed, they laid their hands on them."

We have in the paſſage above quoted, an account of the inſtitution of the order of deacons; from which it appears, 1. That the primary deſign of the order was, that the widows, the aged, the infirm, &c. ſhould be ſufficiently provided for. For we are not to ſuppoſe, that *the widows* only *in this reſpect* were the objects of their care, but all the infirm, and all whoſe temporal ſituation required extraordinary attention.

2. Nor can we with any propriety imagine, that the circle of action of men *like theſe*, who were FULL OF THE HOLY GHOST AND WISDOM, was *confined* to ſuch menial offices. They were men, we doubt not, choſen out of the preachers of the goſpel, who uſed *the gifts of the Holy Ghoſt* and *the wiſdom they had received from above*, not ſo much for miniſtring to the temporal wants of the widows, &c. as to the ſpiritual wants of immortal ſouls, for which principally ſuch invaluable bleſſings were beſtowed upon them. Accordingly we are informed, Acts vi. 8. that " Stephen [the firſt of the deacons] *full of faith and* POWER, did great wonders and miracles among the people." He had alſo the high honour of being the firſt chriſtian martyr, by being ſtoned to death " for the witneſs of Jeſus and for the word of God."* Again, we read of Philip, another of thoſe deacons, who was commanded by an angel of the Lord to " go toward the ſouth," to preach the goſpel to " an eunuch of great authority under Candace, queen of the Ethiopians, who had the charge of all her treaſure, and had come to Jeruſalem for to worſhip;" and after the converſion and baptiſm of the eunuch, " the Lord caught away Philip, that the eunuch ſaw him no more: and he went on his way rejoicing. But Philip" (adds the word of God) " was found at Azotus: and, paſſing through, *he preached in all the cities*, till he came to Ceſarea." See Acts viii. 26—40. It muſt be evident to every candid reader of the above-quoted paſſages, that theſe two deacons were preachers of the goſpel. And we muſt beg leave to repeat, *in reſpect to the whole of them*, that the deſcription which the word of God gives of them, clearly raiſes them above the private members in general of a chriſtian ſociety, in reſpect to *gifts*, and *wiſdom*, and *power*.

3. The directions which the great apoſtle gives to Timothy in reſpect to the *deacons*, are ſo weighty and ſolemn, that it is evident the apoſtle conſidered *thoſe men* as of far greater importance than to be limited in their public offices *merely* to the work of ſer-

---

ving tables, or attending on the poor and infirm: 1 Tim. iii. 8—13. " Likewife muft the *deacons* be grave, not double tongued, not given to much wine, not greedy of filthy lucre : holding the myftery of the faith in a pure confcience. *And let thefe alfo firft be proved; then* let them ufe the office of a deacon, being found blamelefs. Even fo muft their wives be grave, not flanderers; fober, faithful in all things. Let the deacons be the hufbands of one wife, ruling their children and their own houfes well. For they that have ufed the office of a deacon well, purchafe to themfelves *a good degree,* and *great boldnefs* in the faith which is in Chrift Jefus." The laft words are certainly defcriptive of an office of confiderable importance in the church of God.

4. All we have faid in refpect to this office agrees with the accounts given us by the fathers of the church, in the pureft ages of chriftianity. From their writings we are alfo informed, that the deacons were employed to affift thc elder or prefbyter in the adminiftration of the Lord's fupper ; and alfo to carry a part of the confecrated elements to the fick, who were not able to attend at the place of public worfhip. And as we find from the firft quoted text that the deacons were fet apart for their office by the impofition of hands, but not by the impofition of the hands of the elders, as in other cafes; fo we endeavour to come as near to the fcripture-mode as we can, by confining the ceremony of the impofition of hands to the epifcopacy only, in the prefent inftance, without daring to compare ourfelves, as fome of our enemies would moft malicioufly affert, to the holy apoftles; but fimply, and in the fear of God, coming up to the written word as nearly as in our power.

5. This office ferves as an excellent probation for that of an elder. No preacher can be eligible to the office of an elder, till he has exercifed the office of a deacon for two years, except in the cafe of miffions. For we would wifh to fhew the utmoft attention to the order of elders, and to have the fulleft proof of the abilities, grace, and ufefulnefs of thofe, who fhall be, from time to time, propofed for fo important an office as that of a prefbyter in the church of God. And we judge, that the man who has proved himfelf a worthy member of our fociety, and an ufeful clafs-leader, exhorter, and local preacher, who has been approved of for two years as a travelling preacher on trial, and has faithfully ferved in the office of a travelling deacon for at leaft two years more—has offered fuch proofs of fidelity and piety, as muft fatisfy every reafonable mind. But as this continent is exceedingly large, and will continually open to our conferences new miffions for the fpread of the gofpel (perhaps for ages to come) we have, in the cafe of miffions given a difcretionary power to the yearly conferences. We have thus been able, through the grace and providence of God, to conftitute fuch a regular gra-

dation in our miniftry, as, we truft, will contribute highly to its purity, to the dignity of the minifterial office, and to the advantage of our people.

6. We have here alfo made the fame reftriction for the prefervation of our important itinerant plan, in refpect to the deacons' withdrawing themfelves from the general work, without the confent of the yearly conference, which was made before in the cafe of the elders, and which has been fpoken to in the notes on the former fection.

SECTION VIII.

Of the Method of receiving Preachers, and of their Duty.

Queft. 1. HOW is a preacher to be received ?
    Anfw. 1. By the yearly conference.

2. In the interval of the conference, by the bifhop, or prefiding elder of the diftrict, until the fitting of the conference.

3. When his name is not printed in the minutes, he muft receive a written licence from the bifhop or prefiding elder.

Queft. 2. What is the duty of a preacher ?
Anfw. 1. To preach.

2. To meet the focieties, claffes, and bands.

3. To vifit the fick.

4. To preach in the morning, where he can get hearers.

N. B. We are fully determined never to drop morning preaching, and to preach at five o'clock in the fummer, and fix in the winter, wherever it is practicable.

Queft. 3. What are the directions given to a preacher ?
Anfw. 1. Be diligent. Never be unemployed ; never be triflingly employed. Never trifle away time ; neither fpend any more time at any place than is ftrictly neceffary.

2. Be ferious. Let your motto be, *holinefs to the Lord.* Avoid all lightnefs, jefting, and foolifh talking.

3. Converse sparingly and cautiously with women. Timothy, v. 2.

4. Take no step towards marriage without first consulting with your brethren.

5. Believe evil of no one without good evidence; unless you see it done, take heed how you credit it. Put the best construction on every thing. You know the judge is always supposed to be on the prisoner's side.

6. Speak evil of no one; else your word especially would eat as doth a canker. Keep your thoughts within your own breast, till you come to the person concerned.

7. Tell every one under your care, what you think wrong in his conduct and temper, and that plainly, as soon as may be: else it will fester in your heart. Make all haste to cast the fire out of your bosom.

8. Avoid all affectation. A preacher of the gospel is the servant of all.

9. Be ashamed of nothing but sin.

10. Be punctual. Do every thing exactly at the time. And do not mend our rules, but keep them; not for wrath but conscience' sake.

11. You have nothing to do but to save souls. Therefore spend and be spent in this work. And go always not only to those that want, but to those that want you most.

Observe! It is not your business only to preach so many times, and to take care of this or that society: But to save as many souls as you can; to bring as many sinners as you possibly can to repentance, and with all your power to build them up in that holiness, without which they cannot see the Lord. And remember! A Methodist preacher is to mind every point great and small, in the Methodist discipline! Therefore you will need to exercise all the sense and grace you have.

12. Act in all things, not according to your own will, but as a son in the gospel. As such it is your duty to employ your time in the manner which we di-

rect: in preaching and visiting from house to house: in reading, meditation, and prayer. Above all, if you labour with us in the Lord's vineyard, it is needful you should do that part of the work which we advise, at those times and places which we judge most for his glory.

Quest. 4. What method do we use in receiving a preacher at the conference?

Answ. After solemn fasting and prayer, every person proposed shall then be asked, before the conference, the following questions (with any others which may be thought necessary) viz. Have you faith in Christ? Are you going on to perfection? Do you expect to be made perfect in love in this life? Are you groaning after it? Are you resolved to devote yourself wholly to God and his work? Do you know the rules of the society? Of the bands? Do you keep them? Do you constantly attend the sacrament? Have you read the form of discipline? Are you willing to conform to it? Have you considered the rules of a preacher; especially the first, tenth, and twelfth? Will you keep them for conscience' sake? Are you determined to employ all your time in the work of God? Will you endeavour not to speak too long or too loud? Will you diligently instruct the children in every place? Will you visit from house to house? Will you recommend fasting or abstinence, both by precept and example? Are you in debt?

We may then, if he gives us satisfaction, receive him as a probationer, by giving him the form of discipline, inscribed thus: To A. B. "*You think it your duty to call sinners to repentance. Make full proof hereof, and we shall rejoice to receive you as a fellow-labourer.*" Let him then carefully read and weigh what is contained therein; that if he has any doubt, it may be removed. Observe! Taking on trial is entirely different from admitting a preacher. One on trial may be either admitted or rejected, without doing him any wrong; otherwise it would be no trial at all. Let every one that has the charge of a circuit, explain this to those who are on

trial, as well as to thofe who are in future to be propofed for trial.

But no one fhall be received, unlefs he firft procure a
recommendation from the quarterly meeting of his circuit.

After two years' probation, being approved by the
yearly conference, and examined by the prefident of
the conference, he may be received into full connection,
by giving him the form of difcipline infcribed thus:
*As long as you freely confent to, and earneftly endeavour to
walk by thefe rules, we fhall rejoice to acknowledge you as
a fellow-labourer.*

N. B. If any preacher abfent himfelf from his circuit without the leave of the prefiding elder, the prefiding elder fhall, as far as poffible, fill his place with
another preacher, who fhall be paid for his labours out
of the falary of the abfent preacher in proportion to
the ufual allowance.

N O T E S.

If we duly confider the articles containing the duties of a
preacher, and the manner in which he muft fill up thofe duties,
from the nature and fituation of the work in which he is engaged,
we may venture to addrefs him in the words of the great apoftle, 2 Tim. iv. 1, 2. " I charge thee, therefore, before God, and
the Lord Jefus Chrift, who fhall judge the quick and the dead, at
his appearing and his kingdom, preach the word; be inftant in
feafon, out of feafon; reprove, rebuke, exhort, with all long-
fuffering and doctrine."   And we may add, with the wife man,
Ecclef. xi. 6. " In the morning fow thy feed, and in the evening
withhold not thine hand: for thou knoweft not whether fhall prof-
per either this or that, or whether they both fhall be alike good."
To preach almoft every day, and to meet focieties or claffes feveral times in the week, and to vifit the fick, not only in the towns,
but as far as practicable on the plantations, is a work which requires no fmall degree of diligence and zeal: and no perfon is fit
to be a travelling preacher, who cannot fill up thefe duties inceff-
antly all the year round, except occafional indifpofitions incapaci-
tate him for a feafon; or fome reafonable and urgent neceffity call
him away for a little time.

Let us now take a view of the twelve rules for the direction of
a preacher.

1. Let every moment be employed to the glory of God! This is the fubftance of the firft rule. And how agreeable is this to the written Word: Ecclef. ix. 10. "Whatfoever thy hand findeth to do, *do it with thy might* : for there is no work, nor device, nor knowledge, nor wifdom in the grave, whither thou goeft." Eph. v. 15, 16. "See then that ye walk circumfpectly, not as fools, but as wife, *redeeming the time*, becaufe the days are evil." 1 Tim. iv. 15. "Meditate upon thefe things, *give thyfelf wholly to them* , that thy profiting may appear to all." At the fame time that we fhould endeavour to lie fully open, in all our fermons, to the influences of the Holy Spirit of God, "we fhould not offer to the Lord our God of that which doth coft us nothing," 2 Sam. xxiv. 24. Time is one of the moft precious talents man poffeffes : O that thofe words of the poet may be engraven on every preacher's heart,

———————"Pay no
" Moment but for the purchafe of its worth :
" And what's its worth ? Afk death-beds, they can tell !"

2. Let all your deportment be grave, according to thofe commands of the apoftle, Eph. v. 4. "[Let] neither filthinefs, nor foolifh talking, nor jefting, which are not convenient [be once named among you :] but rather giving of thanks." Col iv. 5, 6. "Walk in wifdom toward them that are without, redeeming the time. Let your fpeech be alway with grace, feafoned with falt, that ye may know how ye ought to anfwer every man." 1 Tim. iv. 12. "Let no man defpife thy youth, but be thou an example of the believers, in word, in converfation, in charity, in fpirit, in faith, in purity." A minifter of the gofpel fhould preach, not only by his fermons, but by his actions, his common converfation, his whole example, yea, even by his looks. He fhould be every where a flame of fire. Wherever he is, the eyes of all are upon him. He cannot be neutral, but in every place will do either good or evil.

3. Preferve chaftity even in the moft delicate fenfe of the word. Remember thofe words of our Lord, Matt. v. 28. "Whofoever looketh on a woman to luft after her, hath committed adultery with her already in his heart :" and, therefore, fee that you "make a covenant with your eyes," Job xxxi. 1.——that you "entreat the elder women as mothers, the younger as fifters, with all purity," 1 Tim. v. 2.—— and that you "flee youthful lufts : but follow righteoufnefs, faith, charity, peace, with them that call on the Lord out of a *pure* heart," 2 Tim. ii. 22.

4. What St. Paul fays of the *wives* of the deacons, belongs as much to the wives of preachers, "Even fo muft their wives be grave, not flanderers; fober, faithful in all things," 1 Tim. iii.

11. Preachers certainly, therefore, should not trust in their own judgments, *merely*, in so weighty an affair.

5. Take care that your private sentiments of your brethren be not biassed, or your esteem of them diminished, except by convincing proof. "Judge not that ye be not judged. For with what judgment ye judge, ye shall be judged; and with what measure ye mete, it shall be measured to you again," Matt. vii. 1, 2. "Above all things have fervent charity among yourselves: for charity shall cover the multitude of sins," 1 Pet. iv. 8. Charity " *covereth* all things" (for so should the original word be rendered) " believeth all things, hopeth all things," 1 Cor. xiii. 7.

6. Be exceedingly tender of the characters of others: for to rob another of his character, by rash judgment, is to do him an irreparable injury. Let those words of Scripture be ever kept in view, as of infinite importance to all, but especially to a minister of the gospel, 2 Tim. ii. 16. 17. " Shun profane and vain babblings; for they will increase unto more ungodliness. And their word will eat as doeth a canker." The influence of a travelling preacher is very extensive: and for him to use that influence for the ruin of characters would be terrible indeed! Jam. i. 19, 20. " Wherefore, my beloved brethren, let every man be swift to hear, flow to speak, flow to wrath: for the wrath of man worketh not the righteousness of God." iv. 11, 12. " Speak not evil one of another, brethren. He that speaketh evil of his brother, and judgeth his brother, speaketh evil of the law, and judgeth the law ; but if thou judge the law, thou art not a doer of the law, but a judge. There is one Lawgiver, who is able to save, and to destroy: who art thou that judgest another ?" Tit. iii. 1. 2. " *Put them in mind*——to speak evil of no man, to be no brawlers, but gentle, shewing *all meekness* unto *all men :*" You are not only always thus to bridle your own tongue, but frequently *to put others in mind* of this important duty.

7. At the same time, it is your bounden duty to reprove sin, wherever you meet with it: So says the word of God: Lev. xix. 17. " Thou shalt in any wise rebuke thy neighbour, and not suffer sin upon him." Eph. v. 11. " Have no fellowship with the unfruitful works of darkness, but rather reprove them." Ver. 13. " All things that are reproved, are made manifest by the light : for whatsoever doth make manifest, is light." To reprove the open, presumptuous sinner, or to tell your brother of his faults in private, or even in public, if the sin be gross, and the honour of God and his sacred cause demand it, by no means clashes with the two preceding rules. It must also be remembered, that these three last rules do not relate to the conduct of those who have the oversight of circuits, when they act as *judges : their* duties, in that respect, shall be considered in due place.

8. Labour after that true greatnefs of foul, that genuine humility, of which our adorable Redeemer fets us fo bright an example. "Better it is to be of an humble fpirit," fays the wife man, "than to divide the fpoil with the proud," Prov. xvi. 19. "I fay, through the grace given unto me," obferves the great apoftle, "to every man that is among you, not to think of himfelf more highly than he ought to think; but to think foberly, according as God hath dealt to every man the meafure of faith," Rom. xii. 3. And again, "We preach not ourfelves, but Chrift Jefus the Lord; and *ourfelves, your fervants*, for Jefus' fake," 2 Cor. iv. 5.

9. What a pattern have we before us in our Lord, for all chriftians, but efpecially for thofe whofe one bufinefs is to fave fouls? John xiii. 3—17. "Jefus——rifeth from fupper, and laid afide his garments; and took a towel, and girded himfelf. After that, he poureth water into a bafon and began to wafh the difciples' feet, and to wipe them with the towel wherewith he was girded.——So after he had wafhed their feet, and had taken his garments, and was fet down again, he faid unto them, Know ye what I have done to you? Ye call me mafter and Lord: and ye fay well; for fo I am. If I then, your Lord and Mafter, have wafhed your feet, ye alfo ought to wafh one another's feet. For I have given you an example, that ye fhould do as I have done to you. Verily, verily, I fay unto you, The fervant is not greater than his Lord; neither he that is fent greater than he that fent him. If ye know thefe things, happy are ye if ye do them." Pride is the very fpirit of the devil: he is full of pride. All other graces, without humility, are like a fine powder carried in the wind without a cover, foon blown away and gone. The ftreams of grace flow down, and fink into the vallies of humility, and there *only* fructify, whilft the hills of pride are dry and barren. But at the fame time, the true minifter of Chrift, like his Mafter, can, in the way of duty, when neceffary, "fet his face like a flint,"* and go through the fire and through the water. "The wicked flee, when no man purfueth; but the righteous are bold as a lion," Prov. xxviii. 1.

10. *Punctuality* is of vaft importance in every circumftance of life. Without it, no confidence can exift: and the want of it is productive of innumerable evils to fociety. But how much ftronger are thefe obfervations, when applied to our fituation? The itinerant plan, which we fo much and fo juftly venerate, would be the moft pernicious in the world, without *punctuality*. It would be almoft fufficient to make mankind hate religion. The man who will difappoint a congregation through any world-

---

* *Ifaiah* l. 7.

ly motive, is highly criminal, and anfwerable for all the evil which his negligence has caufed—anfwerable for all the fouls which, through difguft, do afterwards defpife or neglect the ordinances of God. When an appointment is fixed, and cannot be revoked in time, it fhould be confidered as an engagement made to God. "Lord," fays the Pfalmift, "who fhall abide in thy tabernacle, and who fhall dwell in thy holy hill?————He that fweareth to his own hurt, and changeth not." See Pfalm xv. and the word of a preacher of the gofpel, indeed of every chriftian, fhould be the fame as his oath, or he is not even an honeft man. Alas! the good which the beft of us do, is but little, and, therefore, fhould not fuffer any fubtraction. *But when the itinerant preacher frequently proves himfelf deftitute of punctuality*, his life and labours become more hurtful than profitable. He not only prevents a faithful man from filling up the office which he himfelf abufes, but gives continual offence, and imperceptibly drives numbers from the ordinances of God, and thereby out of the way of falvation. "Give," therefore, "none offence, neither to the Jews, nor to the gentiles, nor to the church of God. Even as I," adds the apoftle, "pleafe all men in all things, not feeking mine own profit, but the profit of many, that they may be faved," 1 Cor. x. 32, 33. What a reafon, "*that they may be faved!*" A reafon, which fhould influence the heart of a preacher of the gofpel more than the ftrongeft temptations of fenfe or temporal intereft! Approve yourfelves, therefore, "as the minifters of God, giving no offence in any thing, that the miniftry be not blamed," 2 Cor. vi. 3, 4.

11. The falvation of fouls fhould be your only aim. The zeal of the Lord's houfe fhould eat you up. O that we could but feel a little of what Jefus felt *for immortal fouls*, when he offered up himfelf on Calvary! In fpeculation we acknowledge *their* ineftimable value: but O for the practice! O for a little of the zeal of the great apoftle, when he was going, bound in the fpirit, to Jerufalem, and could fay to the elders of the church of Ephefus, "None of thefe things *move* me; neither count I my life dear unto myfelf, fo that I might finifh my courfe with joy, and the *miniftry* which I have received of the Lord Jefus, to teftify the gofpel of the grace of God!" Acts xx. 24. This fpirit will give us true humility, and make us prefer the meaneft houfes of the poor, when we can benefit immortal fouls, to the moft pompous buildings and moft elegant entertainments, when we have *no accefs* to the fouls of men. "To the weak," fays St. Paul, "became I as weak, that I might gain the weak: I am made all things to all men, that I might *by all means* fave fome," 1 Cor. ix. 22. O let us think it an honour to confume our lives in fo glorious a

work! May we be able to say to our people from the ground of our hearts, with the apostle, " I will very gladly spend and be spent for you; though," adds the apostle, " the more abundantly I love you, the less I be loved," 2 Cor. xii. 15. Even in that trying situation, when despised or disapproved of by many, yet still let us go on, speaking and acting for God, and leaving all consequences to him. Let us not be discouraged: let God do *his* work of blessing, and let us do *our* work of sowing the seed, and of planting and watering, in season and out of season. Then we shall certainly have seals to our ministry, though, perhaps, the Lord may hide many of them, at present, from our eyes, lest we should be exalted above measure: and in due time, if we faint not,—if we lay not down *our* crown, we " shall shine as the stars for ever and ever, having [through grace] turned many to righteousness," Dan. xii. 3.

12. The command given by the apostle, Heb. xiii. 17. " Obey them that have the rule over you, and submit yourselves," is as binding on ministers as on the people. Among us there is no exception. Our bishops are bound to obey and submit to the general conference; and the preachers are bound to obey and submit to the general conference, and also to the yearly conferences, in every thing except the stationing of them for their respective districts and circuits; and in this respect they are bound to obey and submit to the episcopacy. This is the order of our church: and as the New Testament is silent as to the constitutions of states, so is it, in a great measure, in respect to the constitutions of churches. It only requires obedience or submission to the powers that are, without which no order could possibly exist. This does not, in any degree, prevent the due reformation of the constitutions of churches, any more than of those of states. We may add to these considerations the command of St. Peter, 1st Ep. v. 5. " Ye younger, submit yourselves unto the elder."

The due examination of candidates for the ministry is of the utmost importance. The questions proposed for this purpose, in the present section, may be drawn out and enlarged upon by the bishops, as they judge necessary; and, if duly considered will be found to contain in them the whole of christian and ministerial experience and practice. In respect to doctrines, experience, and practice, the preachers will have passed already through various examinations, before they are received into the travelling connection. Let us take a view of the whole, remembering that our societies form our grand nurseries or universities for ministers of the gospel.

1. On application for admission into the society, they must be duly recommended to the preacher who has the oversight of the circuit, by one in whom he can place sufficient confidence, or must have met three or four times in a class, and must be truly awak-

ened to a sense of their fallen condition. Then the preacher who has the oversight of the circuit, gives them notes of admission, and they remain on trial for six months. 2. When the six months are expired, they receive tickets, if recommended by their leader, and become full members of the society. And to prevent any future complaint on the ground of ignorance, the rules of the society must be read to them the first time they meet in clafs. 3. Out of these are chosen, from time to time, *the leaders of classes*, who should not only be deeply experienced in divine things, but have a measure of the gift of preaching, so as to feed the flock of Christ under their care, in due season. 4. Out of these, when they discover in public prayer-meetings an extraordinary gift of prayer and some gift for exhortation, are chosen *the exhorters*. 5. Out of the exhorters, who are employed in the places of least confequence, or to fill up the place of a preacher, in cases of neceffity, are chosen *the local preachers*. These are first to receive a licence signed by the prefiding elder, and by the quarterly meeting,* which is compofed of the local preachers, ftewards, and leaders of the circuit. Without the confent of the prefiding elder, and of the majority of this meeting, which is the moft proper and refpectable reprefentation of the circuit that perhaps can poffibly be devifed, no one can be admitted as a local preacher. And the licence above-mentioned muft be annually renewed, till the local preacher be admitted into the deacon's office. 6. Out of the local preachers are chosen *the travelling preachers*, of whom thofe in full connection form the members of our conferences. These muft be on trial for two years before they can be received into full connection with the conference, their characters being examined at each conference (whether they be prefent or abfent) in refpect to morals, grace, gifts, and fruit. Nor can they be received upon trial as *travelling preachers*, till they have obtained a recommendation from the quarterly meetings of their refpective circuits. The bifhops indeed, and the prefiding elders, have authority to call them to travel, in the intervals of the conferences, when they have received the above recommendation, otherwife the circuits would be frequently deftitute of preachers. But their call to travel, muft afterwards be confirmed by the yearly conference.

From all that has been obferved, it muft be clear to every candid reader, that it is not the yearly conference *only*, or the bifhops or prefiding elders *only*, in the intervals of the conferences, who choofe the local or travelling preachers. On the contrary, *they* have no authority to choofe at all, till the people, through their leaders, ftewards, &c. recommend. And thofe who will

---

* See the 21ft fection of this chapter.

not be fatisfied with this whole procefs of probation, confidered in all its parts, muft be rigid indeed. But we blefs God for the whole of this economy, and do attribute to it, under his grace and providence, the purity of our miniftry. When we confider the importance of *the gofpel miniftry*, this fevere procefs is by no means exceffive. " Now then," fays St. Paul, " *we* are *ambaffadors for Chrift*, as though God did befeech you by us," 2 Cor. v. 20. And again, " Whether any do inquire of Titus, he is my partner and fellow-helper concerning you ; or *our brethren* be inquired of, *they* are *the meffengers of the churches*, and *the* GLORY *of* CHRIST," viii. 23. " Try the fpirits," fays St. John, " whether they are of God ; becaufe many falfe prophets are gone out into the world," 1 John iv. 1.

SECTION IX.

Of the Salaries of the Minifters and Preachers.

Queft. 1. WHAT is the annual falary of the bifhops, elders, deacons, and preachers ?

Anfw. Sixty-four dollars, and their travelling expences.

Queft. 2. What fhall be annually allowed the wives of the married preachers ?

Anfw. The wife of every travelling preacher fhall have the fame claim to a yearly falary of fixty-four dollars, as a travelling preacher.

Queft. 3. What plan fhall we purfue in appropriating the money received by our travelling minifters for marriage-fees ?

Anfw. In all the circuits where the preachers do not receive their full quarterage, let all fuch money be given into the hands of the ftewards, and be equally divided between the travelling preachers of the circuit. In all other cafes the money fhall be difpofed of at the difcretion of the yearly conference.

N. B. No minifter or preacher whatfoever fhall receive any money for deficiencies, or on any other account, out of any of our funds or collections, without firft giving an exact account of all the money, clothes, and other prefents of every kind, which he has received the preceding year.

N O T E S.

The duty which lies upon the people to support their ministers, is established by the following scriptures: viz. 1 Cor. ix. 7, 11, 13, 14. " Who goeth a warfare any time at his own charges? who planteth a vineyard, and eateth not of the fruit thereof? or who feedeth a flock, and eateth not of the milk of the flock? —If we have sown unto you spiritual things, is it a great thing if we shall reap your carnal things?—Do ye not know, that they which minister about holy things, live of the things of the temple? and they which wait at the altar, are partakers with the altar? Even so hath the Lord ordained, that they which preach the gospel, should live of the gospel." Gal. vi. 6. " Let him that is taught in the word, communicate unto him that teacheth, in all good things."

Those who read this section attentively, will see the impossibility of our ministers becoming rich by the gospel, except in grace. And here there is no difference between bishops, elders, deacons, or preachers, except in their travelling expences, and consequently in the greater labours of one than the other. The gifts they have to impart, are not silver and gold, but, through the Divine blessing on their labours, and the operations of the Holy Spirit accompanying their word, " love, joy, peace, long-suffering, gentlenefs, goodnefs, faith, meeknefs and temperance." And we may add, that the impossibility of our enriching ourselves by *our ministry*, is another great preservation of *its* purity. The lovers of this world will not long continue travelling preachers. Indeed, we may add, that a great many of the preachers do not receive the whole of their annual pittance, generally, we believe, through the poverty, but sometimes perhaps through the inattention of our friends.

The clause concerning the allowance for a preacher's wife, may need some explanation. The wife is to have *the fame claim* in respect to salary as the travelling preacher: so that if there be a married and a single preacher in the fame circuit, and the money for the support of the ministry be not sufficient to make up all the salaries, the whole is to be divided into three parts, one part of which belongs to the wife.

S E C T I O N X.

Of the Duties of those who have the Charge of Circuits.

Queft. 1. WHAT are the duties of the elder, deacon, or preacher, who has the special charge of a circuit?

Anfw. 1. To fee that the other preachers in his circuit behave well, and want nothing.

2. To renew the tickets quarterly, and regulate the bands.

3. To meet the ftewards and leaders, as often as poffible.

4. To appoint all the ftewards and leaders, and change them when he fees it neceffary.

5. To receive, try, and expel members according to the form of difcipline.

6. To hold watch-nights and love-feafts.

7. To hold quarterly meetings in the abfence of the prefiding elder.

8. To take care that every fociety be duly fupplied with books.

9. To take an exact account of the numbers in fociety, and bring it to the conference.

10. To fend an account of his circuit every quarter to his prefiding elder.

11. To meet the men and women apart in the large focieties once a quarter, wherever it is practicable.

12. To overlook the accounts of all the ftewards.

13. To appoint a perfon to receive the quarterly collection in the *claffes.*

14. To fee that *public* collections be made quarterly, if need be.

15. To raife a yearly fubfcription in thofe circuits that can bear it, for building churches, and paying the debts of thofe which have been already erected.

16. To choofe a committee of lay-members to make a juft application of the money, where it is moft wanted.

Queft. 2. What other directions fhall we give him?

Anfw. Several:

1. To take a regular catalogue of the focieties in towns and cities, as they live in ftreets.

2. To leave his fucceffor a particular account of the ftate of the circuit.

3. To fee that every band-leader have the rules of the bands.

4. To enforce vigorously, but calmly, all the rules of the society.

5. As soon as there are four men or women believers in any place, to put them into a band.

6. To suffer no love-feast to last above an hour and a half.

7. To warn all, from time to time, that none are to remove from one circuit to another, without a note of recommendation from a preacher of the circuit in these words: " *A. B. the bearer has been an acceptable member of our society in C.*" and to inform them, that, without such a certificate, they will not be received into other societies.

8. To recommend every where decency and cleanliness.

9. To read the rules of the society, with the aid of the other preachers, once a year in every congregation, and once a quarter in every society.

10. On any dispute between two or more of the members of our society, concerning the payment of debts or otherwise, which cannot be settled by the parties concerned, the preacher who has the charge of the circuit, shall inquire into the circumstances of the case; and, having consulted the stewards and leaders, shall, if agreeable to their advice, recommend to the contending parties a reference consisting of one arbiter chosen by the plaintiff, and another chosen by the defendant; which two arbiters so chosen shall nominate a third; the three arbiters being members of our society.

But if one of the parties be dissatisfied with the judgment given, such party may apply to the ensuing quarterly meeting of the circuit, for allowance to have a *second* arbitration appointed; and if the quarterly meeting see sufficient reason, they shall grant a *second* arbitration; in which case, each party shall choose two arbiters, and the four arbiters shall choose a fifth, the judgment of the majorities of whom shall be final; and any party refusing to abide by such judgment, shall be excluded the society.

And if any member of our society shall refuse in cases of debt or other disputes, to refer the matter to arbitration, when recommended by him who has the charge of the circuit, with the approbation of the stewards and leaders; or shall enter into a law-suit with another member before these measures are taken, he shall be expelled.

The preachers who have the oversight of circuits are required to execute all our rules fully and strenuously against all frauds, and particularly against dishonest insolvencies; suffering none to remain in our society, on any account, who are found guilty of any fraud.

11. The preacher who has the charge of a circuit, shall appoint prayer-meetings wherever he can, in his circuit.

12. He shall take care that a fast be held in every society in his circuit, on the Friday preceding every quarterly meeting; and that a memorandum of it be written on all the class-papers.

13. He shall also take care, that no unordained local preacher or exhorter in his circuit shall officiate in public, without first obtaining a licence from the presiding elder or himself. Let every unordained local preacher and exhorter take care to have this renewed yearly: and let him who has the charge of the circuit, insist upon it.

N O T E S.

When we consider the duties of the office described in this section, we shall feel no difficulty in allowing, that it is an office of no small importance.

1. The person who holds it, is to watch over the other travelling preachers in his circuit, not with the eye of a severe judge, but with that of a tender elder brother. He should indeed be faithful to his colleagues, and tell them all their faults: but he has no power to correct them. He is to bear an equal share with them in the toils of a travelling preacher, besides having upon him the care of all the churches in his circuit. But if his colleagues will not observe his reasonable directions, or behave grossly amiss, he must inform his presiding elder, whose duty it is, as soon as possible, to judge of and rectify every thing. He is also to use his influence with the people, that his fellow-labourers may

ftand in need of nothing for the fimple convenience or at leaft neceffities of this tranfitory life. They want but little, and that little they ought to have. This alfo implies, that if his colleague be married, he fhould take care that neither he nor his family ftand in need of any of the neceffaries of life. For his performance of this duty, as well as all the reft, he is bounden to God, as well as to the church of which he is a member. " Jefus called them [the twelve] unto him, and faid, ye know that the princes of the Gentiles exercife dominion over them, and they that are great, exercife authority upon them. But it fhall not be fo among you: but whofoever will be great among you, let him be *your minifter;* and whofoever will be chief among you, let him be your fervant: Even as the *Son of Man* came not be be miniftered unto, but to minifter," Matt. xx. 25—28.

2. He is to deliver tickets quarterly to each member of the fociety, with a portion of the word of God printed on them. This is of no fmall moment for the prefervation of our difcipline and the purity of our church. To admit frequently unawakened perfons to our fociety-meetings and love-feafts, would be to throw a damp on thofe profitable affemblies, and cramp, if not entirely deftroy *that liberty of fpeech*, which is always made a peculiar bleffing to earneft believers and fincere feekers of falvation. Befides, this regulation affords the preacher who holds the office now under confideration, an opportunity of fpeaking clofely to every perfon under his care on the ftate of their fouls. " I know thy works," fays our Lord, " and thy labour, and thy patience, and *how thou canft not bear them which are evil:*—and haft borne, and haft patience, and for my name's fake haft laboured, and haft not fainted," Rev. ii. 2, 3. The other duty of regulating the bands is alfo of great confequence, as will appear when we come to enlarge on the 3d fection of the 2d chapter.

3. He is to watch over the ftewards and leaders of his circuit. He fhould meet them weekly, when in the towns, and as often as may be in the country. He is to recommend to the ftewards the poor of their focieties, to lay before them, if neceffary, the wants of his colleagues, and to ftir them up to fidelity and activity, in their office: but above all, he is to exhort the leaders, to inftruct them in the beft mode of addreffing their claffes, and to fet before them the ineftimable value of the precious fouls refpectively intrufted to their care. His whole foul fhould fay, " Would God that all the Lord's people were prophets, and that the Lord would put his Spirit upon them!" Numb. xi. 29.

4. As he is the leaft likely to be influenced by the various circumftances arifing from neighbourhood, long acquaintance, affection, confanguinity, or any other motives diftinct from offi-

cial talents, he is to appoint the ftewards. And as he is, or fhould be, the beft judge of the gifts and experience of the members of fociety, he alfo is to felect the men, from time to time, who are to fill up the weighty office of leader. And again, as he is the only perfon in the circuit, who is refponfible to the yearly conference for the decline of the work of God in his circuit, and the only one the conference *can make* refponfible, he has the authority invefted in him of changing leaders, when they have loft the life of God, or are incapacitated for or negligent of their duty. But if he ever ufe this power in a capricious or tyranical manner, the people may lay their grievances before the bifhops or prefiding elders, who have authority to fufpend him for ill conduct; or, before the yearly conference, which may proceed even to his expulfion, if he grofsly offend againft that wifdom which is from above, " and which is firft pure, then peaceable, gentle, and eafy to be entreated, full of mercy and good fruits, *without partiality, and without hypocrify*," Jam. iii. 17.

5. He is alfo to receive members upon trial, and into fociety, according to the form of difcipline. If this authority were invefted in the fociety, or any part of it, the great work of revival would foon be at an end. A very remarkable proof of this was given feveral years ago, by a fociety in Europe. Many of the leading members of that fociety, were exceedingly importunate to have the whole government of their fociety invefted in a meeting compofed of the principal preacher, and a number of *lay elders* and *lay deacons*, as they termed them. At laft, the preacher who had the overfight of the circuit, was prevailed upon, through their inceffant importunity, to comply with their requeft. He accordingly nominated all the *leaders* and *ftewards*, as lay elders and lay deacons with the defired powers. But alas! What was the confequence? The great revival which was then in that fociety and congregation, was foon extinguifhed. Poor finners, newly awakened, were flocking into the church of God as doves to their windows. But now, the wifdom and prudence of *the new court* kept them at a diftance, till they had given full proof of their repentance: " if their convictions be fincere," faid they, " they will not withdraw themfelves from the preaching of the word on account of our caution; they themfelves will fee the propriety of our conduct." Thus, whilft the fervent preacher was one hour declaring the willingnefs of Chrift immediately to receive the returning finners, the wifdom of the lay elders and lay deacons would the next hour reject them even from being received upon trial, unlefs they had been before *painted fepulchres, inwardly full of dead men's bones and rottennefs*. The preacher who had the charge of the circuit nearly broke his heart, to fee the precious fouls which God had given him, kept at a diftance from him, and thrown back again upon the wide world by *the prudent lay*

elders and deacons. However, at his earneft entreaty, he was removed into another circuit by the conference, under whofe controul he acted, to enjoy the bleffings *of the Methodift economy.* The revival of the work of God was foon extinguifhed ; and the fociety, from being one of the moft lively, became one of the moft languid in Europe.

Glory be to God, *all* our focieties throughout the world, now amounting to upwards of 160,000 have been raifed, under grace, *by our minifters and preachers.* *They,* and they *only,* are their fpiritual fathers under God ; and none others can feel for them as *they* do. It is true, that on great revivals, the fpiritually halt, and blind, and lame, will prefs in crowds into the church of God ; and they are welcome to all that we can do for their invaluable fouls, till they prove unfaithful to convincing or converting grace. And we will not throw back their fouls on the wicked world, whilft groaning under the burden of fin, becaufe many on the trial quench their convictions, or perhaps were hypocritical from the beginning. We would fooner go again into the highways and hedges, and form new focieties as at firft, than we would give up a privilege fo effential to the minifterial office and to the revival of the work of God.

" The mafter of the houfe [God]——faid to his fervant, Go out quickly into the ftreets and lanes of the city, and *bring in hither* the poor, and the maimed, and the halt, and the blind. And the fervant faid, Lord, it is done as thou haft commanded, and yet there is room." He obeys his God, without afking permiffion of any fociety, whether he fhould obey him or not. " And the Lord faid unto the fervant, Go out into the highways and hedges, and *compel them to come in,* that *my houfe* may be filled," Luke xiv. 21—23. The fervant anfwers not to his God, I will comply with thy command as far as my fociety, or my leaders and ftewards will permit me. Again, the Lord fays to Ezekiel, ch. xxxiv. 1—10, " Son of man, prophefy againft the fhepherds of Ifrael, prophefy, and fay unto them, Thus faith the Lord God unto the fhepherds, Wo be to the fhepherds of Ifrael——the difeafed have ye not ftrengthened, neither have ye healed that which was fick, neither have ye bound up that which was broken, *neither have ye brought again, that which was driven away, neither have ye fought that which was loft.* ——And they were fcattered, becaufe there is no fhepherd : and they became meat to all the beafts of the field, when they were fcattered.——Therefore, ye fhepherds, hear the word of the Lord ; As I live, faith the Lord God, furely becaufe my flock became a prey, and my flock became meat to every beaft of the field, becaufe there was no fhepherd, neither did my fhepherds fearch for my flock—Therefore, O ye fhepherds, hear the word of the Lord, Thus faith the Lord God, Behold I am againft the fhepherds, and I will require my

FLOCK AT THEIR HAND, and caufe them to ceafe from feeding the flock," &c. Now, what paftors, called and owned of God, would take upon themfelves this awful refponfibility, if others could refufe to their fpiritual children the grand external privilege of the gofpel, or admit among them the moft improper perfons to mix with and corrupt them. Truly, whatever the paftors of other churches may do, we truft that ours will never put themfelves under fo dreadful a bondage. It is in vain to fay, that others may be as tender and cautious as *the paftors :* for *the paftors* are the perfons refponfible to God, and, therefore, fhould by no means be thus fettered in their paftoral care. And thofe who are defirous to wreft out of the hands of minifters this important part of their duty, fhould rather go out themfelves to the highways and hedges, and preach the everlafting gofpel, or be contented with their prefent providential fituation.

Befides, the command of our Lord, Matt. xxviii. 19. " Go ye, —and teach all nations, *baptizing* them," &c. is addreffed to *paftors only,*——to his difciples, and through them to all his *miniftring* fervants to the end of the world. But if minifters are to be the judges of the proper fubjects of *baptifm*, which is the grand initiatory ordinance into the vifible church, how much more fhould they have a right to determine, whom they will take under *their own* care, or whom God has given them out of the world by the preaching of his word. For minifters to fpend their ftrength, their tears, their prayers, their lives for the falvation of fouls, and to have both themfelves and THEIRS under the controul of thofe who never travailed in birth for them, and, therefore, can never feel for them as their fpiritual parents do, is a burden we cannot bear. Thus it is evident, that both reafon and fcripture do, in the cleareft manner, make the privilege or power now under confideration effential to the gofpel-miniftry.

The other duty, mentioned under this article, of regulating the band-fociety, is of great confequence, as will appear when we come to enlarge upon the 3d fection of the 2d chapter.

6. As the Lord is a God of order, and not of confufion, it is highly neceffary that *one perfon* fhould be invefted with the regulation of the watch-nights and love-feafts : and who would be fo proper, in the abfence of the prefiding elder, as the preacher who has the overfight of the circuit ? As to watch-nights, we may obferve, Did our Lord fpend whole nights in prayer? Matt. xiv. 23—25. Mark vi. 46—48. Luke vi. 12. " And it came to pafs in thofe days, that he went out into a mountain to pray, and continued *all night* in prayer to God." Did St. Paul alfo employ whole nights in inftructing and praying with the church of God ? Acts xx. 7—11. " When he [Paul] had broken bread, and eaten, and talked a long while, *even till break of day*, fo he departed." And fhall not the minifters and people of God *in thefe*

days imitate fuch great examples ?   Shall the diffipated and profane revel and watch, night after night, in the fervice of Satan,
and fhall we think it too much to watch and pray fometimes for
a few hours together ?

Our venerable leader, Mr. Wefley, was in this, as in moft of
his rules, lead on by divine Providence.   When informed,
about the year 1740, that the congregation at Kingfwood, near
Briftol, frequently continued in exhortation and prayer till mid-
night, he had thoughts of fuppreffing fuch meetings : but when,
after fufficient inquiry, he found that the power of God was re-
markably prefent on thofe occafions, and that many were awakened, juftified, or fanctified, he bowed under the hand of God,
and not only permitted the continuance of them in Kingfwood,
but introduced them through the connection, and was, to his
dying hour, fully convinced of their bleffed effects.

In refpect to our love-feafts, we fhall fpeak of them in our
notes on the 4th fection of the 2d chapter.

7. Though the prefiding elder is far more proper to prefide at
the quarterly meetings than any other who regularly attends, yet
the preacher, who has the overfight of the circuit is, next to
him, the moft likely to be impartial.*   It is on this principle,
that the twelve judges of England make it a rule, that no one of
them fhall take that circuit which includes the place where he
was born.   Befides, every thing is finally determined by a majority of votes.   On thofe extraordinary occafions, therefore,
when through ficknefs, or any other unavoidable hindrance, the
prefiding elder is abfent, the next to him in office muft be the
moderator of the meeting.   See the notes on the 5th fection of
this chapter.   Let us all be willing to fubmit to that due fub-
jection, which is neceffary to the good order of the whole, "yea,
all of you be fubject one to another," 1 Pet. v. 5.

8. Next to the preaching of the gofpel, the fpreading of religious knowledge by the prefs, is of the greateft moment to the
people.   The foul, whilft united to the body, muft be daily fed
with pious ideas, otherwife it will lofe ground in the divine life.
Though the Lord is wonderfully kind to thofe of his children
who are fo unfortunate as not to be able to read, yet we are to

---

* *We do not mean that he is likely to have more grace or more inte-*
grity than the other members of the quarterly meeting, but only that he
is not fo much expofed to the temptations of prejudging *a caufe through*
confanguinity, affection, or a variety of other interefts, as the other mem-
bers are.   We have a high efteem for all our official *members, and*
would not intentionally offend them on any account.

ufe all the means in our power. And though the bible be infinitely preferable to all other books, yet we are, even on that very account, to ftudy the writings of thofe fpiritual and great divines, who have by their comments, effays, fermons, or other labours, explained the bible : otherwife, we ought not to attend the preaching of the gofpel ; for what is *that* but an explanation and application of the great truths contained in the bible. He, therefore, who has the charge of the circuit, is to be diligent in the fale of thofe books, which, according to the judgment of our conferences and bifhops, are deemed profitable for the fouls of our people. St. Paul had need of books, otherwife he would not have carried them with him in his extenfive travels. " The cloak that I left at Troas with Carpus, when thou comeft, bring with thee, *and the books*, but efpecially *the parchments*,"* 2 Tim. iv. 13. And to minds which are influenced by the love of God and man, the confideration that the profit of thefe books is wholly applied to the work of God, will be a further inducement to them to purchafe our books.

9. It is neceffary that the yearly conference fhould have an exact account of the numbers in fociety, and of every thing material relating to each circuit under its controul, otherwife it could not poffibly judge of the progrefs of the work, and the fidelity of the preachers : nor could the epifcopacy have otherwife fuch complete knowledge of every thing for the ftationing of the preachers. " Let all things be done," fays St. Paul, " decently, and in order."

10. It is alfo neceffary, that the prefiding elder fhould receive regular details of the proceedings of thofe who have the overfight of circuits, that he himfelf may have fuch a clear knowledge of the ftate of the diftrict, as may enable him to fill up his important truft, and to give fuch information of his diftrict to the bifhops, as may afford them a complete view of the whole. Thus are many eyes opened upon the great work, and the wifdom of many united for the good of the whole. " In the multitude of counfellers," fays the wife man," there is fafety."

11. The people of our fpecial charge want all the advice we can give them: and their ftations and circumftances are fo different, that the rule of meeting the men and women apart, and, when the fociety is large; and the time will admit of it, the married and fingle men apart, and the married and fingle women apart, has been attended with many bleffings. Mr. Wefley, from happy experience, confidered this as a very profitable means of grace.

---

* i. e. *The books written on parchment, the art of printing not being known in thofe days.*

Ministers of the gospel should think no labour lost, or means in vain, by which they may be enabled to give their whole flock their due spiritual portion. "The Lord said, Who then is that faithful and wise steward, whom his Lord shall make ruler over his houfehold, to give them their portion of meat in due feafon? Bleffed is that fervant, whom his lord, when he cometh, shall find fo doing. Of a truth I fay unto you, That he will make him ruler over all that he hath," Luke xii. 42—44.

12. As the public money fhould be applied with the greateft fidelity, the accounts fhould be examined with the ftricteft fcrutiny : and, therefore, the preacher who has the charge of the circuit is to examine the ftewards' accounts, as a preparative to their being laid before the quarterly meeting : and this not out of difrefpect to the ftewards, whom we highly efteem for their difintereſted labours of love, but to prevent, as far as poffible, even any plaufible pretence for fufpicion. "It is required in ftewards," fays the apoftle, "that a man be found faithful." No perfon of integrity (and fuch we have reafon to believe all our ftewards are, without exception) will object to this rule.

13 & 14. The quarterly collections *in the claffes*, &c. according to the abilities of our friends, are the chief fupport of the work.

15 & 16. One of the greateft charities upon earth is the raifing of buildings for public worfhip and the preaching of the gofpel. "How fhall they call on him," fays the apoftle, "in whom they have not believed? and how fhall they believe in him of whom they have not heard? and how fhall they hear without a preacher? and how fhall they preach except they be fent? as it is written, How beautiful are the feet of them that preach the gofpel of peace, and bring glad tidings of good things," Rom. x. 14, 15. But the preachers who are fent of God, muft have a place to affemble their hearers, otherwife they can but feldom deliver their meffage. Little good will be done, if they can have *only* the open air to preach in : becaufe the Lord will not work unneceffary miracles. Where a few perfons, or many, have raifed a houfe for God, and continue to live to God themfelves, they will receive from the nature of diftributive juftice, *a proportionable fhare of the reward*, for *all the fouls* faved in or by the means of that building and the ordinances adminiftered there, *as long as the building lafts*. And though no finite being could make the due diftribution in fo intricate a cafe, yet he who is infinite Wifdom *can* do it, and *will* do it, when he fits on his great white throne. And the preacher who has the charge of the circuit will alfo have his fhare of the reward, by ufing all his influence on fuch occafions, to fet on foot and recommend the neceffary fubfcriptions and collections.

We are now to give the reasons for the further directions given in this section to him who has the charge of the circuit.

1. A Catalogue of the members of the society in towns, is highly neceffary to enable the preachers to perform the great duty of vifiting our people from houfe to houfe. But concerning this duty fee the 15th fection of this chapter.

2 & 3. If his fucceffor have not an exact account left him of the ftate of the circuit, it will be impoffible for him to be fo extenfively ufeful for a confiderable time as he otherwife might be. Every preacher fhould enter upon his work on the faireft ground, and with the completeft view poffible of what was before him. " Behold," fays the prophet, fpeaking of the Meffiah, " his work is before him," Ifa. lxii. 11. And fo fhould it be with every minifter of Chrift, in his meafure and degree.

4. The fourth direction is exceedingly weighty. It makes the principal part of his office. But on the rules of the fociety we fhall fpeak largely, when we confider the 1ft fection of the 2d chapter.

5. He is alfo to regulate all the bands in his circuit. See chap. 2. fect. 3.

6. In every thing there muft be order; though frequently what the world calls *confufion*, is *order* in the fight of God. However, the zeal of happy, pious fouls may carry them to many extremes, if not under proper reftriction. " Let your moderation be known unto all men," Phil. iv. 5.

7. We are but one body of people, one grand fociety, whether in Europe or America; united in the clofeft fpiritual bonds, and in external bonds as far as the circumftances of things will admit. And as our numbers have increafed exceedingly both in Europe and America, it is neceffary we fhould be particularly cautious in receiving ftrangers into our fociety, under the pretext of their having been members in other places; as the one end of our whole plan is *to raife a holy people*. On this account all our conferences throughout the world mutually require, that every member of our fociety who changes his place of abode, fhall previoufly obtain a certificate from the preacher who has the charge of his circuit, who is moft likely to be acquainted with his character, his own relations excepted; and that without fuch certificate he fhall not be received into any other fociety. Even in the primitive church, St. Paul faw it neceffary to write to his Philipians, " Brethren, —*Mark them* which walk fo, as ye have us for an enfample. For many walk, of whom I have told you often, and now tell you even weeping, that they are the enemies of the crofs of Chrift,' Phil. iii. 17, 18. How much more then is it our duty to ufe every precaution to preferve the purity of our church, in thefe days, when perfecution has ceafed, and it is the intereft of many to be united to a religious party. Nor is it fufficient for the per-

fon removing to carry *his ticket* with him, as he might have been expelled from our communion, and yet have preferved his ticket.

8. The 8th direction is of great moment, efpecially to profeffors of religion, that the gofpel be not blamed—that the world may not have it in their power to accufe pure religion with making men carelefs or negligent of themfelves. " Know ye not that *your body* is the temple of the Holy Ghoft which is in you, which ye have of God? and ye are not your own, for ye are bought with a price, therefore glorify God *in your body*, and in your fpirit, which are God's," 1 Cor. vi. 19, 20.

9. We do nothing fecretly. We wifh the whole world to know every part of our economy, and more efpecially the rules of our fociety, fo neceffary *for every member of it at leaft* to be thoroughly acquainted with. We have alfo enacted this rule, that chriftian fellowfhip in general, and particularly that mode of chriftian communion which has proved fo beneficial to ourfelves and to myriads now in glory, may be ftrongly and repeatedly recommended to all who truly fear God. " Ye know," fays the apoftle to the elders of the church of Ephefus, " how I kept back nothing that was profitable unto you," Acts xx. 18—20. where the apoftle by the word *you* means the whole church, of whom the elders were the chief organs.

10. For chriftians to appeal to the judges of the world in matters of controverfy or litigation, is ftrongly cenfured by the word of God. " Dare any of you," fays the apoftle, " having a matter againft another, go to law before the unjuft, and not before the faints? Do ye not know that the faints fhall judge the world? and if the world fhall be judged by you, are ye unworthy to judge the fmalleft matters? Know ye not that we fhall judge angels? how much more things that pertain to this life? If then ye have judgments of things pertaining to this life, fet them to judge who are leaft efteemed in the church. I SPEAK TO YOUR SHAME. Is it fo that there is not a wife man among you? no, not one that fhall be able to judge between his brethren? But brother goeth to law with brother, and that before the unbelievers. Now, therefore, *there is* UTTERLY *a fault among you*, becaufe ye go to law one with another: why do ye not rather take wrong? why do ye not rather fuffer yourfelves to be defrauded?" 1 Cor, vi. 1—7. But as we would by no means wifh that minifters of the gofpel fhould interfere *as judges* of fuch affairs, it is directed, that the preacher who has the overfight of the circuit fhall (after confulting the leaders and ftewards, *if agreeable to their advice*) recommend a fcriptural arbitration to the contending parties: and as our rules declare that " Brother fhall not go to law with brother," he fhall exclude that party which refufes fo equitable a propofal. And we will take the liberty of adding, that where the contending parties are of two different *religious* focieties, the only *chriftian*

method we know of, on which they could proceed, would be for each of them to choose an arbiter out of his own society, and for those two to choose a third; or to proceed on some similar plan.

11. The authority of appointing prayer-meetings will not, we think, be disputed by any. Many of our greatest revivals have been begun and chiefly carried on in our prayer-meetings. We wish that the utmost zeal might be manifested by those who have the charge of circuits in the execution of this direction. The sacred writer describing the effects of the day of Pentecost, observes, " Then they that gladly received his word were baptized: and the same day there were added unto them about *three thousand souls*. And *they* continued stedfastly in the apostles' doctrine and fellowship, and in breaking of bread, and *in prayers*," Acts ii. 41, 42. There is no doubt but those words refer to *social* worship. O that every family in our connection had occasionally a prayer-meeting at stated times for the benefit of their neighbours! There would be no danger of wanting persons to pray : God would pour forth the spirit of grace and supplication ; and soon the flame of divine love would glow through every civilized part of this vast continent. The Lord hasten the day !

12. Public fasts are to be appointed by him at the regular times, and he is of course to take care, that himself and his helpers not only set the example, but also render those days peculiarly profitable by public meetings for the service of God. 2 Chron. xx. 3. Jehoshaphat—proclaimed *a fast throughout all Judah*. Ezra. viii. 21. Ezra *proclaimed a fast* at the river Ahava. Isa. lviii. 3. *In the day of your fast*, you find pleasure. Jer. xxxvi. 9. They proclaimed *a fast before the Lord* to all the people in Jerusalem, and to all the people that came from the cities of Judah unto Jerusalem. Joel i. 14. Sanctify *a fast*, call an assembly : and ii. 15. Jonah iii. 5. The people of Ninevah believed God, and proclaimed *a fast*. Matt. ix. 15. Jesus said unto them, can the children of the bride-chamber mourn as long as the bridegroom is with them ? but the days will come when the bridegroom shall be taken from them, and *then shall they fast*. See also Mark ii. 18— 20. and Luke 33—35.

13. The whole organization of our church depends on an exact attention to all its distinctions and orders. " I am with you in the Spirit." says St. Paul to his Colossians, " *joying and beholding your order*," Col. ii. 5. The Lord wills that we should fight in his great cause *lawfully* : " if a man also strive for masteries, yet is he not crowned except he strive *lawfully*," 2 Tim. ii. 5. Therefore the church of God is compared to *an army with banners :* Cant. vi. 4. " Thou art beautiful, O my love, as Tirzah; comely as Jerusalem ; terrible as *an army with banners*." It has been, we doubt not, the close order and organization of our

church, under the grace and providence of God, which has enabled us to refift all the fhocks we have lately felt from the fatani-
cal fpirit of divifion, and to remain firm as a rock.

We may juft add, that it is cuftomary for the prefiding elders,
or in their abfence the preachers who have the charge of circuits,
to hold quarterly, or half-yearly conferences with the local preachers and exhorters refpectively under their care, to examine into
their grace, gifts and ufefulnefs, and into the ftate of the work
of God——a cuftom of exceeding great utility, and, therefore,
fuch as, we truft, will never be neglected.

SECTION XI.

Of the Trial of thofe who think they are mov-
ed by the Holy Ghoft to preach.

Queft. 1. HOW fhall we try thofe who profefs to be
moved by the Holy Ghoft to preach?

Anfw. 1. Let the following queftions be afked, viz.
Do they know God as a pardoning God? Have they
the love of God abiding in them? Do they defire and
feek nothing but God? And are they holy in all manner of converfation?

2. Have they gifts (as well as grace) for the work?
Have they (in fome tolerable degree) a clear, found
underftanding, a right judgment in the things of God,
a juft conception of falvation by faith? And has God
given them any degree of utterance? Do they fpeak
juftly, readily, clearly?

3. Have they fruit? Are any truly convinced of fin,
and converted to God, by their preaching?

As long as thefe three marks concur in any one, we
believe he is called of God to preach. Thefe we receive
as fufficient proof that he is moved by the Holy Ghoft.

N O T E S.

We have enlarged on the prefent fubject in our notes on the
8th fection of this chapter. Every reader may from hence per-
ceive the care we take in receiving our preachers and minifters.
As the prefiding elders, or thofe who have the charge of cir-

cuits, are attentive to the examination of the local preachers and exhorters, fo the yearly conferences are attentive to the gifts grace, and ufefulnefs of all the travelling preachers and minif- ters. Nothing will do for us without *the life of God.* Brilliant parts, fine addrefs, &c. are to us but tinkling cymbals, when def- titute of the power of the Holy Ghoft.

At the fame time we are far from defpifing *talents* which may be rendered ufeful to the church of Chrift. We know the worth of improved abilities: and nothing can equal our itinerant plan, in the opportunity it affords of fuiting our various focieties with men of God, who are endued with gifts agreeable to their re- fpective wants.

The following texts may illuftrate the prefent fubject. Gal. i. 15, 16. " When it pleafed God, who feparated me from my mo- ther's womb, and called me by his grace, *to reveal his Son in me,* that I might preach him among the heathen ; immediately I con- ferred not with flefh and blood." You may here obferve, that Chrift *was revealed in* St. Paul, that he might preach. This is an effential requifite for every preacher of the gofpel: and he who attempts to enter into the fheepfold by any other door, than Chrift—Chrift revealed in him, and moving him by his Spirit to preach the word, is a thief and a robber; but, bleffed be God, " the fheep will not follow him, but flee from him !" See the 10th chapter of St. John. Again, St. Paul defires his Ephe- fians to pray " always with all prayer and fupplication in the Spirit, and" to watch " thereunto with all perfeverance and fup- plication for all faints ; *and for me,*" adds he, " that *utterance* may be given unto me, that I may open my mouth boldly, to make known the myftery of the gofpel, for which I am an ambaffador in bonds ; that therein I may fpeak boldly, as I ought to fpeak," Eph. vi. 18—20. If the apoftle had need of the prayers of the faints, that he might have the *fpiritual* gift of *utterance,* how much more need, alas ! have we? Once more, " Ye are our epiftle written in our hearts, known and read of all men ; for- afmuch as ye are manifeftly declared to be the epiftle of Chrift, miniftered by us, written not with ink, but with the Spirit of the living God ; not in tables of ftone, but in flefhly tables of the heart, 2 Cor. iii. 2, 3. Here was *fruit !* The Lord grant us much of *this fruit !*

SECTION XII.

Of the Matter and Manner of Preaching, and of other public Exercifes.

Queft. 1. WHAT is the beft general method of preaching ?

Anſw. 1. To convince: 2. To offer Chriſt: 3. To invite: 4. To build up: And to do this in ſome meaſure in every ſermon.

Queſt. 2. What is the moſt effectual way of preaching Chriſt?

Anſw. The moſt effectual way of preaching Chriſt, is to preach him in all his offices; and to declare his law, as well as his goſpel, both to believers and unbelievers. Let us ſtrongly and cloſely inſiſt upon inward and outward holineſs in all its branches.

Queſt. 3. Are there any ſmaller advices, which might be of uſe to us?

Anſw. Perhaps theſe: 1. Be ſure never to diſappoint a congregation. 2. Begin at the time appointed. 3. Let your whole deportment be ſerious, weighty, and ſolemn. 4. Always ſuit your ſubject to your audience. 5. Chooſe the plaineſt text you can. 6. Take care not to ramble, but keep to your text, and make out what you take in hand. 7. Take care of any thing aukward or affected, either in your geſture, phraſe, or pronunciation. 8. Print nothing without the approbation of the conference, or of one of the biſhops. 9. Do not uſually pray *ex tempore* above eight or ten minutes (at moſt) without intermiſſion. 10. Frequently read and enlarge upon a portion of ſcripture; and let young preachers often exhort without taking a text. 11. Always avail yourſelf of the great feſtivals, by preaching on the occaſion.

N O T E S.

The preaching of the goſpel is of the firſt importance to the welfare of mankind; and, conſequently, *the mode* of preaching muſt be of conſiderable moment. It is not the fine metaphyſical reaſoning: it is not the philoſophical diſquiſitions of the works of nature under the pretext of raiſing up our minds to the great Creator, which regenerate the heart, and ſtamp the image of God upon the ſoul. No. The preacher muſt,

1. Convince the finner of his dangerous condition. He muft "break up the fallow ground."* "Cry aloud, fpare not," fays the Lord to his prophet, "lift up thy voice like a trumpet, and fhew my people their tranfgreffion, and the houfe of Jacob their fins," Ifai. lviii. 1. He muft fet forth the depth of original fin, and fhew the finner how far he is gone from original righteouf-nefs; he muft defcribe the vices of the world in their juft and moft ftriking colours, and enter into all the finner's pleas and ex-oufes for fin, and drive him from all his fubterfuges and ftrong-holds. He muft labour to convince the formalift of the impoffi-bility of being juftified before God by his ceremonial or moral righteoufnefs. Myriads are continually perifhing, yea, thoufands of thofe who acknowledge in fpeculation the great truths of the gofpel, through their dependance upon ordinances or upon an outwardly moral life. "In Chrift Jefus neither circumcifion availeth any thing, nor uncircumcifion, but *a new creature*," Gal. vi. 15. See the texts on the 8th and 9th articles of religion.

2. He muft fet forth the virtue of the *atoning blood*. He muft bring the mourner to a *prefent* Saviour: he muft fhew the wil-lingnefs of Chrift *this moment* to blefs him, and bring a prefent falvation *home* to his foul. Here he muft be indeed *a fon of confo-lation*. He muft fay nothing which can keep the trembling mourner at a diftance: he muft not provide for him a rich feaft, and hand it up to him in difhes too hot to be touched. There muft be nothing now held forth to the view of the penitent but the everlafting arms, and the mercy which is ready to embrace him on every fide. "Come unto me," fays our Lord, "all ye that labour and are heavy-laden, and I will give you reft," Matt. xi. 28. "Him that cometh to me, I will in no wife caft out," John vi. 37. "Having, therefore, brethren, boldnefs to enter into the holieft by the blood of Jefus,——let us draw near with a true heart, in full affurance of faith," &c. Heb. x. 19—22.

3. He muft, like a true fhepherd, feed the lambs and fheep of Chrift. He muft point out to the newly juftified the wiles of Satan, and ftrengthen them if they ftagger through unbelief. He muft fet before them the glorious privileges offered to them in the gofpel. He muft nourifh them with the pure milk of the word. Thofe who are more adult in grace, he muft feed with ftrong meat. He muft fhew them the neceffity of being cruci-fied to the world, and of dying daily: that "if they mortify not the deeds of the flefh, they fhall die." He muft not fpare the remaining man of fin: he muft anatomize the human heart, and follow felf-will and felf-love through all their windings. And all this being addreffed to the children of God, he muft do it

---

* *Jer.* iv. 3. *Hof.* x. 12.

with great tendernefs. " I proteft by your rejoicing which I have in Chrift Jefus our Lord, *I die daily*," fays the apoftle, 1 Cor. xv. 31. " If ye live after the flefh ye fhall die: but if ye, through the Spirit, do mortify the deeds of the body, ye fhall live," Rom viii. 13. — " *Grow in grace*, and in the knowledge of our Lord and Saviour, Jefus Chrift," 2 Pet. iii. 18.

And now he muft again turn the fon of confolation. He muft hold forth Chrift as an all-fufficient Saviour, as " able to fave them to the uttermoft that come unto God by him, feeing he ever liveth to make interceffion for them," Heb. vii. 25. He muft defcribe to them, in all its richeft views, the bleffing of perfect love. He muft now declare how our great Zerubbabel is *this moment* able and willing to reduce the mountain into a plain. And all the above he muft endeavour more or lefs to introduce into every fermon which he delivers to a mixed congregation. " The very God of peace fanctify you wholly, and I pray God your whole fpirit, foul, and body be preferved blamelefs unto the coming of our Lord Jefus Chrift. Faithful is he that calleth you, who alfo *will do it*," 1 Theff. v. 23. " This is the will of God, even your fanctification," iv. 3.

He muft preach the law as well as the gofpel. He muft hold forth our adorable Redeemer as a prophet to teach, a prieft to atone, and a king to reign in us and over us. He muft break the *flony* heart, as well as bind up the *broken*. But ftill *holinefs* inward and outward muft be his end: *holinefs* muft be his aim: and antinomianifm and every doctrine which oppofes *holinefs*, he muft contend with, till he gain the victory, or render his hearers utterly inexcufable. Who is fit for thefe things? O Lord God, help us all! Let us do our utmoft, and leave the bleffing to the Lord.

Acts iii. 22. " A *prophet* fhall the Lord your God raife up unto you of your brethren." Heb. v. 6. " Thou art *a Prieft* for ever." Ifai. xxxii. 1. " Behold *a king* fhall reign in righteoufnefs." O let us never be wearied of exalting Chrift, as *living in us*, as well as *dying for us*.

Some ufeful fmaller advices are now given, 1. Never break an engagement. This we have enlarged upon under the 8th fection of this chapter.

2. The fecond advice belongs only to town-congregations, where they have clocks and watches to direct them. In fuch cafes, if they attend not exactly at the appointed time, they will be equally tardy, if the preacher *habitually* wait for them ever fo long. But every where let *him* be always at the time. It is inexcufable *in one* to make a thoufand, or even a hundred, wait *for him*. Let " no man put a ftumbling-block, or an occafion to fall, in his brother's way," Rom. xiv. 13.

3. The deepest seriousness at all times becomes the minister of the gospel : but in the pulpit there should not be even *the appearance* of a deviation from it. An ambassador of an earthly government, when immediately engaged in the duties of his embassy, would be far from trifling : how much more should an ambassador of God ? " Do the work," therefore, " of an *evangelist*, make *full proof* of thy ministry," 2 Tim. 4. 5.

4. A preacher who seeks the honour which comes from God, and not that which comes from man, will consider the spiritual wants of his audience, and choose his text and subject accordingly. He will not preach to shew his own abilities, but merely *to do good*. And indeed, if he preach not from *this pure motive alone*, he has no right to expect the blessing of God upon his labours. See Luke xii. 42—44.

5. Be cautious of allegorizing. It seldom informs the judgment, and still seldomer warms the heart. It may be called a *pretty way* of talking. The preacher may be admired, but the hearer will be little edified. And what is applause, or any thing but the salvation of souls, to the faithful minister of Christ ? The genuine language of his heart is, ' I ask not riches, honours, or pleasures, gain or applause ; I ask only for the salvation of souls !' " And I, brethren, when I came to you, came not with excellency of speech, or of wisdom, declaring unto you the testimony of God. For I determined not to know any thing among you, save Jesus Christ, and him crucified," 1 Cor. ii. 1, 2.

6. When the preacher has fixed upon the subject which he judges most suitable to the states of the souls he is going to address, he must keep to his point. He must labour to arrange his ideas, and to speak to the understanding as well as the heart. He must first endeavour fully to explain, and then to apply, to " shew" himself " a workman that needeth not to be ashamed, rightly dividing the word of truth," 2 Tim. ii. 15.

7. He must take care, that his good be not evil spoken of, or laughed at, if possible, through any awkward or unmeaning gestures in the pulpit. When the instruction of immortal spirits is his employment, he should mind every thing little and great, which can assist him in this glorious work, in which angels would envy him, if it were possible for them to indulge so base a passion. " These things speak and exhort, and rebuke with all authority. Let no man despise thee," Tit. ii. 15.

8. Be not too forward in writing for the press. Nothing disgraces a cause so much, as to attempt to defend it in a feeble manner. Let not a few friends who are attached to you, and are not in the least degree judges of composition, prevail upon you to become an author. To write well requires a life devoted in a great measure to close and severe study. Preaching the everlasting gospel and spiritual instruction in season and out of season,

are your grand objects. There are so many excellent publications already in the world, which by the means of the press may be put into every hand, that there are fewer necessary to be written than many imagine. A few good writers in one church are quite sufficient, especially in ours, which has already been honoured with a Wesley and a Fletcher. But particularly comply with our express rules on this subject. " Of making many books there is no end," says the wise man, Ecclef. xii. 12.

9. Scarcely any thing tends to damp divine service more than to be praying too long, and in a languid manner. Few things more tend to bring a congregation into a *formal* spirit. Sometimes indeed the minister is led within the vail in an unsual way, and may then justly give full vent to the holy flame. But on other occasions let the prayer be very fervent, and of a moderate length. " When ye pray" says our Lord, " use not vain repetitions, as the heathen do : for they think that they shall be heard for their much speaking. Be not ye therefore like unto them," Matt. vi. 7, 8.

10. A comment on a portion of scripture is sometimes very profitable to the congregation, especially when a warm application is adjoined. And it is exceedingly useful for young preachers to habituate themselves to the giving of warm exhortations, otherwise they may get into a formal way of preaching without a due application of the subject. *A fervent exhortation* is preferable to *a sermon without application.* " Till I come," says St. Paul to Timothy, " give attendance to reading, *to exhortation*, to doctrine," 1 Ep. iv. 13.

11. Souls are of so much value, that we should improve every opportunity for their good. Shall the men of the world have carnal festivals on their birth-days, and shall we not commemorate the birth-day of our Lord? The primitive fathers of the church observed *the day*, which is *now* kept sacred by most of the churches of christendom. Irenæus who was one of the fathers, was a disciple of *St. John;* and the mother of Jesus lived with *that apostle* from the crucifixion of our Lord. There cannot therefore be a doubt but *St. John* knew, and of course his disciples, *Irenæus, Ignatius, and Polycarp*, the day of our Lord's nativity; and *from them* all the fathers of the church. Again, shall states and nations celebrate the day of liberation from slavery or oppression, or some other glorious event, from year to year? And shall *we* not celebrate by a holy festival the crucifixion and resurrection of our Lord, and the mission of the Holy Spirit, to which we are indebted for blessings infinitely more valuable than any which the revolution of states can possibly afford

SECTION XIII.

Of the Duty of Preachers to God, themselves, and one another.

Quest. 1. HOW shall a Preacher be qualified for his charge?

Answ. By walking closely with God, and having his work greatly at heart: And by understanding and loving discipline, ours in particular.

Quest. 2. Do we sufficiently watch over each other?

Answ. We do not. Should we not frequently ask each other, Do you walk closely with God? Have you now fellowship with the Father and the Son? At what hour do you rise? Do you punctually observe the morning and evening hour of retirement? Do you spend the day in the manner which the conference advises? Do you converse seriously, usefully, and closely? To be more particular: Do you use all the means of grace yourself, and enforce the use of them on all other persons? They are either instituted or prudential.

I. The instituted are,

1. Prayer; private, family, public; consisting of deprecation, petition, intercession, and thanksgiving. Do you use each of these? Do you forecast daily wherever you are, to secure time for private devotion? Do you practise it every where? Do you ask every where, Have you family-prayer? Do you ask individuals, Do you use private prayer every morning and evening in particular?

2. Searching the scriptures, by

(1) Reading; constantly, some part of every day: regularly, all the bible in order; carefully, with notes: seriously, with prayer before and after: fruitfully, immediately practising what you learn there?

(2) Meditating: At set times? By rule?

(3) Hearing: Every opportunity? With prayer before, at, after? Have you a bible always about you?

3. The Lord's supper: Do you use this at every

opportunity? With folemn prayer before? With ear-neft and deliberate felf-devotion?

4. Fafting: Do you ufe as much abftinence and faft-ing every week, as your health, ftrength, and labour will permit?

5. Chriftian conference: Are you convinced how important and how difficult it is to order your converfa-tion aright? Is it always in grace? Seafoned with falt? Meet to minifter grace to the hearers? Do you not converfe too long at a time? Is not an hour com-monly enough? Would it not be well always to have a determinate end in view? And to pray before and af-ter it?

II. Prudential means we may ufe, either as chrifti-ans, as Methodifts, or as preachers.

1. As chriftians: What particular rules have you in order to grow in grace? What arts of holy living?

2. As Methodifts: Do you never mifs your clafs or band?

3. As Preachers: have you thoroughly confidered your duty? And do you make a confcience of execut-ing every part of it? Do you meet every fociety? Al-fo, the leaders and bands?

Thefe means may be ufed without fruit. But there are fome means which cannot; namely, watching, de-nying ourfelves, taking up our crofs, exercife of the prefence of God.

1. Do you fteadily watch againft the world? Your-felf? Your befetting fin?

2. Do you deny yourfelf every ufelefs pleafure of fenfe? Imagination? Honour? Are you temperate in all things? Inftance in food. (1) Do you ufe only that kind, and that degree, which is beft both for your body and foul? Do you fee the neceffity of this? (2) Do you eat no more at each meal than is neceffary? Are you not heavy or drowfy after dinner? (3) Do you ufe only that kind and that degree of drink which is beft both for your body and foul? (4) Do you chufe and ufe water for your common drink? And only take wine medicinally or facramentally?

3. Wherein do you take up your crofs daily? Do you cheerfully bear your crofs, however grievous to nature, as a gift of God, and labour to profit thereby?

4. Do you endeavour to fet God always before you? To fee his eye continually fixed upon you? Never can you ufe thefe means, but a blefling will enfue. And the more you ufe them, the more will you grow in grace.

N O T E S.

The prefent fection is full of matter. Sermons might be written upon it without exhaufting it. It includes the whole of chriftianity. We can only give a few leading ideas on each article.

1. A minifter of the gofpel, who has confecrated all he is and has, and all he can do and fuffer, to the fervice of his God, fhould confider himfelf as eminently called *to walk with God*. His peculiar calling is of the moft public nature. It is a public profeffion, that he is a reformer of mankind: it fays more loudly than any words, " I am, or ought to be, one of the beft of men; follow me as I follow Chrift." It is the very depth of hypocrify to preach and not live the gofpel. Of all hypocrites fuch a one is the greateft. Nay, it is in vain to preach, it is in vain to fhew forth the moft fhining talents, if the life of the preacher correfpond not with his doctrines. He may poffibly have the reward he feeks for here below : but the approbation of God he never will receive. " Many will fay to me in that day," obferves our Lord, " Lord, Lord, have we not prophefied in thy name? and in thy name have caft out devils, and in thy name done many wonderful works? And then will I profefs unto them, I never knew you : depart from me, ye that work iniquity," Matt. vii. 22, 23.

The work of God muft alfo lie near his heart: yea, his very foul muft enter into it. Nor muft he be contented to preach, and then leave the fouls he has been bleffed to at the mercy of the world. He muft feek out the awakened. He muft fence in the flock. He muft not only love, but, according to his fphere of action, recommend and enforce chriftian difcipline, efpecially the difcipline of that church of which he is a member; without which there would be nothing but anarchy and confufion ; and the word of God would in general become " like water fpilt upon the ground." " Neither count I my life dear unto myfelf," fays St. Paul, " fo that I might finifh my courfe with joy, and the miniftry which I have received of the Lord Jefus, to teftify the gofpel of the grace of God," Acts xx. 24.

2. The preachers should tell each other in the spirit of love and meekness, and at the same time with humble boldness, all they think and all they fear of each other, in respect to every thing of consequence, particularly in regard to the spiritual life, the practice of devotion, and spiritual conversation. " Faithful are the wounds of a friend," says Solomon, Prov. xxvii. 6.

3. Ministers of the gospel should be eminently attentive to all the means of grace, particularly private prayer. We do rejoice that *our* ministers are examples to the flock in this respect. When in the mountains and wildernesses they have no chamber to themselves, they will retire into the woods and other solitary places, and spend much of their time in that most useful exercise. O that we may continue to preserve this spirit and practice ! " Thou, when thou prayest," says Christ, " enter into thy closet : and, when thou hast shut thy door, pray to thy Father which is in secret ; and thy Father which seeth in secret, shall reward thee openly," Matt. vi. 6. We should also in the families, where we from time to time reside, be examples to all. The whole world is composed of families. A travelling preacher may bring as many souls to glory by his fidelity in the families which he visits, as by his public preaching. See the 15th section of this chapter.

4. Preachers of the gospel should be much conversant in the Scriptures. They should never be without a bible. That invaluable book is like the starry heavens on a clear night : cast your eyes on any given part, and some bright stars will immediately strike your sight ; but the more you gaze, the more stars will appear to your view. It is an inexhaustible mine of the richest treasures. The more infidels despise and oppose it, the more should we love, study, and defend it. It is reproachful to see a minister of God *lounging away* his time, when the word of truth and salvation is within his reach. " I love thy commandments," says the psalmist, " above gold, yea, above fine gold," Psalm cix. 127. " My soul hath kept thy testimonies : and *I love them exceedingly*, ver. 167. " and *thy law is my delight*," ver. 174.

5. Whenever we have opportunity to eat of the bread and drink of the cup of the Lord, we should not only as far as possible make it a blessing to others, but also to ourselves. See the texts quoted in the notes on the 16th and 18th articles of religion.

6. The duty of fasting is strongly recommended in the sacred writings. That or abstinence frequently observed, is highly necessary for the divine life. Pf. xxxv. 13. " I humbled my soul with *fasting*." lxix. 10. " When I wept and chastened my soul with *fasting*." cix. 24. " My knees are weak through *fasting*." Dan. ix. 3. " I set my face unto the Lord God, to seek by prayer and supplications, with *fasting*." Joel ii. 12. " Turn ye even

unto me with all your heart, and with *fasting*, and with weeping, and with mourning." Matt. vi. 16—18. " *When ye fast*, be not as the hypocrites.—But thou, *when thou fastest*, anoint thine head, &c.—that thou appear not unto men to fast, but unto thy Father, which is in secret, &c." Matt. xvii. 14—21. " This kind goeth not out but by prayer and *fasting*." See also Mark ix. 29. Luke ii. 37. " She [Anna] served God with *fastings*, and prayers night and day." Acts x. 30. " Four days ago I [Cornelius] was *fasting* until this hour, &c." 1 Cor. vii. 5. " That ye may give yourselves to *fasting* and prayer." 2 Cor. vi. 5. " In watchings, *in fastings*." xi. 27. " in hunger and thirst, *in fastings often*."

7. How awful are those words of our Lord, " By thy words thou shalt be justified, and by thy words thou shalt be condemned," Matt. xii. 37. When the conversation is always " seasoned with salt," you will never lose a day : your whole life will be a constant blessing to all around you : " only let your conversation be as it becometh the gospel of Christ," Phil. i. 27.

8. What lives should they live, who bear the sacred name of *christian*, and especially of *christian minister*. The infidels themselves, in general, will acknowledge the excellence of the *christian* morality. But where say they is the man who comes up to the model ? They know him not, because to the poor the gospel is preached. They despise the poor and the ministers of the poor. O that the screen of formalism and hypocrisy was but *removed*, that the church of God might become the city set upon a hill ! And it *shall* be removed. The Lord Jesus has already given the outward court to be trodden under foot by the gentiles; and the whole temple of God shall soon be cleansed, and Israel shall dwell alone. How soon would this be brought about, if all the ministers of the gospel did but answer the model, " by pureness, by knowledge, by long-suffering, by kindness, by the Holy Ghost, by love unfeigned, by the word of truth, by the power of God, by the armour of righteousness on the right hand and on the left !" 2 Cor. vi. 6, 7.

9. Methodist preachers should *love* every part of their duty. It is *love* alone which can oil the wheels, and make them run in the paths of duty like the chariots of Aminidab. Where slavish fear is the base motive, all is misery. But when we do every thing in the spirit of love, when " the love of Christ constraineth us," all is delight. 2 Cor. v. 14.

10. A Methodist preacher has raised up his standard, and declared open war against the vices of the world. He must expect to be hated or despised by all men, except the children of God, and those who are seeking so to be. This is his great advantage, if he bear it with patience. The wall of contempt which surrounds him, preserves him from a thousand temptations to which

ether minifters are expofed. But he has a world within him far more dangerous,—" the luft of the eye, the luft of the flefh, and the pride of life," 1 John ii. 16. Every converted perfon knows his befetting fin; and this will attack him, and conquer him, among profeffors, among poffeffors of grace, yea, in the moft folitary place, *unlefs he watches unto prayer.* " Be not conformed to this world," Rom. xii. 2. " Let us lay afide every weight, and the fin which doth fo eafily befet us," Heb. xii. 1.

11. The true minifter of Chrift delights in the crofs. His adorable Lord has confecrated it, and he takes it up with cheer-fulnefs, and " follows the Lamb whitherfoever he goeth." The love of God in his heart makes bitter things fweet, and difficult things eafy. " He is temperate in all things." He eyes God in every thing, and " walks with God." God is the joy of his heart, and the delight of his eyes, and his all-fufficient portion. " Thou, God, feeft me," is written upon his inmoft foul. " Whether he eats or drinks, or whatfoever he doth, he doth it all to the glory of God," 1 Cor. x. 31. " If any man will come after me," fays Chrift, " let him deny himfelf, and take up his crofs, and follow me," Matt. xvi. 24. See alfo Mark viii. 34, and Luke 9. 24.

SECTION XIV.

Rules by which we fhould continue, or defift from, Preaching at any Place.

Queft. 1. IS it advifable for us to preach in as many places as we can, without forming any focieties?

Anfw. By no means: We have made the trial in various places; and that for a confiderable time. But all the feed has fallen by the way-fide. There is fcarce any fruit remaining.

Queft. 2. Where fhould we endeavour to preach moft?

Anfw. 1. Where there are the greateft number of quiet and willing hearers.

2. Where there is the moft fruit.

Queft. 3. Ought we not diligently to obferve, in what places God is pleafed at any time to pour out his Spirit more abundantly?

Anfw. We ought : And at that time, to fend more labourers than ufual into that part of the harveft.

N O T E S.

1. The anfwer to the firft queftion of this feคtion, given in Europe by Mr. Wefley, after long experience and extenfive travels, is a proof of the importance of chriftian difcipline. Where the people defpife or neglect chriftian difcipline or fellowfhip, little or no good is ever done. It is indeed a proof that few in fuch cafes are awakened. The awakened foul is ready to embrace every affiftance, which the word of God recommends, and the circumftances of things will admit of. Mal. iii. 16—18. " Then *they that feared the Lord fpake often one to another :* and the Lord hearkened, and heard it : and a book of remembrance was written before him for *them that feared the Lord,* and that thought upon his name. And *they fhall be mine,* faith the Lord of hofts, in that day when I make up my jewels; and I will fpare them, as a man fpareth his own fon that ferveth him. *Then* fhall ye return, and DISCERN between the righteous and the wicked; between him that ferveth God, and him that ferveth him not."

2. Our life is fhort. We muft not only do good, but *the moft* in our power. As we fhould, on the one hand, prefer a fmall congregation to a large one, if the fmall one produces a company of precious fouls united in love to God and each other, whilft the large one affords none but thofe who live in the fpirit of the world: fo, on the other hand, we fhould prefer the largeft congregation with proportionable fruit to any other confideration. In fhort, nothing fhould, *nothing will,* influence the true minifter of Chrift but the glory of God, the falvation of fouls, crucifixion to the world and all things in it, and the life of God in the foul of man. Comfortable lodgings, agreeable food, or the company of perfons of improved minds, will never for a moment *by him* be put into the balance. *His* fingle queftion at all times and in all places will be, " Where fhall I bring moft fouls to Jefus Chrift ?" " Say not ye," obferves our Lord, " There are yet four months, and then cometh harveft ? behold, I fay unto you, Lift up your eyes, and look on the fields ; for they are white already to harveft," John iv. 35. *That* is the gofpel-call for the labourer.

3. He will, therefore, above all things, attend to the out-pourings of grace. He will labour moft, where the Lord moft abundantly pours forth his Spirit. And this will be the conduct not only of a fingle individual, but of general bodies of faithful minifters. Our yearly conferences conftantly take this point into confideration. The ftationing of the preachers is in the epifco-

pacy; but the determination of the number of preachers to be sent to a circuit is in the yearly conference; with powers invested in the epifcopacy and prefiding-elderfhip to meet the openings of grace and Providence in the intervals of the conference. We muft in all things follow, and not run before the Lord. It is a great thing to ftudy the will of God in his word and providence unitedly confidered. " I will tarry at Ephefus until Pentecoft," fays St. Paul; " for *a great and effectual door* is opened unto me, and there are many adverfaries." However numerous or great his oppofers may be, the true minifter of Chrift improves the gracious opportunity God is pleafed to put into his hands, with thankfulnefs and zeal.

SECTION XV.

Of visiting from House to House, guarding against those Sins that are so common to Professors, and enforcing Practical Religion.

Quest. 1. HOW can we further affift thofe under our care?

Anfw. By inftructing them at their own houfes. What unfpeakable need is there of this! The world fays, " *The Methodifts are no better than other people.*" This is not true in the general: But, 1. Perfonal religion. either toward God or man, is too fuperficial amongft us. We can but juft touch on a few particulars. How little faith is there among us? How little communion with God? How little living in heaven, walking in eternity, deadnefs to every creature? How much love of the world? Defire of pleafure, of eafe, of getting money? How little brotherly love? What continual judging one another? What goffipping, evil-fpeaking, tale-bearing? What want of moral honefty? To inftance only one particular;—who does as he would be done by, in buying and felling?

2. Family religion is wanting in many branches, And what avails public preaching alone, though we could preach like angels? We muft, yea, every travelling preacher muft inftruct the people from houfe to

houfe. Till this is done, and that in good earneft, the Methodifts will be no better.

Our religion is not deep, univerfal, uniform : but fu-perficial, partial, uneven. It will be fo till we fpend half as much time in this vifiting, as we now do in talk-ing ufelefsly. Can we find a better method of doing this than Mr. Baxter's? If not, let us adopt it without delay. His whole tract, entitled, *Gildas Salvianus*, is well worth a careful perufal. Speaking of this vifiting from houfe to houfe, he fays (p. 351.)

• " We fhall find many hindrances, both in ourfelves and the people.

1. In ourfelves, there is much dulnefs and lazinefs, fo that there will be much ado to get us to be faithful in the work.

2. We have a bafe, man-pleafing temper, fo that we let men perifh rather than lofe their love : we let them go quietly to hell, left we fhould offend them.

3. Some of us have alfo a foolifh bafhfulnefs. We know not how to begin, and blufh to contradict the devil.

4. But the greateft hindrance is weaknefs of faith. Our whole motion is weak, becaufe the fpring of it is weak.

5. Laftly, we are unfkilful in the work. How few know how to deal with men, fo as to get within them, and fuit all our difcourfe to their feveral conditions and tempers : To choofe the fitteft fubjects, and follow them with a holy mixture of ferioufnefs, terror, love, and meeknefs ?"

But undoubtedly this private application is implied in thofe folemn words of the apoftle, *I charge thee before God and the Lord Jefus Chrift, who fhall judge the quick and dead at his appearing, preach the word ; be inftant in feafon, out of feafon : Reprove, rebuke, exhort, with all long-fuffering.*

O brethren, if we could but fet this work on foot in all our focieties, and profecute it zealoufly, what glory would redound to God ! If the common lukewarmnefs were banifhed, and every fhop and every houfe bufied in fpeaking of the word and works of God; furely God would dwell in our habitations, and make us his delight.

And this is abfolutely neceffary to the welfare of our people, fome of whom neither repent nor believe to this day. Look round, and fee how many of them are ftill in apparent danger of damnation. And how can you walk, and talk, and be merry with fuch people, when you know their cafe? Methinks when you look them in the face, you fhould break forth into tears, as the prophet did when he looked upon Hazael, and then fet on them with the moft vehement exhortations. O, for God's fake, and the fake of poor fouls, beftir yourfelves, and fpare no pains that may conduce to their falvation!

What caufe have we to bleed before the Lord this day, that we have fo long neglected this good work! If we had but engaged in it fooner, how many more might have been brought to Chrift? And how much holier and happier might we have made our focieties before now? And why might we not have done it fooner? There were many hindrances: And fo there always will be. But the greateft hindrance was in ourfelves, in our littlenefs of faith and love.

But it is objected, I. " This will take up fo much time, we fhall not have leifure to follow our ftudies."

We anfwer, 1. Gaining knowledge is a good thing, but faving fouls is a better. 2. By this very thing you will gain the moft excellent knowledge, that of God and eternity. 3. You will have time for gaining other knowledge too. Only fleep not more than you need: " and never be idle, or triflingly employed." But, 4. If you can do but one, let your ftudies alone. We ought to throw by all the libraries in the world, rather than be guilty of the lofs of one foul.

It is objected, II. " The people will not fubmit to it." If fome will not, others will. And the fuccefs with them, will repay all your labour. O let us herein follow the example of St Paul. 1. For our general bufinefs, *Serving the Lord with all humility of mind* · 2. Our

ſpecial work, *Take heed to yourſelves, and to all the flock:*
3. Our doctrine, *Repentance towards God, and faith towards our Lord Jeſus Chriſt:* 4. The place, *I have
taught you publicly, and from houſe to houſe:* 5. The object
and manner of teaching, *I ceaſed not to warn every one,
night and day, with tears:* 6. His innocence and ſelf-de-
nial herein, *I have coveted no man's ſilver or gold:* 7. His
patience, *Neither count I my life dear unto myſelf.* And
among all other motives, let theſe be ever before our
eyes: 1. *The church of God, which he hath purchaſed with
his own blood.* 2. *Grievous wolves ſhall enter in: yea, of
yourſelves ſhall men ariſe, ſpeaking perverſe things.*

Write this upon your hearts, and it will do you more
good than twenty years ſtudy. Then you will have no
time to ſpare: You will have work enough. Then
likewiſe no preacher will ſtay with us who is as ſalt that
has loſt its ſavour. For to ſuch this employment would
be mere drudgery. And in order to it, you will have
need of all the the knowledge you can procure, and
grace you can attain.

The ſum is, Go into every houſe in courſe, and teach
every one therein, young and old, to be chriſtians inwardly and outwardly; make every particular plain to
their underſtandings; fix it in their minds; write it on
their hearts. In order to this, there muſt be line upon
line, precept upon precept. What patience, what love,
what knowledge is requiſite for this! We muſt needs do
this, were it only to avoid idleneſs. Do we not loiter
away many hours in every week? Each try himſelf: No
idleneſs is conſiſtent with a growth in grace. Nay, without exactneſs in redeeming time, you cannot retain the
grace you received in juſtification.

Queſt. 2. Why are we not more holy, why do we not
live in eternity? Walk with God all the day long?
Why are we not all devoted to God? Breathing the
whole ſpirit of miſſionaries?

Anſw. Chiefly becauſe we are enthuſiaſts; looking
for the end without uſing the means. To touch only
upon two or three inſtances: Who of you riſes at four

Or even at five, when he does not preach? Do you know the obligation and benefit of fasting or abstinence? How often do you practise it? The neglect of this alone is sufficient to account for our feebleness and faintness of spirit. We are continually grieving the Holy Spirit of God by the habitual neglect of a plain duty. Let us amend from this hour.

Quest. 3. How shall we guard against sabbath-breaking, evil-speaking, unprofitable conversation, lightness, expensiveness or gaiety of apparel, and contracting debts without due care to discharge them?

Answ. 1. Let us preach expressly on each of these heads. 2. Read in every society the sermon on evil-speaking. 3. Let the leaders closely examine and exhort every person to put away the accursed thing. 4. Let the preachers warn every society, that none who is guilty herein, can remain with us. 5. Extirpate buying or selling goods which have not paid the duty laid upon them by government, out of every society. Let none remain with us who will not totally abstain from this evil in every kind and degree. Extirpate bribery, receiving any thing directly or indirectly, for voting at any election. Shew no respect to persons herein, but expel all that touch the accursed thing. And strongly advise our people to discountenance all treats given by candidates before or at elections, and not to be partakers in any respect of such iniquitous practices.

Quest. 4. What shall we do to prevent scandal, when any of our members fail in business, or contract debts which they are not able to pay?

Answ. Let him who has the charge of the circuit, desire two or three judicious members of the society to inspect the accounts of the supposed delinquent; and if he has behaved dishonestly, or borrowed money without a probability of paying, let him be expelled.

N O T E S.

We need not enlarge on the great duty of visiting from house to house. The section so far explains itself, and is full of the moſt pathetic exhortation. We will, therefore, only make a few brief obſervations, and proceed.

In the plantations, which make the chief part of theſe ſtates, and in which, of courſe, the chief part of our ſocieties reſide, the preachers cannot viſit many of our competent families in a day. But they may almoſt daily viſit many of the poor—many of thoſe who moſt want their help. Various diſagreeable circumſtances ariſing from the inattention of *the poor* to cleanlineſs, &c. may attend our zealous obſervance of the directions given in this ſection on the preſent ſubject, as far as it reſpects *them*. But where is our zeal for God, where our crucifixion to the world, where our regard for ſouls, if ſuch conſiderations move us in the leaſt? Our Lord gives it as one grand proof of his being the Meſſiah, that " the poor have the goſpel preached to them," Matt. xi. 5. O then, if we love Chriſt, if we wiſh to be his miniſters and diſciples, let us not forget the poor. We have but little ſilver or gold to offer them; but we have what is infinitely more precious, even grace, pardon, holineſs, Chriſt, heaven. Let us, therefore, labour *at leaſt* as much in the houſes of the poor as of the rich or competent: and *this we certainly ſhall*, if we he not intereſted by carnal or temporal motives—if we breathe the true ſpirit of miſſionaries.

The following texts of Scripture are applicable to the duties enforced, or the ſins condemned, in this ſection.

1. On the relative duties. Epheſ. vi. 4. *Ye fathers*, provoke not *your children* to wrath; but bring them up in the nurture and admonition of the Lord. See alſo Col. iii. 21. Ver. 20. *Children*, obey *your parents* in all things, for this is well-pleaſing unto the Lord. See alſo Epheſ. vi. 1. Col. iii. 19. *Huſbands*, love *your wives*, and be not bitter againſt them. See alſo Epheſ. v. 25—31. Ver. 22. *Wives*, ſubmit yourſelves unto *your own huſbands*, as unto the Lord. See alſo Col. iii. 18. Col. iv. 1. *Maſters*, give unto *your ſervants* that which is juſt and equal, knowing that ye alſo have a Maſter in heaven. See alſo Epheſ. vi. 9. Col. i. 22. *Servants*, obey, in all things, *your maſters*, according to the fleſh, not with eye-ſervice, as men-pleaſers; but in ſingleneſs of heart, fearing God. See alſo Epheſ. vi. 6.

2. On the obſervance of the ſabbath. Gen. ii. 3. God bleſſed the ſeventh day, and ſanctified it. Exod. xx. 10, 11. But the ſeventh day is the ſabbath of the Lord thy God.—Wherefore the Lord bleſſed the ſabbath-day, and hallowed it. xxiii. 12. On the ſeventh day thou ſhalt reſt. Numb. xv. 32—35. They found a man that gathered ſticks on the ſabbath-day.——And the Lord ſaid unto Moſes, The man ſhall be ſurely put to death. See alſo Neh. xiii. 15—22. Iſai. lviii. 13, 14. If thou turn away thy foot from the ſabbath, from doing thy pleaſure on my holy day, and call the ſabbath a delight, the holy of the Lord, honourable,

and shalt honour him, not doing thine own ways, nor finding thine own pleasure, nor speaking thine own words: then shalt thou delight thyself in the Lord; and I will cause thee to ride upon the high places of the earth, and feed thee with the heritage of Jacob thy father: for the mouth of the Lord hath spoken it. lvi. 2. Blessed is the man that doeth this, and the son of man that layeth hold on it; that keepeth the sabbath from polluting it, and keepeth his hand from doing any evil. Mark ii. 28. The Son of man is Lord also of the sabbath. See also Luke vi. 5. Luke xiii. 10. He was teaching in one of the synagogues on the sabbath. Acts xiii. 42—44. When the Jews were gone out of the synagogue, *the gentiles* besought that these words might be preached *unto them* the next *sabbath-day.*——And *the next sabbath-day*, came almost the whole city together to hear the word of God. xvi. 13. *On the sabbath* we went out of the city by a river-side, *where prayer was wont to be made;* and we sat down, and spake unto the women which resorted thither. xviii. 4. He reasoned in the synagogue every sabbath, and persuaded the Jews and Greeks. Rev. i. 10. I was in the spirit *on the Lord's day.* Acts xx. 7. *On the first day of the week*, when the disciples came together to break bread, Paul preached unto them. John xx. 19. Then the same day at evening, being *the first day of the week*, when the doors were shut, where the disciples were assembled, for fear of the Jews, came Jesus, and stood in the midst, &c. I Cor. xvi. 2. *Upon the first day of the week* let every one of you lay by him in store, as God hath prospered him.

3. Against *gossiping.* I Tim. v. 13. Withal they learn to be idle, wandering about from house to house; and not only idle, but tattlers also, and busy-bodies, speaking things which they ought not. I Thess. iv. 11. Study to be quiet, and to do your own business, and to work with your own hands, as we commanded you.

4. Against speaking evil. Tit. iii. 1, 2. Put them in mind—to speak evil of no man.

5. Against buying or selling goods which have not paid the legal duty. Matt. xxii. 21. Then saith he [Jesus] unto them, Render, therefore, unto Cæsar the things which are Cæsar's. See also Mark xii. 17. Luke xx. 25. and Rom. xiii. 6, 7.

6. Against bribery in elections. Isai. xxxiii. 15, 16. He that walketh righteously, and speaketh uprightly; he that despiseth the gain of oppressions, *that shaketh his hands from holding of bribes*, &c. he shall dwell on high; his place of defence shall be the munition of rocks.

7. Against contracting debts without being able to pay them. Rom. xiii. 8. Owe no man any thing, but to love one another. Lev. xix. 13. Thou shalt not defraud thy neighbour. I Thess. iv. 3—6. This is the will of God,——that no man go beyond and

defraud his brother *in any matter;* becaufe that the Lord is the avenger *of all fuch,* as we alfo have forewarned you, and teftified:

SECTION XVI.

Of the Inftruction of Children.

Queft. WHAT fhall we do for the rifing generation?

Anfw 1. Let him who is zealous for God and the fouls of men begin now.

2. Where there are ten children whofe parents are in fociety, meet them an hour once a week; but were this is impracticable, meet them once in two weeks.

3. Procure our inftructions for them, and let all who can, read and commit them to memory.

4. Explain and imprefs them upon their hearts.

5. Talk with them every time you fee any at home.

6. Pray earneftly for them: And diligently inftruct and exhort all parents at their own houfes.

7. Let the elders, deacons, and preachers, take a lift of the names of the children; and if any of them be truly awakened, let them be admited into fociety.

8. Preach exprefsly on education: "But I have no gift for this." Pray earneftly for the gift, and ufe every other means to attain it.

NOTES.

The proper education of children is of exceeding great moment to the welfare of mankind. About one half of the human race are under the age of fixteen, and may be confidered, the infants excepted, as capable of inftruction. The welfare of the ftates and countries in which they live, and, what is infinitely more, the falvation of their fouls, do, under the grace and providence of God, depend in a confiderable degree upon their education. But, alas! the great difficulty lies in finding men and women of genuine piety as inftructors. Let us, however, endeavour to fupply thefe *fpiritual* defects. Let us follow the directions of this fection, and we fhall meet many on the day of judgment, who will acknowledge before the Great Judge, and an affembled univerfe, that their firft defires after Chrift and falvation were received in their younger years by our inftrumentality. In town's we may, without difficulty, meet the children weekly, and in the plantations advife and pray with them every time we vifit their houfes : Nay, in the country, if we give notice that at fuch a time we fhall fpend an hour or two in fuch a houfe with thofe children who fhall attend, many of the neighbours will efteem it a privilege to fend their children to us at the time appointed. But we muft exercife much patience, as well as zeal, for the fuccefsful accomplifhment of this work. And if we can with love and delight condefcend to their ignorance and childifhnefs, and yet endeavour continually to raife up their little minds to the once dying but now exalted Saviour, we fhall be made a bleffing to thoufands of them.

But let us labour *among the poor* in this refpect, as well as among the competent. O if our people in the cities, towns, and villages were but fufficiently fenfible of the magnitude of this duty, and its acceptablenefs to God—If they would eftablifh fabbath-fchools, wherever practicable, for the benefit of the children *of the poor*, and facrifice a few public ordinances every Lord's-day to this charitable and ufeful exercife, God would be to them inftead of all the means they lofe; yea, they would find, to their prefent comfort and the increafe of their eternal glory, the truth and fweetnefs of thofe words, " Mercy is better than facrifice," Matt. ix. 13. and xii. 7. and Hof. vi. 6. But there is fo much of the crofs in all this ! O when fhall we be the true followers of a crucified Saviour !

The following fcriptures enforce the prefent duty : Gen. xviii. 19. I [Jehovah] know him [Abraham] that he will command his children and his houfehold after him, and they fhall keep the way of the Lord. Deut. vi. 6, 7. Thefe words, which I command thee this day, fhall be in thine heart. And thou fhalt teach them diligently unto thy children, and fhalt talk of them when thou fitteft in thine houfe, and when thou walkeft by the way, and when thou lieft down, and when thou rifeft up. Prov. xxii. 6. Train up a child in the way he fhould go; and when he is old he will not depart from it. Mark x. 14. Suffer the little children to come unto me, and forbid them not. 2 Tim. iii. 15. *From a child* thou haft known the holy fcriptures, which are able to make thee wife unto falvation, which is in Chrift Jefus.

N. B. We particularly recommend our fcripture-catechifm for the ufe of children.

SECTION XVII.

Of employing our Time profitably, when we are not travelling, or engaged in public Exercises.

Queſt. 1. WHAT general method of employing our time would you adviſe us to?

Anſw. We adviſe you, 1. As often as poſſible to riſe at four. 2. From four to five in the morning, and from five to ſix in the evening, to meditate, pray, and read the ſcriptures with notes, and the cloſely practical parts of what Mr. Weſley has publiſhed. 3. From ſix in the morning till twelve (allowing an hour for breakfaſt) read, with much prayer, ſome of our beſt religious tracts.

Queſt. 2. Why is it that the people under our care are not better?

Anſw. Other reaſons may concur; but the chief is, becauſe we are not more knowing and more holy.

Queſt 3. But why are we not more knowing?

Anſw. Becauſe we are idle. We forget our firſt rule, " Be diligent. Never be unemployed. Never be triflingly employed: neither ſpend any more time at any place than is ſtrictly neceſſary." We fear there is altogether a fault in this matter, and that few of us are clear. Which of us ſpends as many hours a day in God's work, as he did formerly in man's work? We talk, talk—or read what comes next to hand. We muſt, abſolutely muſt, cure this evil, or betray the cauſe of God. But how? 1. Read the moſt uſeful books, and that regularly and conſtantly. 2. Steadily ſpend all the morning in this employment, or at leaſt five hours in four and twenty. " But I have no taſte for reading." Contract a taſte for it by uſe, or return to your former employment. " But I have no books." Be diligent to ſpread the books, and you will have the uſe of them.

N O T E S.

We have already enlarged so much on the public and private duties of ministers, that on the limited plan and laconic mode we have adopted in these annotations, it may not be necessary to say much more on this subject. We would just recommend to our ministers and preachers, agreeably to the directions given in this section, *much reading and study.* We have various ranks of men to deal with, and as far as possible should be prepared for them all; that as scribes instructed unto the kingdom of heaven, we may, like unto a man that is an householder, bring forth out of our treasures things new and old. See Matt. xiii. 52. A taste for reading profitable books is an inestimable gift. It adds to the comfort of life far beyond what many conceive, and qualifies us, if properly directed, for very extensive usefulness in the church of God. It takes off all the miserable listlessness of a sluggish life; and gives to the mind a strength and activity it could not otherwise acquire. But to obtain and preserve this taste for, this delight in, profitable reading, we must daily resist the natural tendency of man to indolence and idleness. And when we consider the astonishing activity of the enemies of revealed truth, to disseminate their pernicious doctrines, we must allow that it behoves every minister of Jesus Christ, not only to be able to " give an answer to every man that asketh him a reason of the hope that is in him, with meekness and fear," (I Pet. iii. 15.) but to answer and silence the most subtle arguments of the professed enemies of our adorable Lord. "Till I come," says St. Paul, " GIVE ATTENDANCE TO READING," I Tim. iv. 13. Heb. vi. 11, 12. We desire—that ye be not slothful. See also Ephes. v. 16. Col. iv. 5. 2 Tim. ii. 15. and iv. 13.

S E C T I O N XVIII.

Of the Necessity of Union among ourselves.

LET us be deeply sensible (from what we have known) of the evil of a division in principle, spirit, or practice, and the dreadful consequences to ourselves and others. If we are united, what can stand before us? If we divide, we shall destroy ourselves, the work of God, and the souls of our people.

Quest. What can be done in order to a closer union with each other?

Anſw. 1. Let us be deeply convinced of the abſolute neceſſity of it.

2. Pray earneſtly for, and ſpeak freely to each other.

3. When we meet, let us never part without prayer.

4. Take great care not to deſpiſe each other's gifts.

5. Never ſpeak lightly of each other.

6. Let us defend each other's character in every thing, ſo far as is conſiſtent with truth.

7. Labour, in honour, each to prefer the other before himſelf.

N. B. We recommend a ſerious peruſal of *The Cauſes, Evils, and Cures of Heart and Church Diviſions.*

N O T E S.

We have already in our notes on the 4th and 5th ſections, enlarged on the great conſequence of our union to the preſervation and extenſion of the gracious work of God, in which we are engaged. We have alſo given a collection of moſt pointed ſcriptures againſt diviſion and contention in our notes on the 22d article of religion, to which we particularly refer the reader. And we muſt alſo very ſtrongly recommend all our miniſters and preachers to read with the greateſt attention the book which is noticed in this ſection, intitled *The Cauſes, Evils, and Cures of Heart and Church Diviſions.* We could write a volume on this weighty ſubject. Let us preſerve our union, and with the Prince of Peace at our head, we ſhall bear down the oppoſition of all our ſpiritual and temporal enemies. We ſhall imperceptibly gain ground on every hand, and be ourſelves from time to time aſtoniſhed at the progreſs of the work of God. *Love,* when properly directed by united hearts and united endeavours, is the ſtrongeſt thing in the univerſe. But we muſt conclude this ſubject, and only leave upon your minds ſome additional ſuitable paſſages of THE WORD OF GOD.

Pſ. cxxxiii. 1. Behold, how good and how pleaſant it is for brethren to dwell together in unity! See the whole Pſalm. Rom. xii. 10. Be kindly affectioned one to another with brotherly love; in honour preferring one another. Ver. 18. If it be poſſible, as much as lieth in you, live peaceably with all men. Rom. xii. 4, 5. As we have many members in one body, and all members have not the ſame office; ſo we, being many, are *one body in Chriſt,* and every one members one of another. 1 Cor. xii. 12—14. As the body is one, and hath many members, and all the members of that one body, being many, are one body; ſo alſo is Chriſt.

For by one Spirit are we all baptized into one body, whether we be Jews or Gentiles, whether we be bond or free; and have been all made to drink into one Spirit, for the body is not one member, but many. Ver. 25—27. That there should be no schism in the body; but that the members should have the same care one for another. And whether one member suffer, all the members suffer with it: or one member be honoured, all the members rejoice with it. Now ye are the body of Christ, and members in particular. 2 Cor. xiii. 11. Be perfect, be of good comfort, *be of one mind, live in peace;* and the God of love and peace shall be with you. Eph. ii. 20—22. [Ye] are built upon the foundation of the apostles and prophets, Jesus Christ himself being the chief corner-stone: in whom all the building, fitly framed together, groweth unto an holy temple in the Lord: in whom *ye* also *are builded together* for an habitation of God through the Spirit. iv. 3—6. Endeavouring to keep the unity of the Spirit in the bond of peace. There is one body, and one Spirit, even as ye are called in one hope of your calling; one Lord, one faith, one baptism, one God and Father of all, who is above all, and through all, and in you all. Phil. ii. 1, 2. If there be, therefore, any consolation in Christ, if any comfort of love, if any fellowship of the Spirit, if any bowels and mercies, fulfil ye my joy, *that ye be like-minded, having the same love, being of one accord, of one mind.*

SECTION XIX.

*Of the Method by which immoral travelling Ministers or Preachers shall be brought to trial, found guilty, and reproved or suspended in the Intervals of the Conferences.**

Quest. 1. WHAT shall be done when an elder, deacon, or preacher, is under the report of being guilty of *some crime,* expresly forbidden in the word of God, as an unchristian practice sufficient to exclude a person from the kingdom of grace and glory, and to make him a subject of wrath and hell?

Answ. Let the presiding elder, in the absence of a bishop, call as many ministers as he shall think fit, at

K

* For the trial of a bishop, see section IV.

leaſt three, and if poſſible bring the accuſed and accuſer face to face. If the perſon be clearly convicted, he ſhall be ſuſpended from all official ſervices in the church, till the enſuing yearly conference; at which his caſe ſhall be fully conſidered and determined. But if the accuſed be a *preſiding* elder, the preachers muſt call in the preſiding elder of the neighbouring diſtrict, who is required to attend, and preſide at the trial.

If the accuſed and accuſer cannot be brought face to face, but the ſuppoſed delinquent flees from trial, it ſhall be received as a preſumptive proof of guilt; and out of the mouth of two or three witneſſes he ſhall be condemned. Nevertheleſs, even in that caſe, the yearly conference ſhall re-conſider the whole matter and determine.

Queſt. 2. What ſhall be done in caſes of improper tempers, words, or actions?

Anſw. The perſon ſo offending ſhall be reprehended by his ſenior in office. Should a ſecond tranſgreſſion take place, one, two or three miniſters or preachers are to be taken as witneſſes. If he be not then cured, he ſhall be tried at the next yearly conference, and, if found guilty and impenitent, ſhall be expelled from the connection, and his name ſo returned in the minutes of the conference.

Queſt. 3. What ſhall be done with thoſe miniſters or preachers, who hold and preach doctrines which are contrary to our articles of religion?

Anſw. Let the ſame proceſs be obſerved as in caſes of groſs immorality: but if the miniſter or preacher ſo offending do ſolemnly engage, neither to preach nor defend ſuch erroneous doctrines in public or in private, he ſhall be borne with, till his caſe be laid before the next yearly conference, which ſhall determine the matter.

Provided nevertheleſs, that in all the above-mentioned caſes of trial and conviction, an appeal to the enſuing general conferen' ſhall be allowed.

N O T E S.

The section now under confideration is of very great moment. Let us take a view of it under the three heads into which it divides itfelf.

1. The anfwer to the firft queftion ferves to remove every reafonable objection to the *fufpending* power of the prefiding elder. See fection the 5th of this chapter. The trial of a minifter or preacher for grofs immorality fhall be in the prefence of at leaft three minifters. Thefe minifters have, of courfe, full liberty to fpeak their fentiments either in favour or difavour of the perfon accufed. This muft always ferve as a ftrong check on the prefiding elder, refpecting the abufe of his power. An act of tyranny would be fo oppofed by the minifters prefent, and fo reprefented afterwards in favour of the oppreffed, that the prefiding elder who would venture upon an arbitrary ftep, would find himfelf dreadfully embarraffed. Befides, thofe minifters could lay the whole affair before the general conference, if near at hand; or before the enfuing yearly conference; or, as foon as poffible, before a bifhop: in which cafes, the injured perfon might have complete redrefs, and the prefiding elder cenfured or punifhed according to his deferts: and thofe minifters could give all poffible information, having been prefent at the whole of the trial.

The paffage in St. Matthew, ch. xviii. 15—17. " If thy brother fhall trefpafs againft thee, go and tell him his fault between thee and him alone," &c. has nothing to do with the prefent fubject. We are now fpeaking of *grofs* immoralities committed by preachers of the gofpel. This does not concern the *trefpafs* of a private perfon, but the *grofs offence* of a minifter againft the church of God. Undoubtedly, a minifter *fo* offending fhould not be fuffered to remain in his office till the next yearly conference, as *many* fouls might be ruined thereby in the interval. There is certainly as much mercy due to the people as to the minifter; and in the prefent inftance more, as he is but one, and they are many: and he is invefted with his office, not for their *deftruction*, but for their *edification*. See 2 Cor. x. 8. and xiii. 10. But fcarcely any thing can be more deftructive to the caufe of God than the immoral life of a minifter. *Such* an Achan in the camp muft, more or lefs, bring down a curfe upon the caufe. 1 Sam. ii. 27—29. " There came a man of God unto Eli, and faid unto him, Thus faith the Lord,——Wherefore kick ye at my facrifice and at mine offering, which I have commanded in my habitation; *and honoureft thy fons above me*," &c. Ver. 12. "Now the fons of Eli were fons of Belial; they knew not the Lord." iii. 11—14. " The Lord faid to Samuel, Behold, I will do a thing in Ifrael, at which both the ears of every one that heareth it fhall tingle. In that day I will perform againft *Eli* all things which I have fpoken concerning his houfe: when I begin, I will alfo make an end. For I have told him, that I will judge his houfe for ever, for the iniquity *which he knoweth ; becaufe his fons made themfelves vile, and he reftrained them not,*" &c. See that whole hiftory. Matt. vii. 22, 23. " Many will fay to me in that day, Lord, Lord, have we not prophefied in thy name ? and in thy name have caft out devils ? and in thy name done many wonderful works ? And then will I profefs unto them, I never knew you: depart from me, *ye that work iniquity.*" Rom. ii. 3. " Thinkeft thou this, O man, that judgeft them which do fuch things, and *doeft the fame,* that thou fhalt efcape the judgment of God ? 1 Tim. v. 19. "Againft an elder receive not an accufation, but *before two or three witneffes.*"

2. The mode of procefs directed in the anfwer to the fecond queftion, is nearly according to our Lord's directions, concerning the offences of the private members of a church, in Matt. xviii. 15—17. " If thy brother fhall treffpafs againft thee, go and tell him his fault, between thee and him alone: if he fhall hear thee, thou haft gained thy brother. But if he will not hear thee, then take with thee one or two more, that in the mouth of two or three witneffes every word may be eftablifhed. And if he fhall neglect to hear them, tell it unto the church : but if he neglect to hear the church, let him be unto thee as an heathen man and a publican." 1ft, The preacher is to be reproved by his fenior in office. On a fecond offence, the minifter reprehending, is to take with him one, two, or three witneffes: and if ftill incurable, the offender is to be brought before that part of the church, to which he is particularly refponfible, namely, the yearly conference. He is not to be tried by the members of his circuit or diftrict, for *they* are the complainants—the perfons fuppofed to be aggrieved,——but by his elders and equals. There is, however, a confiderable difference between the perfons concerned, in the directions given by our Lord in the portion of Scripture quoted above, and thofe who are adverted to in the prefent fection. *That fcripture* evidently refers to the private members of a church ; and *the minifter himfelf,* after private reproof and public reprehenfion, firft before two or three witneffes, and then before the church, is to exclude the perfon, if impenitent. But of this we fhall treat largely, when we come to confider the 8th fection of the 2d chapter. *Improper tempers,* manifefted in the converfation or conduct of a minifter of the gofpel, may be productive of more evil, than all his public labours can poffibly compenfate. But at the fame time, he may not be fo criminal, but that he may be borne with for a time, in hope of reformation.

N. B. The reafon why the expreffion *one, two, or three witneffes* is mentioned in the fection under this head, is, becaufe it

may, in some instances, be impossible to have more than one besides the reprehending minister, without sending to a neighbouring circuit: and as no public censure can pass upon the offending
preacher in this case till the sitting of the yearly conference, it
would not be proper to take a minister of the gospel from his labours in another circuit, for two or three days, to answer the present purpose.

" The servant of the Lord," says St. Paul, " must not strive;
but be gentle unto all men, apt to teach, patient; in meekness
instructing those that oppose themselves," 2 Tim. ii. 24, 25.
" He [Christ] turned, and rebuked them, and said, Ye know
not what manner of spirit ye are of," Luke ix. 55.

3. It will, we believe, be allowed by all who love the truth as
it is in Jesus, that the heretical doctrines are as dangerous, at least
to the hearers, as the immoral life of a preacher ; and, therefore,
the same process is provided for both cases. Those must indeed
be blind, who can sit for any time under the ministry of an ari-
an, socinian, universalian, or any other heretical minister : " and
if the blind lead the blind, both shall fall into the ditch," Matt.
xv. 14. and Luke vi. 39. But as we would guard against a hasty
and arbitrary measure in a matter which sometimes, perhaps, it
may be difficult to determine, the case alluded to at present shall
lie over to the yearly conference, if the preacher be perfectly
silent, in public and private, on the subjects objected to. But if
he will go on to dishonour Christ, or to oppose the doctrines of
holiness, or to introduce novel sentiments or " vain jangling" (1
Tim. i. 6.) to draw our people from *the one thing needful*,—
CHRIST DYING FOR AND LIVING IN US, an immediate stop
must be put to such dangerous, such pernicious proceedings.

Matt. vii. 15, 16. " Beware of false prophets, which come to
you in sheeps' clothing, but inwardly they are ravening wolves."
Tit. iii. 10, 11. " A man that is an heretick, after the first and
second admonition, reject ;" (here the authority of *judging* and
rejecting is invested in Timothy) " knowing that he that is such
is subverted, and sinneth, being condemned of himself." 2 Pet.
ii. 1—3. " But there were false prophets also among the people,
even as there shall be false teachers among you, who privily shall
bring in damnable heresies, even denying the Lord that bought
them, and bring upon themselves swift destruction. And many shall follow their pernicious ways; by reason of whom the
way of truth shall be evil spoken of. And through covetous-
ness shall they, with feigned words, make merchandise of you:
whose judgment now of a long time lingereth not, and their
damnation slumbereth not." Rev. ii. 2. " I know thy works, and
thy labour, and thy patience, and how thou canst not bear them

which are evil: and *thou* haft tried them which fay they are apoſtles, and are not, and haſt found them lyars." ii. 20. " Not-withſtanding I have a few things againſt thee, becauſe *thou* [the angel of the church in Thyatira] ſuffereſt that woman, Jezebel, which calleth herſelf a propheteſs, to teach and to ſeduce my ſervants to commit fornication, and to eat things ſacrificed unto idols."

Before we conclude our notes on this ſection, we muſt entreat our reader to notice, not only here, but throughout the whole of our economy, *the appeals* which are allowed upon all occaſions, as far as the nature and circumſtances of things will poſſibly allow of them, without making our economy intricate and bur-denſome.

SECTION XX.

How to provide for the Circuits in the Time of Conference, and to preſerve and increaſe the Work of God.

Queſt. WHAT can be done to ſupply the circuits during the ſitting of the conference ?

Anſw. 1. Let all the appointments ſtand according to the plan of the circuit.

2. Engage as many local preachers and exhorters as will ſupply them ; and let them be paid for their time in proportion to the ſalary of the travelling preachers.

3. If preachers and exhorters cannot attend, let ſome perſon of ability be appointed in every ſociety to ſing, pray, and read one of Mr. Weſley's ſermons.

4. But if that cannot be done, let there be prayer-meetings.

NOTES.

If the reader compare this ſection with the third queſtion of the third ſection of this chapter, and the notes upon it, it will appear that we have taken every ſtep in our power, conſiſtently with the well-being of our conferences, to ſupply the circuits with the miniſtry of the word, whilſt the conferences are ſitting. And, we truſt, our people are too well acquainted with the im-portance of our conferences to the general work, not to be willing to make some facrifices on their account. And we have no doubt but every member of our conferences can, with heart-felt affection, addrefs their brethren with whom they are acquainted refpectively, in the words of the apoftle, " Only let your converfation be as it becometh the gofpel of Chrift; that, whether I come and fee you, or elfe be abfent, I may hear of your affairs, that ye ftand faft in one fpirit, with one mind, ftriving together for the faith of the gofpel; and in nothing terrified by your adverfaries," Phil. i. 27, 28.

SECTION XXI.

Of the Local Preachers.

Queft. 1. WHAT directions fhall be given concerning our brethren the local preachers, in refpect to their being received as preachers, or admitted into the order of deacons?

Anfw. 1. No local preacher fhall receive a licenfe to preach, till he has been examined and approved at the quarterly meeting of his circuit; which licenfe fhall be drawn up in the following words, figned by the prefident of the meeting, viz. " N. M. has applied to us for liberty to preach as a local preacher in our circuit: and after due inquiry concerning his gifts, grace, and ufefulnefs, we judge he is a proper perfon to be licenfed for this purpofe; and we accordingly authorize him to preach."

2. Before any perfon fhall be licenfed as a local preacher by a quarterly meeting, he fhall bring a recommendation from the fociety of which he is a member.

3. A local preacher fhall be eligible to the office of a deacon, after he has preached for four years from the time he received a regular licenfe, and has obtained the teftimonial which is directed in the fourth fection of the firft chapter of the form of difcipline.

Queft. 2. Shall any regulations be made in refpect to allowing a recompence to local preachers for their work in given cafes?

Anfw. 1. Whenever a local preacher fills the place of a travelling preacher, he fhall be paid for his trouble a fum proportionable to the falary of a travelling preacher; which fum fhall be paid by the circuit at the next quarterly meeting, if the travelling preacher whofe place he filled up, was either fick or neceffarily abfent; or, in other cafes, out of the falary of the travelling preacher himfelf.

2. If a local preacher be diftreffed in his temporal circumftances on account of his fervice in the circuit, he may apply to the quarterly meeting who may give him what relief they judge proper, after the falaries of the travelling preachers, and of their wives, and all other regular allowances to the travelling preachers, be difcharged.

Queft. 3. What directions fhall be given concerning the trial of local preachers, local deacons, or local elders?

Anfw. If a charge be brought againft a local preacher, or local deacon, or elder, the preacher who has the overfight of the circuit, fhall fummon three or more local preachers of the neighbourhood, or, for want of local preachers, fo many leaders or exhorters. And if they, or the majority of them, on due examination, judge that the local preacher, deacon, or elder aforefaid, has been guilty of fuch a crime, or has preached fuch falfe doctrines, as require his fufpenfion from all public offices in our church, till the enfuing quarterly meeting, the preacher who has the overfight of the circuit, fhall accordingly fufpend him from all public offices till the enfuing quarterly meeting.

And in fuch cafe, and in every cafe where a meeting affembled as above defcribed, fhall deem the faid local preacher, deacon, or elder, culpable, the next quarterly meeting fhall proceed upon his trial, and fhall have authority to clear, cenfure, fufpend, or expel him according to their judgment. And the prefiding elder, or the preacher who has the overfight of the circuit, fhall at the commencement of the trial, appoint a fecretary, who shall take down regular minutes of the evidence and proceedings of the trial, which minutes, when read and approved, shall be signed by the said presiding elder or preacher, and also by the members of the said quarterly meeting, or by the majority of them.

And in case of condemnation, the local preacher, deacon, or elder condemned, shall be allowed an appeal to the next yearly conference, provided that he fignify to the said quarterly meeting his determination to appeal; in which case the said presiding elder, or preacher who has the oversight of the circuit, shall lay the minutes of the trial above mentioned, before the said yearly conference, at which the local preacher, deacon or elder, so appealing, may appear: and the said yearly conference shall judge and finally determine from the minutes of the said trial, so laid before them.

N O T E S.

By this mode of trial we are desirous of showing the most tender regard towards our local brethren. We are all but men. The best of us may fall into sin, or be drawn into dangerous and pernicious errors; and it is sometimes necessary to stop the plague by an immediate stroke of discipline.—But we would not have so important a character as that of one of our local brethren, even touched to its disadvantage, by only one preacher, who possibly might be younger than the accused. We have, therefore, provided, that a small meeting of respectable persons shall be held, before a single step be taken in the business. The trial will then come before the most weighty assembly in the circuit.

We have directed the yearly conference, upon an appeal, to determine upon the merits of the cause from the memorial of the quarterly meeting, on account of the difficulty, if not impossibility, of bringing the necessary witnesses, perhaps thirty, fifty, or a hundred miles from their home: Nor have we any right or authority to lay such a burden on any of our people. In short, we have done the best we can, according to the nature of the circumstances in which we are placed.

SECTION XXII.

Of Baptifm.

1. LET every adult perfon, and the parents of eve-ry child, to be baptized, have the choice either of immerfion, fprinkling, or pouring.

2. We will on no account whatever receive a prefent for adminiftering baptifm, or for burying of the dead.

N O T E S.

1. In refpect to the facrament of baptifm, we muft refer our reader to our fcripture references on the 16th and 17th articles of religion. We need only obferve here, that we are confcious that *fprinkling, pouring,* and *immerfing* have been practifed by different churches, in each of which the pure gofpel was preached, and the life of God, more or lefs, experienced; and that all thefe modes are, more or lefs, acceptable to God, when adminiftered with fincerity. At the fame time, we know well, that as much or more may be faid in favour of *fprinkling* than of immerfion, from the account given us in Scripture of the baptifm of *John himfelf:* and the primitive churches *in general,* we believe, favoured the practice of *fprinkling.* However, we would meet the tender mind, and *in matters uneffential* condefcend as far as we confcientioufly can, to the feelings and fentiments of all. Rom. xiv. 1—5. "Him that is weak in the faith receive ye, but not to doubtful difputations. For one believeth that he may eat all things: another, who is weak, eateth herbs. Let not him that eateth, defpife him that eateth not; and let not him which eateth not, judge him that eateth: for God hath received him.——One man efteemeth one day above another: another efteemeth every day alike. Let every man be fully perfuaded in his own mind." Rom. xv. 2, 3. Let every one of us pleafe his neighbour for his good to edification: for even Chrift pleafed not himfelf." 1 Cor. ix. 22, 23. "To the weak became I as weak, that I might gain the weak: I am made all things to all men, that I might by all means fave fome. And this I do for the gofpel's fake, that I might be partaker thereof with you." x. 33. "Even as I pleafe all men in all things, not feeking mine own profit, but the profit of many, that they may be faved."

2. As we have before obferved our aim is to fave fouls, and not to enrich ourfelves: therefore, Mr. Wefley and our general

conference placed *our whole economy* as far diftant as poffible from *that* of a lucrative miniftry. We are determined not to fell the ordinances of God: in this no man fhall make our glorying void. Matt. x. 8. " Freely ye have received," fays our Lord, " freely give." 1 Cor. ix. 11—18. " If we have fown nnto you fpiritual things, is it a great thing if we fhall reap your carnal things? If others be partakers of this power over you, are not we rather? Neverthelefs, *we have not ufed this power;* but fuffer all things, left we fhould hinder the gofpel of Chrift.——I have ufed *none of thefe things;* neither have I written thefe things that it fhould be fo done unto me: for it were better for me to die than that any man fhould make my glorying void.——What is my reward then? Verily, that, when I preach the gofpel, I may make the gofpel of Chrift without charge, that I abufe not my power in the gofpel." 2 Cor. xi. 7. " Have I committed an offence, in abafing myfelf that ye might be exalted, becaufe I have preached to you the gofpel of God *freely?*" 1 Pet. v. 2. " Feed the flock of God which is among you,——not for filthy lucre, but of *a ready mind.*" 3 John 7. " For his name's fake they went forth, taking nothing of the gentiles."

SECTION XXIII.

Of the Lords's Supper.

Queft. ARE there any directions to be given concerning the adminiftration of the Lord's fupper?

Anfw. 1. Let thofe who have fcruples concerning the receiving of it kneeling, be permitted to receive it either ftanding or fitting.

2. Let no perfon that is not a member of our fociety, be admitted to the communion, without examination, and fome token given by an elder or deacon.

3. No perfon fhall be admitted to the Lord's fupper among us, who is guilty of any practice for which we would exclude a member of our fociety.

NOTES.

Our readers muft here be referred to the fcripture-references on the 16th, 18th, and 19th articles of religion, and our obfervations on the preceding fection. As the Scripture is filent about the posture of the communicants, we prefer *the most humble,* whatever our Saviour might have permitted when he instituted the sacred ordinance. Besides, as we always receive the elements *in prayer,* we for that reason also prefer the kneeling posture. We must also observe, that our elders should be very cautious how they admit to the communion persons who are not in our society. It would be highly injurious to *our brethren,* if we suffered any to partake of the Lord's supper with them, whom we would not readily admit into our society on application made to us. Those whom we judge unfit to partake of our profitable, *prudential* means of grace, we should most certainly think improper to be partakers of an ordinance which has been expressly instituted by Christ himself.

1 Cor. v. 11. " Now I have written unto you *not to keep company,* if any man that is called a brother be a fornicator, or covetous, or an idolater, or a railer, or a drunkard, or an extortioner ; *with such an one, no, not to eat.*" 2 Thess. iii. 6—15. " Now we command you, brethren, in the name of our Lord Jesus Christ, that ye *withdraw yourselves* from every brother that walketh disorderly, and not after the tradition which he received of us. For yourselves know how ye ought to follow us ; for we behaved not ourselves disorderly among you.——For we hear that there are some which walk among you *disorderly,* working not at all, but are busy-bodies. Now them that are such we command and exhort by our Lord Jesus Christ, that with quietness they work, and eat their own bread. And if any man obey not our word by this epistle, *note that man, and have no company with him,* that he may be ashamed. Yet count him not as an enemy, but admonish him as a brother." 1 Tim. iv. 8. " *Bodily exercise* profiteth little : but godliness is profitable unto all things, having promise of the life that now is, and of that which is to come."

SECTION XXIV.

Of Public Worship.

Quest. WHAT directions shall be given for the establishment of uniformity in public worship amongst us, on the Lord's-day.

Answ. 1. Let the morning-service consist of singing, prayer, the reading of a chapter out of the Old Testament, and another out of the New, and preaching.

2. Let the afternoon-fervice confift of finging, prayer, the reading of one chapter out of the bible, and preaching.

3. Let the evening-fervice confift of finging, prayer, and preaching.

4. But on the days of adminiftering the Lord's fupper, the two chapters in the morning-fervice may be omitted.

5. Let the fociety be met, wherever it is practicable, on the fabbath-day.

N O T E S.

This fection needs little more than fome pointed texts of facred writ for its confirmation to all chriftian perfons. Our church infifts on the reading of the Scriptures in the congregation, and gives directions accordingly. This is of the utmoft confequence, and we truft will be moft facredly obferved by all our minifters and preachers. A peculiar bleffing accompanies the public rea ing as well as preaching the word of God to attentive, believing fouls. And in thefe days of infidelity, nothing fhould be omitted, which may lead the people to the love of the holy bible.

The meeting of the fociety alfo, wherever practicable, is of confiderable moment. There are various weighty fubjects, peculiarly fuitable to religious focieties, which cannot be fo well enlarged upon to a mixed congregation. Brotherly union and fellowfhip, chriftian difcipline in all its branches, and various other particulars may be enlarged upon and enforced with great propriety and fuccefs on fuch occafions. At thefe times alfo we may enter more minutely into the different parts of the relative duties, than we can to unawakened fouls, whofe whole life is fin, and who are at the beft only " like unto whited fepulchres, which indeed appear beautiful outward, but are within full of dead men's bones, and of all uncleannefs."

(1) Exod. xx. 24. In all places where I record my name, I will come unto thee, and I will blefs thee. Ifai. lx. 13. And I will make the place of my feet glorious. Mal. i. 11. For from the rifing of the fun, even unto the going down of the fame, my name fhall be great among the gentiles; and in every place incenfe fhall be offered unto my name, and a pure offering. Pfalm xxii. 25. My praife fhall be of thee *in the great congregation:* I will pay my vows before them that fear him. xxxv. 18. I will give thee thanks *in the great congregation:* I will praife thee *among*

much people. xl. 9. *I have preached righteoufnefs in the great congregation.* lxviii. 26. Blefs *ye* God *in the congregations,* even the Lord, from the fountain of Ifrael. Matt. xviii. 20. Where two or three are gathered together in my name, there am I in the midft of them. Luke iv. 16, 17. He [Chrift] came to Nazareth, where he had been brought up: and AS HIS CUSTOM WAS, he went into the fynagogue on the fabbath-day, and ftood up FOR TO READ. And there was delivered unto him the book of the prophet Efaias. Acts xiii. 14—16. When they departed from Perga they came to Antioch in Pifidia, and went into the fynagogue on the fabbath-day, and fat down. And, *after the reading of the law and the prophets,* the rulers of the fynagogue fent unto them, faying, Ye men and brethren, if ye have any word of exhortation for the people, fay on. Then Paul ftood up, &c. Ver. 27. They knew him not, nor yet *the voices of the prophets which are read every fabbath-day.* I Cor. xi. 20. When *ye come together*—into one place, &c. See alfo the 14th chapter on public prayer, thankfgiving, and prophecy or preaching. Col. iv. 16. When this epiftle is read *among you,* caufe that it be read alfo *in the church* of the Laodiceans. I Theff. v. 27. I charge you, by the Lord, *that this epiftle be read unto all the holy brethren.* Rev. i. 3. Bleffed is he that readeth, *and they that hear the words of this prophecy,* and keep thofe things which are written therein.

(2) Acts xi. 26. It came to pafs, that a whole year they affembled themfelves *with the church,* &c. xiv. 27. When they were come, and had gathered the church together, &c.

SECTION XXV.

Of the Spirit and Truth of Singing.

Queft. HOW fhall we guard againft formality in finging?

Anfw. 1. By choofing fuch hymns as are proper for the congregation?

2. By not finging too much at once; feldom more than five or fix verfes.

3. By fuiting the tune to the words.

4. By often ftopping fhort, and afking the people, " Now! Do you know what you faid laft? Did you fpeak no more than you felt?"

5. Do not suffer the people to sing too flow. This naturally tends to formality; and is brought in by thofe who have either very ftrong or very weak voices.

6. In every large fociety let them learn to sing; and let them always learn our tunes firft.

7. Let the women conftantly sing their parts alone. Let no man sing with them, unlefs he underftands the notes, and sings the bafs as it is compofed in the tune-book.

8. Introduce no new tune till they are perfect in the old.

9. Recommend our tune-book. And if you cannot sing yourfelf, choofe a perfon or two at each place to pitch the tune for you.

10. Exhort every perfon in the congregation to sing, not one in ten only.

11. Sing no hymns of your own compofing.

12. If a preacher be prefent, let him alone give out the words.

13. When the fingers would teach a tune to the congregation, they muft sing only the tenor.

14. The preachers are defired not to encourage the finging of fuge-tunes in our congregations.

15. Let it be recommended to our people, not to attend the finging-fchools which are not under our direction.

N. B. We do not think that fuge-tunes are finful, or improper to be ufed in private companies: but we do not approve of their being ufed in our public congregations, becaufe public finging is a part of divine worfhip in which all the congregation ought to join.

N O T E S.

The finging of pfalms and hymns and fpiritual fongs in the congregation, has been allowed by all the churches of God in all ages (one modern fociety excepted) to be a part of divine worfhip; and, *from its very nature*, it evidently belongs to the *whole* congregation. It would be unfeemly for the minifter *alone* to sing: but if this be the duty of *one* member of the congregation, it muſt be the duty of all who have voices for ſinging; and there are very few who may not join in the *tenor* part, all the defects of their voices being ſwallowed up in the general ſound. Few things can be more pleaſing to the Lord, than a congregation, with one heart and one voice, praiſing his holy name. It is indeed to be feared, that there is ſeldom a large congregation, where *every* individual is *ſincere*. However, all who do in ſincerity deſire a bleſſing, ſhould ſtrive to join in the general chorus— we mean, in every part of the hymn. If one part of it be above the experience of the ſinger, he ſhould adjoin a ſilent prayer, that the Lord may give him the grace he needs; for the Lord liſtens to hear what the heart ſpeaks, and takes all as nothing, if the heart be ſilent. Again, when his experience riſes above the hymn, his ſecret prayer ſhould be in behalf of that part of the congregation which it ſuits: but in the *proper* hymns of praiſe he may throw off all reſerve, for we are *all* infinitely indebted to our good God. From theſe remarks we ſurely muſt be ſenſible of the neceſſity of confining ourſelves to *ſimple* tunes, as the *fuge-tunes* have an unavoidable tendency to confine *to a few* this part of divine worſhip, which belongs to the whole. And thoſe, we think, have made few remarks on public worſhip, who have not obſerved, on the one hand, how naturally the fuge-tunes puff up with vanity thoſe who excel in them; and on the other hand, how it deadens devotion, and only at the beſt raiſes an admiration of the ſingers, and not of Chriſt.

When it is recommended in this ſection to the preacher ſometimes to ſtop and addreſs the people in the courſe of ſinging, *the ſubſtance* only of what he ſhould ſay is mentioned there. It is not intended, that he ſhould ſpeak *abruptly* on ſuch occaſions, but with ſoftneſs and due reſpect on the neceſſity of ſinging and of performing every act of devotion from the heart.

1 Chron. xvi. 7—9. On that day David delivered firſt this pſalm, to thank the Lord, *into the hand of Aſaph and his brethren.* Give thanks unto the Lord, call upon his name, make known his deeds *among the people.* Sing unto him, *ſing pſalms* unto him, talk ye of all his wondrous works. Pſalm xcv. 1, 2. O come, let *us* ſing unto the Lord; let *us* make *a joyful noiſe* to the rock of our ſalvation. Let *us* come *before his preſence* with thankſgiving, and make *a joyful noiſe* unto him with pſalms. xcvi. 1. O ſing unto the Lord a new ſong: ſing unto the Lord *all the earth.* civ. 33. I will ſing unto the Lord as long as I live; I will ſing praiſe unto my God while I have my being. Pſalm cxxxviii. 1. I will praiſe thee with my whole heart; *before the gods* will I ſing praiſe unto thee. Matt. xxvi. 30. When they [Chriſt and his diſciples] *had ſung an hymn,* they went out into the mount of Olives. See alſo Mark xiv. 26. 1 Cor. xiv. 15. I will ſing with the Spirit, and I will ſing with the underſtanding alſo.

Ephef. v. 18, 19. Be filled with the Spirit; fpeaking to yourfelves in pfalms, and hymns, and fpiritual fongs, finging and making melody in your heart to the Lord. Col. iii. 16. Let the word of Chrift dwell in you richly in all wifdom; teaching and admonifhing ONE ANOTHER *in pfalms, and hymns, and fpiritual fongs,* finging, with grace in your hearts, to the Lord. Jam. v. 13. Is any among you afflicted? let him pray. Is any merry [joyful]? let him fing pfalms.

SECTION XXVI.

*

Of the Method of raifing a Fund for the Su-perannuated Preachers, and the Widows and Orphans of Preachers.

Queft. HOW can we provide for fuperannuated preachers, and the widows and orphans of preachers?

Anfw. 1. Let every preacher, when firft admitted into full connection, pay two dollars and two thirds, at the yearly conference.

2. Let every other preacher in full connection, contribute two dollars every year; except the conference difpenfe with the payment in cafes of diftrefs: in which inftances the preachers fo indulged, fhall be entitled to all the privileges of the fund, in the fame manner as if they had paid their fubfcription.

3. Out of this fund, let provifion be made, firft, for the worn-out preachers, and then for the widows and children of thofe who are dead.

4. Every worn-out preacher fhall receive, if he need it, not ufually more than fixty-four dollars annually.

5. Every widow of a preacher fhall receive annually, if fhe need it, during her widow-hood, fifty-three dollars and one third.

6. Every orphan of a preacher fhall receive once for all, if needed, fifty-three dollars and one third.

7. But no one shall be entitled to any thing from this fund, till he has paid six dollars and two thirds.

8. Nor any who neglects to pay his subscription and arrears for three years together, unless he be employed on foreign missions, or has received a dispensation as above mentioned.

9. Let every preacher who has the care of a circuit, bring to the conference, as far as possible, the contribution of every preacher left behind in his circuit.

10. Every person who desires support from the fund shall first make his case known to the yearly conference, which shall determine how far he is a proper subject of relief.

11. The president of the yearly conference shall give an order on the general steward of the fund or any of his agents, for any sum of money allowed by the conference, agreeably to these rules.

12. The receipts and disbursements of the fund shall be printed annually in the minutes of the conference.

13. The presiding elder of each district shall keep a regular account of all the concerns of the fund, as far as they relate to his district, in a proper book which he shall hand down to his successor.

14. Each member of the fund shall from time to time receive a certificate from his yearly conference for the payment of his subscription.

15. This fund shall be reserved for extraordinary cases, which the chartered fund may not reach. And no travelling preacher shall have a vote in the disposal of the travelling preachers' annual subscription, unless he be himself an annual subscriber.

16. The fund shall never be reduced to less than six hundred dollars.

N O T E S.

This institution is not to be considered as a charity, but as an agreement among brethren for their mutual support when old or worn-out in the work of the ministry ; and also for the support of their surviving widows and orphans. The chartered fund allows no more than sixty-four dollars a year to an unmarried, superannuated, or worn-out preacher, which is far from being sufficient to supply him with the necessaries of life, if he have nothing of his own. The same may be observed concerning all the other objects of this institution. *This* fund, therefore, is intended to supply the defects of the *chartered* fund, in respect to those who have so richly and specially served the connection with their strength and lives. And as it is supported *only* by the subscriptions of the preachers out of their little annual pittance, no one has any right or ground to object to it.

John xiii. 34, 35. A new commandment *I* give unto you, That ye love one another; as I have loved you, that ye also love one another. By this shall all men know that ye are my disciples, if ye have love one to another. xv. 12. This is MY commandment, That ye love one another, as I have loved you. Ver. 17. These things *I command you*, that ye love one another. Rom. xii. 10. Be kindly affectioned one to another with brotherly love. Gal. v. 13. By love serve one another. 1 Thess. iv. 9. But as touching brotherly love, ye need not that I write unto you: for ye yourselves are taught of God to love one another. Heb. xiii. 1. Let brotherly love continue. 1 Pet. i. 22. See that ye love one another, with a pure heart, fervently. iii. 8. Love as brethren. 1 John iii. 11. This is the message that ye heard from the beginning, that we should love one another. iv. 7. Beloved, let us love one another; for love is of God. Ver. 11. Beloved, if God so loved us, we ought also to love one another. See also 2 Kings iv. 1—7. concerning the miracle wrought by Elisha, for the relief of a widow of one of the sons of the prophets.

SECTION XXVII.

Of raising a general Fund for the Propagation of the Gospel.

Quest. HOW may we raise a general fund for carrying on the whole work of God?

Answ. By a yearly collection, and if need be, a quarterly one, to be raised by every one who has the charge of a circuit, in every principal congregation in his circuit. To this end, he may then read and enlarge upon the following hints:

" How shall we send labourers into those parts where they are most of all wanted? Many are willing to hear, but not to bear the expence. Nor can it as yet be expected of them: Stay till the word of God has touched their hearts, and then they will gladly provide for them that preach it. Does it not lie upon us in the mean time to supply their lack of service? To raise a general fund, out of which from time to time, that expence may be defrayed? By this means those who willingly offer themselves, may travel through every part, whether there be societies or not, and stay wherever there is a call, without being burdensome to any. Thus may the gospel, in the life and power thereof, be spread from sea to sea. Which of you will not rejoice to throw in your mite to promote this glorious work?

" Beside this, in carrying on so large a work through the continent, there are calls for money in various ways and we must frequently be at considerable expence, or the work must be at a full stop. Many too are the *occasional* distresses of our preachers, or their families, which require an immediate supply.—Otherwise their hands would hang down, if they were not constrained to depart from the work.

" The money contributed will be brought to the ensuing conference.

" Men and brethren, help! Was there ever a call like this since you first heard the gospel found? Help to relieve your companions in the kingdom of Jesus, who are pressed above measure. Bear ye one another's burdens, and so fulfil the law of Christ. Help to send forth able, willing labourers into your Lord's harvest: So shall ye be assistant in saving souls from death, and hiding a multitude of sins. Help to propagate the gospel of your salvation to the remotest corners of the earth, till the knowledge of our Lord shall cover the land as the waters cover the sea. So shall it appear to ourselves and all men, that we are indeed one body, united by one spirit; so shall the baptized heathens be yet again constrained to say, " See how these christians love one another?"

N O T E S.

The addrefs to the people given in this fection is itfelf both an explanation and application of the whole fubject. The following fcriptures alfo will ferve to illuftrate the fubject:

Luke viii. 1—3. He [Chrift] went throughout every city and village, preaching and fhewing the glad tidings of the kingdom of God; and the twelve were with him, and certain women,— Mary, called Magdalene,—and Joanna the wife of Chuza, Herod's fteward, and Sufanna, and many others, *which miniftered unto him of their fubftance.* 1 Cor. ix. 9. It is written in the law of Mofes, Thou fhalt not muzzle the mouth of the ox that treadeth out the corn. 2 Tim. i. 16—18. The Lord give mercy unto the houfe of Onefiphorus; for he oft refrefhed me, and was not afhamed of my chain. But when he was in Rome, he fought me out very diligently, and found me. The Lord grant unto him, that he may find mercy of the Lord in that day: and in how many things he miniftered unto me at Ephefus thou knoweft very well. See alfo the fcripture-references in the notes on the 9th fection of this chapter.

S E C T I O N XXVIII.

Of the Chartered Fund.

Queft. 1. WHAT further provifion, fhall be made for the diftreffed travelling preachers, for the families of travelling preachers, and for fuperannuated and worn-out preachers, and the widows and orphans of preachers?

Anfw. There fhall be a chartered fund, to be fupported by the voluntary contributions of our friends; the principal ftock of which fhall be funded under the direction of truftees, and the intereft applied under the direction of the general conference, according to the following regulations, viz.

1. THAT no fum exceeding fixty-four dollars, fhall in any one year be applied to the ufe of an itinerant, fuperannuated, or worn-out *fingle* preacher.

2. That no fum exceeding one hundred and twenty-eight dollars in any one year, fhall be applied to the

ufe of any itinerant, fuperannuated, or worn-out *mar-ried* preacher.

3. That no fum exceeding fixty-four dollars in any one year, fhall be applied for the ufe of each widow of itinerant, fuperannuated, or worn-out preachers.

4. That no fum exceeding fixteen dollars fhall be applied in any one year, for the ufe of each child or orphan of itinerant, fuperannuated, or worn-out preachers.

5. That the elders, and thofe who have the overfight of circuits, fhall be the collectors and receivers of fubfcriptions, &c. for this fund.

6. The money fhall, if poffible, be conveyed by bills of exchange, through the means of the poft, to John Dickins, our general book-fteward, in Philadelphia, who fhall pay it in to the truftees of the fund: Otherwife it fhall be brought to the enfuing yearly conference.

7. There fhall be no money drawn out of the fund till the firft day of Auguft, 1798.

8. The intereft fhall then be divided into fix parts, and each of the yearly conferences fhall have authority to draw that fixth part out of the fund, according to the regulations before prefcribed: And if in one or more conferences, a part lefs than one fixth be drawn out of the fund in any given year, then, in fuch cafe or cafes, the other yearly conferences held in the fame year, fhall have authority, if they judge it neceffary, to draw out of the fund, according to the above regulation, fuch furplus of the intereft, which has not been applied by the former conferences: And the bifhops fhall bring the neceffary information of the ftate of the intereft of the fund, refpecting the year in queftion, from conference to conference.

9. The prefent ftock of the preachers' fund, fhall be thrown into the chartered fund.

10. The produce of the fale of our books, after the book-debts are paid, and a fufficient capital is provided for carrying on the bufinefs, fhall be regularly paid into th chartered fund.

11. The money subscribed for the chartered fund, may be lodged, on proper securities, in the states respectively in which it has been subscribed, under the direction of deputies living in such states respectively: *Provided*, Such securities and such deputies be proposed, as shall be approved of by the trustees in Philadelphia; and the stock in which it is proposed to lodge the money, be sufficiently productive to give satisfaction to the trustees.

N O T E S.

* We need not be urgent on our benevolent friends to promote this great charity. Their own feelings, we well know, will sufficiently prevail, when proper light is given them on the subject. Our brethren who have laboured on the mountains, on the western waters, and in the poorer circuits in general, have suffered unspeakable hardships, merely for the want of some established fund, in which the competent members of our society might safely lodge what their benevolent hearts would rejoice to give, for the spread of the gospel. On the same account, many of our worn-out preachers, some of whom quickly consumed their strength by their great exertions for the salvation of souls, have been brought into deep distress; and the widows and orphans of our preachers have been sometimes reduced to extreme necessity, who might have lived in comfort, if not in affluence, enjoying the sweets of domestic life, if the preachers who were the husbands on one hand, and the fathers on the other, had not loved their Redeemer better than wife or children, or life itself. And it is to be lamented, if possible, with tears of blood, that we have lost scores of our most able married ministers—men who like good householders, could upon all occasions, bring things new and old, out of their treasury, but were   liged to retire from the general work, because they saw noth   before them for their wives and children, if they continu   .tinerants, but misery and ruin. But the present institution wil   we trust, under the blessing of God, greatly relieve us in, if i   entirely deliver us from, these mighty evils. For we have fu i confidence, that the hearts of our friends will be engaged, and their hands stretched forth on this important occasion; and a provision will be made, sufficient to preserve the objects of the charity from want, which is all that is aimed at or desired.

C H A P. II.

S E C T I O N I.

The Nature, Design, and general Rules of the United Societies.

1. IN the latter end of the year 1739, eight or ten perfons came to Mr. Wefley in London, who appeared to be deeply convinced of fin, and earneftly groaning for redemption. They defired (as did two or three more the next day) that he would fpend fome time with them in prayer, and advife them how to flee from the wrath to come; which they faw continually hanging over their heads. That he might have more time for this great work, he appointed a day when they might all come together, which from thence forward they did every week, namely on *Thurfday* in the evening. To thefe, and as many more as defired to join with them (for their number increafed daily) he gave thofe advices from time to time which he judged moft needful for them; and they always concluded their meeting with prayer fuited to their feveral neceffities.

2. This was the rife of the UNITED SOCIETY, firft in *Europe* and then in *America*. Such a fociety is no other than " *a company of men* having the form and feeking the power *of godlinefs, united in order to pray together, to receive the word of exhortation, and to watch over one another in love, that they may help each other to work out their falvation.*"

3. That it may the more eafily be difcerned, whether they are indeed working out their own falvation, each fociety is divided into fmaller companies, called claffes, according to their refpective places of abode. There are but twelve perfons in every clafs; one of whom is ftiled *The Leader.*——It is his duty,

1. To fee each perfon in his clafs once a week at leaft, in order,

    1. To enquire how their fouls profper;

    2. To advife, reprove, comfort, or exhort, as occafion may require;

    3. To receive what they are willing to give, towards the relief of the preachers, church and poor.*

II. To meet the minifter and the ftewards of the fociety once a week; in order,

    1. To inform the minifter of any that are fick, or of any that walk diforderly, and will not be reproved.

    2. To pay to the ftewards what they have received of their feveral claffes in the week preceding.

    3. There is one only condition previoufly required of thofe who defire admiffion into thefe focieties, *a defire to flee from the wrath to come, and to be faved from their fins.* But wherever this is really fixed in the foul, it will be fhewn by its fruits. It is therefore expected of all who continue therein, that they fhould continue to evidence their defire of falvation,

Firft, By doing no harm, by avoiding evil of every kind: efpecially that which is moft generally practifed: Such as

The taking the name of God in vain:

The profaning the day of the Lord, either by doing ordinary work thereon, or by buying or felling.

Drunkennefs: or drinking fpirituous liquors, unlefs in cafes of neceffity:

The buying or felling of men, women, or children, with an intention to enflave them:

Fighting, quarrelling, brawling, brother *going to law* with brother; returning evil for evil; or railing for railing: the *ufing many words* in buying or felling:

The *buying or felling goods that have not paid the duty:*

The *giving or taking things on ufury,* i. e. unlawful intereft:

M

---

* This part refers wholly to towns and cities, where the poor are generally numerous, and church-expences confiderable.

Uncharitable or *unprofitable* converfation : particularly fpeaking evil of magiftrates or of minifters :

Doing to others as we would not they fhould do unto us :

Doing what we know is not for the glory of God : As

The *putting on of gold and coftly apparel :*

The *taking fuch diverfions* as cannot be ufed in the name of the Lord Jefus :

The *finging* thofe *fongs*, or *reading* thofe *books*, which do not tend to the knowledge or love of God :

Softnefs and needlefs felf-indulgence :

Laying up treafure upon earth :

Borrowing without a probability of paying ; or taking up goods without a probability of paying for them.

4. It is expected of all who continue in thefe focieties, that they fhould continue to evidence their defire of falvation,

Secondly, By doing good, by being in every kind merciful after their power, as they have opportunity, doing good of every poffible fort, and as far as is poffible, to all men :

To their bodies, of the ability which God giveth, by giving food to the hungry, by clothing the naked, by vifiting or helping them that are fick or in prifon.

To their fouls, by inftructing, reproving, or exhorting all we have any intercourfe with ; trampling under foot that enthufiaftic doctrine, that " we are not to do good, unlefs *our hearts be free to it.*"

By doing good, efpecially to them that are of the houfehold of faith, or groaning fo to be ; employing them preferably to others, buying one of another, helping each other in bufinefs : and fo much the more, becaufe the world will love its own and them *only.*

By all poffible *diligence* and *frugality,* that the gofpel be not blamed.

By running with patience the race which is fet before them, *denying themfelves, and taking up their crofs daily :* fubmitting to bear the reproach of Chrift, to be as the filth and off-fcouring of the world; and looking that men fhould *fay all manner of evil of them falfely for the Lord's fake.*

5. It is expected of all who defire to continue in thefe focieties, that they fhould continue to evidence their defire of falvation,

Thirdly, By attending upon all the ordinances of God: Such are

The public worfhip of God:

The miniftry of the word, either read or expounded;.

The fupper of the Lord;

Family and private prayer;

Searching the fcriptures; and

Fafting or abftinence.

6. Thefe are the general rules of our focieties: all which we are taught of GOD to obferve, even in his written word, which is the only rule, and the fufficient rule both of our faith and practice. And all thefe we know his Spirit writes on truly awakened hearts. If there be any among us who obferve them not, who habitually break any of them, let it be known unto them who watch over that foul, as they who muft give an account. We will admonifh him of the error of his ways. We will bear with him for a feafon.—But then, if he repent not, he hath no more place among us. We have delivered our own fouls.

N O T E S.

* The prefent fection forms, perhaps, one of the completeft fyftems of chriftian ethics or morals, for its fize, which ever was publifhed by an uninfpired writer. We fpeak this the more readily, becaufe it was the work of the firft divine, we believe, fince the time of the apoftles, the late Mr. Wefley, after matured experience, with only a fmall addition, which the circumftances of thefe ftates required. The rules are fo clear, and fo obvioufly approve themfelves to every candid mind, that we need only touch briefly upon them, proving them by quotations from the facred writings.

1. Of clafs-meeting we fhall fpeak hereafter: We would here only explain a few particulars concerning the office of a leader.

We have found it neceffary in innumerable inftances to enlarge the number of the clafs, from the impoffibility of providing a fufficiency of clafs-leaders, if the number were always limited to *twelve*. The office is of vaft confequence. The revival of the work of God does perhaps depend as much upon *the whole body of leaders*, as it does *upon the whole body of preachers*. We have almoft conftantly obferved, that when a leader is dull or carelefs or inactive—when he has not abilities or zeal fufficient to reprove with courage though with gentlenefs, and to prefs a prefent falvation upon the hearts of the fincere, the clafs is, in general, languid: but, on the contrary, when the leader is much alive to God and faithful in his office, the clafs is alfo, in general, lively and fpiritual. This arifes from the nature of the chriftian plan of falvation. It is the fame, in general, with a minifter and his flock; and every leader, as we have before intimated, is, *in fome degree*, a gofpel minifter: though we may add, that among us a fpiritual body of leaders may counteract the otherwife pernicious confequences of a languid miniftry.

At the beginning of Methodifm, the leader called weekly upon each of his clafs, in which cafe twelve were quite fufficient for his infpection. But very foon it was found abundantly preferable for the whole clafs to meet the leader *together*, not only for the fake of the leader, but for the good of the people, who, by that means, enjoy the unfpeakable advantages of chriftian fellowfhip. At the fame time the leader is expected to vifit the members of his clafs at their own houfes, efpecially when they are fick or confined, as often as his circumftances will admit.

Numb. xi. 14—17. "I am not able to bear all this people alone, becaufe it is too heavy for me. And if thou deal thus with me, kill me, I pray thee, out of hand, if I have found favour in thy fight; and let me not fee my wretchednefs. And the Lord faid unto Mofes, Gather unto me feventy men of the elders of Ifrael, whom thou knoweft to be the elders of the people, and officers over them; and bring them unto the tabernacle of the congregation, that they may ftand there with thee. And I will come down and talk with thee there: and I will take of the Spirit which is upon thee, and will put it upon them; and they fhall bear the burden of the people with thee, that thou bear it not thyfelf alone." Ver. 24, 25. "And Mofes went out, and told the people the words of the Lord, and gathered the feventy men of the elders of the people, and fet them round about the tabernacle: and the Lord came down in a cloud, and fpake unto him, and took of the fpirit that was upon him, and gave it unto the feventy elders: and it came to pafs, that when the Spirit refted upon them, they *prophefied*, and did not ceafe." Exod. xii. 18. "Moreover, thou fhalt provide, out of all the people, able men, *fuch as fear God, men of truth, hating covetouf-*

nefs; and place fuch over them, to be rulers of thoufands, and rulers of hundreds, rulers of fifties, *and rulers of tens.*" [It is, we think, evident from the context, that thefe men were appointed not only to determine on civil queftions, but in refpect to every difficulty relating to the ceremonial law, and " all the ftatutes of God, and his laws," ver. 16. in fhort, to act in every thing in the place of Mofes, except in matters of great moment.] 1 Cor. xii. 28. God hath fet fome in the church; firft, apoftles; fecondarily, prophets; thirdly, *teachers;* after that miracles; then gifts of healing, *helps,* governments, diverfities of tongues." See the whole chapter. Ephef. iv. 11. " And he gave fome, apoftles; and fome, prophets; and fome, evangelifts; and fome, paftors *and teachers.*"

2d. *The defire to flee from the wrath to come,* and *to be faved from their fins,* is expreffed as the *fingle* condition of being admitted into our fociety, becaufe thefe two are infeparably united. There never was a foul which truly defired to flee from the wrath of God, but at the fame time defired real falvation. They both come from God: and his Spirit never gives the facred wifh to avoid the one, but he beftows an equally ardent defire to obtain the other. The nature of God and the whole plan of falvation by Jefus Chrift require this. The creation and redemption of man, and all the operations of the Divine Spirit, have no other end but the making us like to God, and preparing us for his fervice, and for the eternal enjoyment of himfelf. Matt. xi. 28. " Come unto me," fays Chrift, " all ye that labour and are heavy laden, and I will give you reft." Luke xviii. 13, 14. " The publican, ftanding afar off, would not lift up fo much as his eyes unto heaven, but fmote upon his breaft, faying, God be merciful to me, a finner. I tell you, This man went down to his houfe juftified rather than the other."

3d. The foul which fees its danger, and longs for falvation, will not intentionally offend the God it fears—the God it defires to love. At leaft, if it have not power over inward fin, it will abhor the vices and criminal amufements of the world. All its former pleafures are embittered to it. It now feeks a happinefs which the world cannot afford it, and, therefore, loaths every thing which tends to keep it from the object of its wifhes. Matt. iii. 8. " Bring forth fruits meet for repentance." See alfo Luke iii. 8. 2 Cor. 7, 10. " Godly forrow worketh repentance *to falvation* not to be repented of."

1. The taking of God's name in vain is fo grofs a vice, that thofe muft be wholly given up to Satan, who will commit it. Exod. xx. 7. " Thou fhalt not take the name of the Lord thy God *in vain;* for the Lord will not hold him guiltlefs that taketh

his name in vain." See alfo Deut. v. 11. Lev. xix. 12. " Neither fhalt thou profane the name of thy God." See alfo the fcripture-references taken from the New Teftament in the notes on the 25th article of religion.

2. Sabbath breaking is a vice which may be committed under various fpecious pretences, though it is the forerunner of all evil. In this day efpecially it is a vice inexcufable in thofe who make the leaft profeffion of chriftianity ; when the entire rejection of the fabbath is looked upon by the enemies of revealed religion, in general, as the moft effectual means to deftroy chriftianity itfelf. O let us all come out to the help of the Lord againft the mighty (Judges v. 23.) and love the fabbath for the fake of its Divine Founder and the ineftimable bleffings flowing from the due obfervance of it. It has been already honoured by the divine reft from creation, and is an emblem of that fpiritual and eternal reft which remains for the people of God. (Heb. iv. 9.) See particularly the numerous fcripture-references in the notes on the 15th fection of the firft chapter, as alfo the references on the 23d fection.

3. The fin of drunkennefs fhould be particularly guarded againft in a country where the materials for diftilled liquors fo much abound. Senfuality, alas ! of every kind, but particularly that which arifes from intemperance in the ufe of diftilled liquors, foils and defiles the foul, fills it full of impure defires, and turns the human nature, capable of the image of God, into a loathfome beaft. Luke xxi. 34, " Take heed to yourfelves, left at any time your hearts be overcharged with furfeiting, and drunkennefs, and cares of this life, and fo that day come upon you unawares." Rom. xiii. 13. " Let us walk honeftly as in the day, not in rioting and drunkennefs." 1 Cor. v. 1. " —A drunkard—with fuch an one no not to eat." vi. 10. "—Nor drunkards—fhall inherit the kingdom of God." Gal. v. 19—21. " Now, the works of the flefh are manifeft, which are thefe :—drunkennefs, &c. Ephef. v. 18. " Be not drunk with wine, wherein is excefs ; but be filled with the Spirit."—1 Theff. v. 7. " They that be drunken, are drunken in the night.' Tit. ii. 1—3. " Speak thou,— that the aged women [be] not given to much wine."

✱ 4. The buying and felling the fouls and bodies of men (for what is the body without the foul but a dead carcafe) is a complicated crime.* It was indeed, *in fome meafure*, overlooked in'

---

* *Are there not many proprietors to be found on this continent, who reftrain their flaves from enjoying the privileges of the gofpel, and thereby invade the rights of* the fouls *and* confciences *of their flaves, as well as* their bodies? *At the fame time we muft give the credit due to multitudes who do not thus enflave* the minds *of their fervants, but allow them full liberty to attend the preaching of the gofpel, wherever they think they are moft profited.*

the Jews by reafon of the wonderful hardnefs of their hearts, as
was the keeping of concubines and the divorcing of wives at
pleafure, but it is totally oppofite to the whole fpirit of the gofpel. It has an immediate tendency to fill the mind with pride
and tyranny, and is frequently productive of almoft every act of
luft and cruelty which can difgrace the human fpecies. Even
the moral philofopher will candidly confefs, that if there be a
God, every perfection he poffeffes muft be oppofed to a practice
fo contrary to every moral idea which can influence the human
mind. Nehem. v. 8, 9. " I faid unto them, We, after our ability, have redeemed our brethren, the Jews, which were fold
unto the heathen ; *and will ye even fell your brethren ? or fhall they
be fold unto us ?* Then held they their peace, and found nothing
to anfwer. Alfo I faid, It is not good that ye do : ought ye not
to walk in the fear of our God, becaufe of the reproach of the
heathen our enemies ?" Ifai. lviii. 6. Is not this the faft that I
have chofen ? to loofe the bands of wickednefs, *to undo the heavy
burdens,* and *to let the oppreffed go free,* and that *ye break every yoke.*"
Ezek xxvii. 13, (This chapter is written on the deftruction of
Tyrus, and the caufes of it) " Javan, Tubal, and Mefhech,
they were thy merchants : they *traded the perfons of men.*" Acts
xvii. 24—26. " *God—hath made of one blood all nations of men* for
to dwell on all the face of the earth." 1 Tim. i. 9, 10. " Knowing this, that the law is not made for a righteous man, but for
the lawlefs and difobedient, for the ungodly and for finners, for
unholy and profane, for murderers of fathers, and murderers of
mothers, for man-flayers,——for *men-ftealers,*" &c. Rev. xiii.
10. " He that leadeth into captivity fhall go into captivity."
Rev. xviii. (On the fall of Babylon, and the caufes of it) ver.
1 —13. " No man buyeth their merchandife any more : the
merchandife of gold, and filver,——and *flaves,* and *fouls of
men.*"

5. " The fruit of the Spirit is love, joy, peace, long-fuffering,
gentlenefs, goodnefs, faith, meeknefs, temperance," Gal. v. 22,
23. Thefe are directly oppofite to *fighting, quarrelling, brawling,
litigioufnefs, revenge, and railing.* It is, therefore, impoffible for
the holy Spirit of God to dwell in a heart which is a cage of
* fuch unclean birds—to have any connection with a foul, which
indulges thofe tempers which are fo contrary to his own holy
nature. Thofe, therefore, who manifeft fuch difpofitions cannot
be even under the convictions of the Spirit of God, and are, of
confequence, unfit for any chriftian fociety. Col. iii. 12, 13.
" Put on, therefore, as the elect of God, holy and beloved, bowels of mercies, kindnefs, humblenefs of mind, meeknefs, long-
fuffering ; forbearing one another, and forgiving one another, if
any man have a quarrel againft any ; even as Chrift forgave you,
fo alfo do ye." Tit. iii. 1, 2. " Put them in mind—to be no

brawlers, but gentle, ſhewing all meekneſs unto all men." Jam. iv. 1. " From whence come wars and fightings among you ? come they not hence, even of your luſts, that war in your members ?" See alſo the notes on ſection 10. chapter 1. concerning going to law with each other.

We alſo conceive it ſcarcely poſſible to uſe many words in buying and ſelling, without being frequently guilty of lying, and no lyar can inherit the kingdom of God. John viii. 44. " When he [the devil] ſpeaketh a lye, he ſpeaketh of his own : for he is a lyar, and the father of it." Epheſ. iv. 25. " Wherefore, putting away lying, ſpeak every man truth with his neighbour." Col. iii. 9. " Lie not one to another, ſeeing that ye have put off the old man with his deeds." Rev. xxi. 8. " —All liars ſhall have their part in the lake which burneth with fire and brimſtone; which is the ſecond death." xxii. 15. " Without are dogs, &c. and whoſoever loveth and maketh a lie."

6. We are debtors to the conſtitution under which we live *(we, eſpecially in theſe United States)* for all the bleſſings of law and liberty which we enjoy : and without a government to ſupport that conſtitution, all would be anarchy and comfuſion. It is, therefore, our duty to ſupport it by bearing, with our fellow-citizens, an equal proportion of its expences; and it is as great a crime to rob our country, as to rob a private individual; and the blindneſs of too many to this truth injures not, in the leaſt, the veracity of it. See the ſcripture-references on the 23d article of religion, and thoſe alſo on the 15th ſection of the firſt chapter, 5th article.

7. Uſury has been condemned in all civilized nations of the world. It is the offspring of covetouſneſs arrived to its height. It is a vice which belongs only to the baſeſt of the human race ; and the mind which is under its government is in danger of being led on, by degrees, to the higheſt exceſs. Exod. xxii. 25. " If thou lend money to any of my people that is poor by thee, thou ſhalt not be to him *as an uſurer*, neither ſhalt thou lay upon him *uſury*." See alſo Lev. xxv. 35—37. Jer. xv. 10. " I have neither lent on *uſury*, nor men have lent to me on *uſury*." Ezek. xviii. 5—9. " If a man be juſt, and do that which is lawful and right,——he that hath not given forth upon *uſury*, &c. he is juſt, he ſhall ſurely live, ſaith the Lord God." Jam. v. 1—3. " Go to now, ye rich men, weep and howl for your miſeries that ſhall come upon you. Your riches are corrupted, and your garments are moth eaten. Your gold and ſilver is cankered : and the ruſt of them ſhall be a witneſs againſt you, and ſhall eat your fleſh as it were fire. Ye have heaped treaſure together for the laſt days."

8. If " our converſation is to be alway with grace, ſeaſoned with ſalt" (Col. iv. 6.) how oppoſite to this is the ſlandering our

neighbours, or fpeaking evil of any. We are not in our converfation to fpeak *evil* of another, however true it may be : nothing can juftify it, but the cautioning of a friend from fome *immediate* danger. It will, in every other cafe, be condemned on
the day of judgment, not merely as an idle but as a criminal
word. If this be the cafe, it is ftill more criminal to fpeak evil
of public characters. It is taking the moft unjuft advantage of
them : and we may, perhaps, without intention, ruin the characters and ufefulnefs of much better men than ourfelves. This
is a vice which we fhould particularly guard againft, becaufe the
temptations to it are fo frequent and various ; and fo many *profeffors* (we can fcarcely fay *poffeffors*) are guilty of it. Follow
always the rule of good bifhop Beveridge, " Speak of men's vices
only to their faces, and of their virtues *only* behind their backs."
Acts xxiii. 25. " It is written, Thou fhalt not fpeak evil of the
ruler of thy people." See the fcripture references in the notes on
the 23d article of religion, and chap. 1. fect. 15.

9. To do to others as we would wifh they fhould do to us
(See Matt. vii. 12, and Luke vi. 21) includes in it the whole of
our duty to our neighbour—even the difinterefted love of man,
which can flow alone *from the love of God.* It is natural for the
men of the world to imagine that all mankind are influenced by
private motives, becaufe they know nothing of the love God,
and efteem the profeffors of grace as enthufiafts. It is the love
of God alone which can raife the foul above every thing on earth,
and crucify it entirely to the world, and, confequently, to every
object which could intereft it here below. *It is only this* which
can enable us to act to others continually according to that gold-
en rule, on which hang all the law and the prophets. See 1
Cor. xiii.

10. To do all to the glory of God, is the fpring of all religion. Every thing is finful which proceeds from any other principle : but every thing is an acceptable facrifice to God, through
Chrift, which proceeds from this heavenly motive—the glory of
God. He, who thus acts, has found out the philofopher's ftone,
the art of turning every thing into the true gold of the fanctuary.
He is bleffed in his bafket and ftore, in his going out and coming
in, and in his lying down and rifing up. But the very reverfe is the
cafe with all who act from any other principle, however fpecious
their outward conduct may be. *Without this,* every thing is carnal or devilifh, finful and accurfed. 1 Cor. x. 31. " Whether
therefore ye eat, or drink, or whatfoever ye do, do all to the
glory of God." 1 Cor. vi. 19, 20. " What? know ye not that
your body is the temple of the Holy Ghoft which is in you, which
ye have of God, and ye are not your own? For ye are bought
with a price: therefore glorify God in your body, and in your
fpirit, which are God's."

The man who acts from this heavenly principle,

(1.) Cannot wear any apparel which tends to feed his own pride, or to prevent his liberality to the poor. See the 7th section of this chapter.

(2.) He cannot indulge himself in the carnal diversions of the world. What blasphemy would it be for men or women, when they were throwing themselves about in a dance, to cry " I do this in the name of the holy Jesus!" What insolence would it be for the card-player, when he is tossing about his cards, or the horse-racer when he is driving furiously, to say, " I do this to the glory of God!" These diversions have been pronounced *by the spiritual ministers of Christ*, of all denominations in all ages, as inconsistent with true religion: and we shall find on the day of judgment, that *they* were better acquainted with the mind of God in these respects, than the children of Satan. 1 Tim. v. 6. " She that liveth in pleasure, is dead while she liveth." 2 Tim. iii. 1—4. " This know also, that in the last days perilous times shall come. For men shall be lovers of pleasures more than lovers of God." Job xxi. 7—11. " Wherefore do the wicked live, become old, yea, are mighty in power:——they send forth their little ones like a flock, *and their children dance.*

(3.) He sings and reads for the glory of God—for the sole purposes of gaining clearer light in the truths of God, inflaming his heart with more of the ove of God, and promoting the temporal, spiritual, and eternal interests of his fellow-creatures. Psal. cxix. 54. " Thy statutes have been *my songs* in the house of my pilgrimage." Ver. 99. " I have more understanding than all my teachers: for thy testimonies are *my meditation.*" Ver. 148. " Mine eyes prevent the night watches, *that I might meditate* on thy word."

(4.) He is well aware, how all that is carnal draws him from God. He therefore daily takes up his cross. He feels a delight (though perhaps mixed with some natural reluctance) to restrain and oppose his fleshly affections. He keeps at a distance from self-indulgence, and draws not too near to the brink of the precipice. He feels his own weakness: and though he lives by faith upon the Son of God, yet he would not *presume* upon him. Matt. x. 38. " He that taketh not his cross and followeth after me, is not worthy of me." xvi. 24. " Then said Jesus unto his disciples, If any man will come after me, let him deny himself, and take up his cross and follow me." Mark viii. 34. " And when he had called the people unto him, with his disciples also, he said unto them, Whosoever will come after me, let him deny himself, and take up his cross, and follow me." x. 21. " Come, take up the cross, and follow me." Luke ix. 23. " And he said to them all, if any man will come after me, let him deny himself, and take up his cross daily, and follow me." xiv. 27. " And whosoever doth not bear his cross, and come after me, cannot be my disciple."

(5.) He is a faithful steward of the manifold blessings of his God. He provides for his family with *christian* wisdom and *christian* prudence; and all the rest he lays out for the relief of the poor and afflicted, and for the advancement of the kingdom of God upon earth. He does not wish to have his good things in this world, and afterwards in hell to lift up his eyes in torments: but his highest ambition is to enjoy the sovereign good, the God of his salvation, to the utmost capacity of his renewed nature and to all eternity. Matt. vi. 9—21. " Lay not up for yourselves treasures upon earth, where moth and rust doth corrupt, and where thieves break through and steal: but lay up for yourselves treasures in heaven, where neither moth nor rust doth corrupt, and where thieves do not break through, nor steal. For where your treasure is, there will your heart be also." 1 Tim. vi. 9, 10. " They that will be rich fall into temptation, and a snare, and into many foolish and hurtful lusts, which drown men in destruction and perdition. For the love of money is the root of all evil; which while some coveted after, they have erred from the faith, and pierced themselves through with many sorrows."

(6.) He is strictly honest. He abhors the iniquitous attempt of getting money at his neighbour's risk. But alas! this is too common a practice even among many who call themselves professors. A man is poor, and wishes to be rich; or he is rich, and wishes to be richer; he accordingly takes up a great quantity of goods to form a large but false capital; or he borrows money of his friends for the same purpose : if he succeed, he has his ambition gratified, and becomes a man of fortune; if he fail, he is only where he was before, or at least suffers but little; whilst those who have in confidence sold him goods, or advanced to him money, are the only or chief sufferers. He is, what he would call tolerably safe at all events. This is an unjust, an iniquitous practice: and the more so, because the whole is carried on under the mask of honour and honesty, of friendship or integrity. Such persons should have no admission among us; or, if they have, should, when discovered, be expelled as some of the greatest enemies of civil society; whose practice has an immediate tendency to break all the bonds of social union, and to destroy all confidence among men. Mark x. 18, 19. " Jesus said unto him, Defraud not." 1 Cor. vi. 8. " Nay, ye do wrong and defraud, and that your brethren." Isa. xxi. 2. " A grievous vision is declared unto me; The treacherous dealer dealeth treacherously, and the spoiler spoileth" xxxiii. 1. " Woe to thee that dealeth treacherously, and they dealt not treacherously with thee;—when thou shalt make an end to deal treacherously, they shall deal treacherously with thee." See also the scripture references, in the notes on sect. 15th. chap. 1.

4th. True conviction of fin and an earneft longing for falvation will alfo be accompanied with every outward fruit of righteoufnefs. The love of God may not yet have become the governing principle of the whole foul, fo as to make obedience flow as from a fecond nature; but yet the *contrite* foul will have a conftant fear of offending God, and this will be accompanied with a conftant defire of pleafing him. Dan. iv. 27. " Break off thy fins by righteoufnefs, and thine iniquities by fhewing mercy to the poor," Matt. iii. 8. " Bring forth, therefore, fruits meet for repentance," See alfo Luke iii. 8. Acts xxvi. 19, 20. " I was not difobedient to the heavenly vifion; but fhewed—that they fhould repent and turn to God, *and do works meet for repentance.*"

1. This principle will make us feel for the infirmities of others, and fympathize with them. We fhall delight to afford to the hungry and naked, the ftranger, the fick and imprifoned, the neceffaries or comforts they ftand in need of. And in all this, we fhall confider the poor as the reprefentatives of Jefus Chrift, and that in doing it to *them* we do it to *him.* See Matt. xxv. 31—46.

2. It is a perfect miftake to fuppofe, that a real penitent cannot or is not called to do good *to the fouls of others.* Many in their awakened ftate have done confiderable good in this refpect. But when the love of God is become the reigning principle of the foul, we hunger and thirft for the falvation of others. Our cry is, " Come and hear, all ye that fear God, and I will declare what he hath done for my foul," Pfal. lxvi. 16.

3. Though he does good to all according to his ability, yet he particularly feels for the members of Chrift's myftical body. *They* are to him as his own foul. With them he experiences an union which the world is utterly unacquainted with. They are like the members of his own family: they are bone of his bone, and flefh of his flefh. " As we have, therefore, opportunity let us do good unto all men, efpecially unto them *who are of the houfehold of faith,*" Gal. vi. 10. " We know that we have paffed from death unto life, becaufe we love the brethren," 1 John iii. 14.

4. It is frequently one of the devices of Satan, to tempt the children of God to be negligent in their bufinefs, under the pretext that they will be able to live more in heaven by having nothing to do with earthly things. But the believer, when called to labour in a profeffion or trade for the fupport of his family, or to fill up fome ufeful ftation in fociety, may fo intermix pious ejaculations with his ftudies or labours, and improve fo many fhort intervals in private prayer, as not only to preferve his grace, but to increafe daily in the divine life. Ejaculations are fwift meffengers, which foon enter heaven, and foon bring down a gracious anfwer. Rom. xii. 11. " *Not flothful in bufinefs;* fervent in fpirit; ferving the Lord." Ver. 17. " Provide things

honeft in the fight of all men." 1 Tim. v. 8. " If any provide not for his own, and fpecially for thofe of his own houfe, he hath denied the faith, and is worfe than an infidel."

5. We have already enlarged on the great duty of taking up our crofs, and therefore fhall only obferve, that if we will be real difciples of our crucified Lord, we muft expect to meet with contempt and perfecution from the carnal world. Rom. viii. 7. "The carnal mind is enmity againft God: for it is not fubject to the law of God neither indeed can be." John xv. 18—21. " If the world hate you, ye know that it hated me, before it hated you. If ye were of the world, the world would love his own: but becaufe ye are not of the world, but I have chofen you out of the world, therefore the world hateth you. Remember the word that I faid unto you, The fervant is not greater than his lord. If they have perfecuted me, they will alfo perfecute you: if they have kept my faying, they will keep yours alfo. But all thefe things they will do unto you *for my name's fake*, becaufe they know not him that fent me." O what *chriftian* would refufe to fuffer *for the fake of his Redeemer*. Matt. v. 10—12. " Bleffed are they which are perfecuted for righteoufnefs' fake; for theirs is the kingdom of heaven. Bleffed are ye when men fhall revile you, and perfecute you, and fhall fay all manner of evil againft you falfely for my fake. Rejoice, and be exceeding glad: for great is your reward in heaven: for fo perfecuted they the prophets which were before you."

5th. We have alfo fpoken largely on all the ordinances of the gofpel, and the neceffity of being conftant partakers of them; and have proved this by a great variety of fcriptures. Although the ordinances are but *means* of grace, their end, which is the falvation of our fouls, cannot be attained without them. Such is the order of God, except when unavoidable hindrances prevent our attending of them; in which cafe, God will himfelf be to the fincere foul inftead of all ordinances, yea, will turn *the very hindrances themfelves* into the moft profitable of all means.

6th. Thus have we briefly explained *the regulations* by which the members of our fociety are governed. When thefe rules were once in a particular fuit at law read in a full court of juftice, in Europe, " I wifh," faid the judge, lifting up his hands, " that all the world kept them." O what a happy world would it become, *if they were written by the Spirit of God on every heart*. Surely " the Lord God would then dwell among us," (Pfal. lxviii. 18.) yea, his delight would be among the children of men. " The wolf would then dwell with the lamb, and the leopard lie down with the kid," (Ifa. xi. 6.) " They would not hurt nor deftroy in all God's holy mountain: for the earth would be full of the knowledge of the Lord, as the waters cover the fea," (ver. 9.)

SECTION II.

Of Clafs-Meeting.

Queft. 1. HOW may the leaders of claffes be rendered more ufeful?

Anfw. 1. Let each of them be diligently examined concerning his method of meeting a clafs. Let this be done with all poffible exactnefs, at leaft once a quarter. In order to this, take fufficient time.

2. Let each leader carefully inquire how every foul in his clafs profpers: Not only how each perfon obferves the outward rules, but how he grows in the knowledge and love of God.

3. Let the leaders converfe with thofe who have the charge of their circuits, frequently and freely.

Queft. 2 Can any thing more be done in order to make the clafs-meetings lively and profitable?

Anfw. 1. Change improper leaders.

2. Let the leaders frequently meet each other's claffes.

3. Let us obferve which leaders are the moft ufeful: And let thefe meet the other claffes as often as poffible.

4. See that all the leaders be not only men of found judgment, but men truly devoted to God.

Queft. 3. How fhall we prevent improper perfons from infinuating themfelves into the fociety?

Anfw 1. *Give tickets to none until they are recommended by a leader, with whom they have met at leaft fix months on trial.*

2. Give notes to none but thofe who are recommended by one you know, or until they have met three or four times in a clafs.

3. Read the rules to them the firft time they meet.

Queft.. 4. How fhall we be more exact in receiving and excluding members?

Anfw. The official minifter or preacher fhall, at every quarterly meeting, read the names of thofe that are received and excluded.

Queſt. 5. What ſhall we do with thoſe members of ſociety, who wilfully and repeatedly neglect to meet their claſs?

Anſw. 1. Let the elder, deacon, or one of the preachers, viſit them, whenever it is practicable, and explain to them the conſequence if they continue to neglect, viz. Excluſion.

2. If they do not amend, let him who has the charge of the circuit exclude them in the ſociety; ſhewing that they are laid aſide for a breach of our rules of diſcipline and not for immoral conduct.

N O T E S.

1. So much has been already ſpoken concerning the office of a leader in the notes on the preceding ſection and on the 10th of the 1ſt chapter, that we have hardly room to enlarge without tautology. But from the whole we may obſerve, how careful our miniſters ſhould be in their choice of leaders. For our leaders under God are the ſinews of our ſociety, and our revivals will ever, in a great meaſure, riſe or fall with them. Our miniſters and preachers ſhould therefore conſider no time better employed than that which they beſtow on the leaders, in examining them, directing them, and ſtirring them up to their holy and momentous duty.

2. We have made many remarks in the courſe of our work on the neceſſity of chriſtian fellowſhip: but this cannot be carried on to any conſiderable advantage without ſtated ſolemn times of aſſembling. The meetings held for this purpoſe muſt have a name to diſtinguiſh them. We call ours *Claſs-meetings*, and *Band-meetings;* but of the former we are to ſpeak at preſent. Here we muſt notice, that it is *the thing itſelf, chriſtian fellowſhip* and not the name, which we contend for. The experience of about ſixty-years has fully convinced us of its neceſſity; and we ourſelves can ſay that in the courſe of an extenſive acquaintance with men and things, and the church of God, for about twenty or thirty years we have rarely met with one who has been much devoted to God, and at the ſame time not united in cloſe chriſtian fellowſhip to ſome religious ſociety or other. Far be it from us to ſuppoſe that no fellowſhip-meetings, except ours, are owned of God: ſo illiberal a ſentiment never entered our minds. But we muſt ſay, that thoſe who entirely neglect this *divinely inſtituted* ordinance (however various the names given to it, or the modes of conducting it, may be) manifeſt, that they are either aſhamed to acknowledge *as their brethren,* the true children of God, or " are enemies of the croſs

of Chrift," Phil. 3. 18. They wifh to keep up a correfpondence with the world, which chriftian difcipline could not long tolerate: or they cannot bear to have their wounds probed to the bottom, that the balm of Gilead, the healing wine and oil of the gofpel, may be applied by the Divine Phyfician, " and the blood of Jefus Chrift the fon of God cleanfe them from all fin," 1 John i. 7.

We have no doubt, but meetings of chriftian brethren for the expofition of fcripture-texts, may be attended with their advantages. But.the moft profitable exercife of any is a free inquiry into the ftate of the. heart. We therefore confine thefe meetings to *chriftian experience*, only adjoining finging and prayer in the introduction and conclufion. And we praife the Lord, they have been made a bleffing to fcores of thoufands. And we muft add with gratitude to the Moft High, that after an accurate attention to the point ourfelves, and from the impartial account of feveral of our oldeft and moft ufeful minifters in different parts of the globe, we have caufe to believe, that out of thofe who have *died members of our fociety*, far the greateft part have entered into glory in the triumph of faith. In fhort, we can truly fay, that through the grace of God our claffes form the pillars of our work, and, as we have before obferved, are in a confiderable degree our univerfities for the miniftry. Mal. iii. 16, 17. " Then they that feared the Lord, fpake often one to another, and the Lord hearkened, and heard it, and a book of remembrance was written before him for them that feared the Lord, and that thought upon his name. And they fhall be mine, faith the Lord of hofts, in that day when I make up my jewels, and I will fpare them as a man fpareth his own fon that ferveth him." Heb. x. 23—25. " Let us hold faft the profeffion of our faith, &c. *not forfaking the affembling of ourfelves together*, as the manner of fome is; but exhorting *one another:* and fo much the more, as ye fee the day approaching." Matt. xviii. 20. " Where two or three are gathered together *in my name*, there am I in the midft of them."

SECTION III.

Of the Band Societies.

Two, three, or four true believers, who have confidence in each other, form a Band. Only it is to be obferved, that in one of thefe Bands all muft be men, or all women; and all married, or all fingle.

[Rules of the Band Societies, drawn up *Dec.* 25, 1738.]

THE defign of our meeting is to obey that command of God, *Confefs your faults one to another, and pray one for another, that ye may be healed: Jam.* v. 16.

To this end, we agree,

1. To meet once a week, at the leaft.

2. To come punctually at the hour appointed, with-out fome extraordinary reafon.

3. To begin exactly at the hour with finging or pray-er.

4. To fpeak, each of us in order, freely and plainly, the true ftate of our fouls, with the faults we have com-mitted in tempers, words, or actions, and the tempta-tions we have felt fince our laft meeting.

5. To end every meeting with prayer, fuited to the ftate of each perfon prefent.

6. To defire fome perfon among us to fpeak *his* own ftate firft, and then to afk the reft in order, as many and as fearching queftions as may be, concerning their ftate, fins, and temptations.

Some of the queftions propofed to every one before he is admitted among us, may be to this effect:

1. Have you the forgivenefs of your fins?

2. Have you peace with God, through our Lord Jesus Christ?

3. Have you the witnefs of God's Spirit with your fpirit, that you are a child of God?

4. Is the love of God fhed abroad in your heart?

5. Has no fin, inward or outward, dominion over you?

6. Do you defire to be told of your faults?

7. Do you defire to be told of *all* your faults, and that plain and home?

8. Do you defire, that every one of us fhould tell you, from time to time, whatfoever is in his heart con-cerning you?

9. Confider! Do you defire we fhould tell you what-foever we think, whatfoever we fear, whatfoever we hear concerning you?

10. Do you defire, that in doing this we fhould come as clofe as poffible, that we fhould cut to the quick, and fearch your heart to the bottom?

11. Is it your defire and defign to be on this and all other occafions entirely open, fo as to fpeak without difguife, and without referve?

Any of the preceding queftions may be afked as often as occafion requires: The four following at every meeting.

1. What known fins have you committed fince our laft meeting?

2. What particular temptations have you met with?

3. How were you delivered?

4. What have you thought, faid, or done, of which you doubt whether it be fin or not?

Directions given to the Band-Societies. December 25th, 1744.

YOU are fuppofed to have the *Faith that overcometh the world.* To you therefore it is not grievous,

I. Carefully to abftain from doing evil: in particular,

1. Neither to *buy* nor *fell* any thing at all on the Lord's-day.

2. To tafte no fpirituous liquor, *no dram* of any kind, unlefs prefcribed by a phyfician.

3. To be *at a word* both in buying and felling.

4. Not to *mention the fault* of any *behind his back*, and to ftop thofe fhort that do.

5. To wear no *needlefs ornaments*, fuch as rings, ear-rings, necklaces, lace, ruffles.

6. To ufe no *needlefs felf-indulgence.*

II. Zealoufly to maintain good works; in particular,

1. To *give alms* of fuch things as you poffefs, and that according to your ability.

2. To *reprove* thofe who fin in your fight, and that in love and meeknefs of wifdom.

3. To be patterns of *diligence* and *frugality,* of *felf-denial,* and taking up the crofs daily.

III. Conftantly to attend on all the ordinances of GOD; in particular,

1. To be at church, and at the Lord's table, and at every public meeting of the bands, at every opportunity.

2. To ufe private prayer every day; and family prayer, if you are the head of a family.

3. Frequently to read the fcriptures, and meditate thereon. And,

4. To obferve, as days of fafting or abftinence, all *Fridays* in the year.

NOTES.

Our fociety may be confidered as a fpiritual hofpital, where fouls come to be cured of their fpiritual difeafes. The members therefore who compofe our clafs meetings vary exceedingly in the ftate of their minds and the degrees of their experience. On this account it was thought neceffary by our venerable leader Mr. Wefley, to eftablifh a fociety of evangelical believers within the fociety compofed of the whole body of Methodifts, to which he gave the name of *the band-fociety*. This inftitution he borrowed from the practice of the primitive churches, as indeed he did almoft every thing he eftablifhed.

The heart of man *by nature* is fuch a cage of unclean birds, that few are to be found who will lay before their brethren all its fecret movements, unlefs the love of God be the ruling principle of their fouls. And even then they are not called upon to exercife this confidence, except towards a fmall confidential company of true believers like themfelves. When bands can be formed on this plan (and on no other do we form them) they become one of the moft profitable means of grace in the whole compafs of chriftian difcipline. There is nothing we know of, which fo much quickens the foul to a defire and expectation of the perfect love of God as this. It includes in it all the fpiritual benefits of focial intercourfe. For thefe little families of love, not only mutually weep and rejoice, and in every thing fympathize with each other, as genuine friends, but each of them poffeffes a meafure of " that unction of the Holy One," (1 John ii. 20.) which teaches all fpiritual knowledge. And thus are they enabled to " build up themfelves [and each other] on their moft holy faith," Jude 20. and to " confider *one another*, to provoke unto love and good works," Heb. x. 24

The regularity and order, which fhould be obferved in every folemn meeting, requires, that one of the band fhould be the leader, to open and clofe the ordinance with finging, and prayer, though all may be here confidered nearly upon an equality. Each inuft be at full liberty to follow the leader in prayer, whenever they kneel down together before God.

In large focieties, all the members of thofe little bands are to meet together once a week with the preacher, and to fpend an hour in fpeaking their experience one after another, as in our love-feafts: and thefe meetings have been rendered a great blefling to many.

* In very large focieties, there fhould be a quarterly love-feaft for the bands, as well as for the whole fociety (which always includes the members of the bands.)

Wherever alfo it is practicable. there fhould be formed *a felect fociety* chofen out of the members of the bands. This fhould be compofed of believers who enjoy the perfect love of God, or who are earneftly feeking that great blefling. In London, Briftol, &c. &c. in Europe, and in New-York, &c. on this continent, thefe felect focieties have been very profitable. *They* alfo meet once a week for an hour, and the preacher prefides among them. Each member is at liberty to fpeak his or her experience, the preacher giving fuch advice refpecting the grand point their fouls are aiming at, as he fees expedient.

Thus does our economy by its prudential ordinances, under the grace of God, tend to raife the members of our fociety from one degree of grace to another. And we have invariably obferved, that where thefe meetings of the bands have been kept up in their life and power, the revival of the work of God has been manifeft both in the addition of members to the fociety, and in the deepening of the life of God in general.

We earneftly wifh, that our elders, deacons and preachers be peculiarly attentive to thefe blefled ordinances in their refpective fpheres of action. They probably may find earneft believers in almoft every circuit, who will be willing to meet in band, if properly advifed and encouraged. And when many of thefe bands are formed, the other meetings may eafily be eftablifhed and regulated. And we believe, hardly any thing will promote the general work more than this.

The propriety of feparating the men and women in thefe bands, muft be evident to every one who confiders the account here given of this means of grace. The feparating of the married and fingle arifes from the peculiar circumftances in which they are fituated, and from the clofer union which is likely to fubfift between thofe who are circumftanced alike. Widowers or widows may have their choice of me ting either with the married or the fingle, unlefs a band can be formed of them alone refpectively.

The focial principle is one of the grand fprings in the foul of man. It was not the defign of chriftianity to annihilate this principle, but the very contrary—to improve it, to fpiritualize it, and ftrengthen it. O then let us exercife it in fpiritual intercourfe, as we well know that one part of our heavenly felicity will flow from friendſhip and union with our brethren the redeemed of the Lord to all eternity! Gal. vi. 2. " Bear ye one another's burdens, and ſo fulfil the law of Chriſt." 1 Cor. xii. 26, 27. " Whether one member ſuffer, all the members ſuffer with it : or one member be honoured, all the members rejoice with it. Now ye are the body of Chriſt, and members in particular." Phil. ii. 1, 2. " If there be therefore any conſolation in Chriſt, if any comfort of love, if any fellowſhip of the Spirit, if any bowels and mercies : fulfil ye my joy, that ye be like-minded, having the ſame love, being of one accord, of one mind." We have perhaps one hundred thouſand believers in our church throughout the world; and if all were thus of one accord, " walking by the ſame rule, minding the ſame thing." Phil. iii. 16. What a glorious church ſhould we make : and God would hear our prayers, and look down upon us with the ſame delight, as if we were all aſſembled in the ſame room, or in the ſame temple.

Obſerve, here is nothing of auricular confeſſion or prieſtly abſolution : the whole is the fruit of holy confidence and chriſtian love.

The directions for the bands are included in the rules of the ſociety, and have been already conſidered, excepting the laſt, " To obſerve, as days of faſting or abſtinence, all *Fridays* in the year." In every thing the true believer ſhould be a pattern of piety and crucifixion to the world. The times of abſtinence are therefore fixed, as being more eaſily obſerved than if they were uncertain; that at all events the diſciple of Chriſt may keep his body under, and bring it into ſubjection.

SECTION IV.

Of the Privileges granted to ſerious Perſons who are not of the Society.

Queſt. 1. HOW often ſhall we permit ſtrangers to be preſent at the meeting of the ſociety?

Anſw. At every other meeting of the ſociety in every place, let no ſtranger be admitted. At other times they may; but the ſame perſons not above twice or thrice.

Queſt. 2. How often ſhall we permit ſtrangers to be preſent at our love-feaſts?

Anſw. Let them be admitted with the utmoſt caution ; and the ſame perſon on no account above twice or thrice, unleſs he become a member.

N O T E S.

It is manifeſtly our duty to fence in our ſociety, and to preſerve it from intruders; otherwiſe we ſhould ſoon become a deſolate waſte. God would write *Ichabod* upon us, and the glory would be departed from Iſrael. At the ſame time we ſhould ſuffer thoſe who are apparently ſincere, if they requeſt it, to ſee our order and diſcipline twice or thrice, that they themſelves may judge, whether it will be for their ſpiritual advantage to caſt in their lot among us. But we ſhould by no means exceed the indulgence here allowed; otherwiſe we ſhould make our valuable meetings for chriſtian fellowſhip cheap and contemptible, and bring a heavy burden on the minds of our brethren. Gal. ii. 4, 5. " Becauſe of falſe brethren unawares brought in, who came in privily to ſpy out our liberty, which we have in Chriſt Jeſus, that they might bring us into bondage: to whom we gave place by ſubjection, no, not for an hour." Eph. v. 11. " Have no fellowſhip with the unfruitful works of darkneſs."

S E C T I O N V.

Of the Qualification and Duty of the Stewards of Circuits.

Queſt. 1. WHAT are the qualifications neceſſary for ſtewards?

Anſw. Let them be men of ſolid piety, who both know and love the Methodiſt doctrine and diſcipline; and of good natural and acquired abilities to tranſact the temporal buſineſs.

Queſt. 2 What are the duties of ſtewards?

Anſw. To take an exact account of all the money, or other proviſion collected for the ſupport of preachers in the circuit ; to make an accurate return of every expenditure of money, whether to the preachers, the ſick, or the poor ; to ſeek the needy and diſtreſſed,. in order to relieve and comfort them; to inform the preach-

ers of any fick or diforderly perfons ; to tell the preachers what they think wrong in them ; to attend the
quarterly meetings of their circuit ; to give advice, if
afked, in planning the circuit ; to attend committees
for the application of money to churches ; to give
counfel in matters of arbitration ; to provide elements
for the Lord's Supper ; to write circular letters to the
focieties in the circuit to be more liberal, if need be ;
as alfo to let them know, when occafion requires, the
ftate of the temporal concerns at the laft quarterly
meeting ; to regifter the marriages and baptifms, and
to be fubject to the bifhops, the prefiding elder of their
diftrict, and the elder, deacon, and travelling-preach-
ers of their circuit.

Queft. 3. What number of ftewards is neceffary in
each circuit ?

Anfw. Not lefs than two, nor more than four.

N O T E S.

The office of a fteward of a circuit is of confiderable magnitude
in our connection. For a full proof of this we need only recapi-
tulate the different branches of his office. 1. He is to keep regular accounts of the receipts and expenditures of money. This will
not require much of his time, if he be qualified to keep books of
accounts. 2. He is to find out the poor and afflicted, which is a
truly charitable employment, whether he has any thing of his
own to give them, or not. And here he will have an opportunity
of exercifing the gift of prayer or exhortation, if the Lord has
bleffed him with fpiritual talents; but this is not neceffary for his
office. 3. He is to fpeak his mind freely to the preachers concerning their conduct either in public or private life, if he have any
fears in his mind concerning them, not in the way of accufation
(which is a diftinct matter from the prefent) but in tendernefs,
friendfhip, and love. 4. He is to be always at the quarterly-
meetings of his circuit, unlefs ficknefs or fome other juft and abfolutely unavoidable hindrance prevents him. This is a very
confiderable part of his duty. 5. He is to attend all other important meetings for the regulation of the temporal affairs of the circuit. 6. He is to be a peace-maker between contending parties,
or to ufe his endeavours to bring matters to an amicable fettlement. 7. He is to fee that every thing is in order for the regular
adminiftration of the ordinances. 8. He is to promote liberality

among the people; and to afford them all neceffary information in writing or otherwife concerning the temporal affairs of the circuit. 9. He is to keep the regifters. Laftly, He is to be ready to promote the work of God in every thing which relates to his office, under the direction of the travelling minifters and preachers of his circuit. When we confider all thefe branches of his charge, we may truly fay, that his office is effential to the good order of the fociety, and highly honourable in the church of God.

In each large fociety, there are generally two or four ftewards of that particular fociety, for the management of its temporal concerns. Thefe are appointed as well as the circuit-ftewards, by the preacher who has the charge of the circuit. He is himfelf to have as little as poffible to do with temporal affairs, but has the appointment of the officers of the fociety invefted in him, as being likely to be the beft judge of the fociety at large, and of each member in particular. Neverthelefs, he is to advife with the quarterly-meeting on the appointment of *circuit-ftewards*, and with the leaders of each fociety refpectively on the appointment of *fociety-ftewards*.

Prov. xxviii. 20. " A faithful man fhall abound with bleffings." 1 Cor. iv. 2. " It is required in ftewards, that they be found faithful." See alfo James i. 27. and Matt. v. 9.

SECTION VI.

Of unlawful Marriages.

Queft. 1. DO we obferve any evil which has prevailed among our focieties with refpect to marriage.

Anfw. Many of our members have married with *unawakened* perfons. This has produced bad effects; they have been either hindered for life, or have turned back to perdition.

Queft. 2. What can be done to put a ftop to this?

Anfw. 1. Let every preacher publicly enforce the apoftle's caution, " Be ye not unequally yoked together with unbelievers."

2. Let him openly declare, whoever does this, will be expelled the fociety.

3. When any fuch is expelled, let a fuitable exhortation be fubjoined.

4. Let all be exhorted to take no ftep in fo weighty a matter, without advifing with the moft ferious of their brethren.

Queſt. 3. Ought any woman to marry without the confent of her parents?

Anſw. In general fhe ought not. Yet there may be exceptions. For if, 1. A woman be under the neceffity of marrying: If, 2. Her parents abfolutely refufe to let her marry any chriftian: Then fhe may, nay, ought to marry without their confent. Yet even then a Methodift preacher ought not to be married to her.

N. B. By the word *unawakened,* as ufed above, we mean one whom we could not in confcience admit into fociety. We do not prohibit our people from marrying perfons who are not of our fociety, provided, fuch perfons have the form, and are feeking the power of godlinefs; but if they marry perfons who do not come up to this defcription, we fhall be obliged to purge our fociety of them: And even in a doubtful cafe, the member of our fociety fhall be put back upon trial.

N O T E S.

We are well affured that few things have been more pernicious to the work of God, than the marriage of the children of God with the children of this world. We therefore think ourfelves obliged to bear our teftimony, both in doctrine and difcipline, againft fo great an evil. We have added the explication in the nota bene, hoping that thereby the preachers who have the overfight of circuits, will be eafily enabled to determine on every point which may come before them, to the fatisfaction of the truly pious, and to the prevention of a practice fo exceedingly injurious to vital religion.

We need only add a few texts out of the word of God for the confirmation of it. Gen. vi. 1—7. " And it came to pafs, when men began to multiply on the face of the earth, and daughters were born unto them; that the fons of God faw the daughters of men, that they were fair; and they took them wives of all which they chofe. And the LORD faid, My Spirit fhall not always ftrive with man, for that he alfo is flefh: yet his days fhall be an hundred and twenty years. There were giants in the earth in thofe days; and alfo after that, when the fons of God came in unto the daughters of men, and they bare children to them: the fame became mighty men, which were of old men of renown. And God faw that the wickednefs of man was great in the earth, and that every imagination of the thoughts of his heart was only evil continually. And it repented the LORD that he had made man on the earth, and it grieved him at his heart. And the LORD faid, I will deftroy man, whom I have created, from the face of the earth, both man and beaft, and the creeping things, and the fowls of the air: for it repenteth me that I have made them." We have given this long quotation, as it evidently fhews, that one grand caufe of the univerfal and entire depravity of the human race juft before the deluge, and of the univerfal deluge itfelf, was the intermixture by marriage of the children of God with the children of this world. Gen. xxiv. 2—4. " And Abraham faid unto his eldeft fervant of his houfe,—I will make thee fwear by the LORD, the God of heaven and the God of the earth, that thou fhalt not take a wife unto my fon of the daughters of the Canaanites amongft whom I dwell: but thou fhalt go unto my country, and to my kindred, and take a wife unto my fon Ifaac." xxvii. 46. " And Rebeckah faid to Ifaac, I am weary of my life, becaufe of the daughters of Heth; if Jacob take a wife of the daughters of Heth, fuch as thefe which are of the daughters of the land, what good fhall my life do me?" xxviii. 1. " And Ifaac called Jacob, and bleffed him, and charged him, and faid unto him, Thou fhalt not take a wife of the daughters of Canaan." Ver. 6—9. " When Efau faw that Ifaac had bleffed Jacob, and fent him away to Padan-aram, to take him a wife from thence; and that as he bleffed him, he gave him a charge, faying, Thou fhalt not take a wife of the daughters of Canaan; and that Jacob obeyed his father, and his mother, and was gone to Padan-aram; and Efau feeing that the daughters of Canaan pleafed not Ifaac his father: Then went Efau unto Ifhmael, and took unto the wives which he had, Mahalath, the daughter of Ifhmael Abraham's fon, &c." Efau therefore married his *firft coufin*. But did he pleafe Ifaac thereby? No, nor God. Ifaac wanted his fons to marry thofe, who fincerely waited for the Meffiah, the promifed feed of the woman. See Gen. iii. 15. Matt. xix. 5, 6. " For this caufe fhall a man leave father and mother, and fhall cleave to his wife; and they twain fhall be *one flefh*. Wherefore they are no more twain, but *one flefh*." See alfo Gen. ii. 24. and Eph. v. 31. 2 Cor. vi. 14—18. " Be ye not unequally yoked together with unbelievers: for what fellowfhip hath righteoufnefs with unrighteoufnefs? and what communion hath light with darknefs? and what concord hath Chrift with Belial? or what part hath he that believeth with an infidel? and what agreement hath the temple of God with idols? for ye are the temple of the living God; as God hath faid,

I will dwell in them, and walk in them; and I will be their God, and they shall be my people. *Wherefore come out from among them, and be ye separate,* saith the Lord, and touch not the unclean thing; and I will receive you, and will be a father unto you, and ye shall be *my sons and daughters,* saith the Lord Almighty."

SECTION VII.

Of Dress.

Quest. SHOULD we insist on the rules concerning dress?

Answ. By all means. This is no time to give any encouragement to superfluity of apparel. Therefore give no tickets to any, till they have left off superfluous ornaments. In order to this, 1. Let every one who has the charge of a circuit, read the thoughts upon dress, at least once a year in every large society. 2. In visiting the classes, be very mild, but very strict. 3. Allow of no exempt case: Better one suffer than many. 4. Give no tickets to any that wear high heads, enormous bonnets, ruffles, or rings.

N O T E S.

As our one aim, in all our economy and ministerial labours, is to raise *a holy people,* crucified to the world, and alive to God, we cannot allow of any thing which has an immediate tendency to defeat our main design, and to strengthen and puff up the carnal mind. Few things, perhaps, have a greater tendency to this than gay apparel, which is expresly and repeatedly forbidden by the scriptures. We endeavour to follow the Word of God; and whilst we have *that* on our side, we must go on, and leave all consequences to the Lord. 1 Tim. ii. 8—10. " I will—in like manner also, that women adorn themselves in modest apparel, with shame-facedness and sobriety: *not with broidered hair,* or *gold,* or *pearls,* or *costly array;* but (which becometh women professing godliness) with good works." 1 Pet. iii. 3—5. " Whose adorning, let it not be *that outward adorning of plaiting the hair, and of wearing of gold,* or *of putting on of apparel:* but let it be the hidden man of the heart, in that which is not corruptible, even the ornament of a meek and quiet spirit, which is in the fight of God of great price. For after this manner in the old time, *the holy women also, who trusted in God,* adorned themselves," &c. Ifai. iii. 16—24. " Moreover, the LORD faith, Becaufe the daughters of Zion are haughty, and walk with ftretched-forth necks and wanton eyes, walking, and mincing as they go, and making a tinkling with their feet: Therefore, the LORD will fmite with a fcab the crown of the head of the daughters of Zion.——In that day the LORD will take away the bravery of their tinkling ornaments about their feet, and their cauls, and their round tires like the moon, the chains, and the bracelets, and the mufflers, the bonnets, and the ornaments of the legs, and the head-bands, and the tablets, and the ear-rings, the rings, and nofe-jewels, the changeable fuits of apparel, and the mantles, and the wimples, and the crifping-pins, the glaffes, and the fine linen, and the hoods, and the vails. And it fhall come to pafs, that inftead of fweet fmell, there fhall be ftink; and inftead of a girdle, a rent; and inftead of well-fet hair, baldnefs; and inftead of a ftomacher, a girding of fackcloth; and burning inftead of beauty." In this laft quotation we have, 1. the crimes of luxury and wanton haughtinefs defcribed; and, 2. the punifhment denounced, with which God would purfue thefe crimes. There is a peculiar emphafis in referring thefe vices of haughtinefs, luxury, wantonnefs, and the love of fuperfluous ornament, to the *daughters of Sion*, that is, to the matrons and virgins of the holy city, chofen by God the hater of luxury and vanity; a mountain and city, which thofe *daughters* of Abraham inhabited, whom, above all others, *outward adorning* became not;——the *plaiting of the hair,* &c. but *the hidden man of the heart,* modefty and humility.

SECTION VIII.

Of bringing to Trial, finding Guilty, and reproving, fufpending, or excluding diforderly Perfons from Society and Church Privileges.

Queft. HOW *fhall a fufpefted member be brought to trial?*

Anfw. Before the fociety of which he is a member, or a felect number of them, in the prefence of a bifhop, elder, deacon, or preacher, in the following manner; Let the accufed and accufer be brought face to face:

but if this cannot be done, let the next beſt evidence be procured. If the accuſed perſon be found guilty, and the crime be ſuch as is expreſsly forbidden by the word of God, ſufficient to exclude a perſon from the kingdom of grace and glory, and to make him a ſubject of wrath and hell, let the miniſter or preacher who has the charge of the circuit, expel him. If he evade a trial by abſenting himſelf after ſufficient notice given him, and the circumſtances of the accuſation be ſtrong and preſumptive, let him be eſteemed as guilty, and be accordingly excluded. Witneſſes from without, ſhall not be rejected.

But in caſes of neglect of duties of any kind, imprudent conduct, indulging ſinful tempers or words, or diſobedience to the order and diſcipline of the church,——Firſt, let private reproof be given by a preacher or leader; and if there be an acknowledgement of the fault and proper humiliation, the perſon may remain on trial. On a ſecond offence, the preacher or leader may take one or two faithful friends. On a third offence, let the caſe be brought before the ſociety or a ſelect number; and if there be no ſign of real humiliation, the offender muſt be cut off.

If there be a murmur or complaint from any excluded perſon in any of the above-mentioned inſtances, that juſtice has not been done, he ſhall be allowed an appeal to the next quarterly meeting; and the majority of the miniſters, travelling and local preachers, exhorters, ſtewards and leaders preſent, ſhall finally determine the caſe.

After ſuch forms of trial and expulſion, ſuch perſons ſhall have no privileges of ſociety or of ſacraments in our church, without contrition, confeſſion, and proper trial.

N. B. If a member of our church ſhall be clearly convicted of endeavouring to ſow diſſentions in any of our ſocieties, by inveighing againſt either our doctrines or diſcipline, ſuch perſon ſo offending ſhall be firſt reproved by the fenior minifter or preacher of his circuit, and, if he afterwards perfift in fuch pernicious practices, he fhall be expelled the fociety.

N O T E S.

The prefent fection requires a very full explication : not becaufe fcripture and reafon do not fully difcover to us the truth on the prefent fubject, but becaufe many have objected to our difcipline in the inftance before us.

The grand point to be determined, is this : whether the final judgment of an offender in refpect to both the guilt and the cenfure, fhould be invefted in the minifter, or the people. We fhall therefore take a view of this part of our economy, firft, in the light of fcripture, and, fecondly, in that of reafon.

Firft, in the light of fcripture. Here we muft confine ourfelves of courfe to the New Teftament, as living under the chriftian difpenfation. 1. The firft fcripture we fhall confider is the declaration of our Saviour in Matt. xviii. 15—17. " Moreover, if thy brother fhall trefpafs againft thee, go and tell him his fault between thee and him alone : if he fhall hear thee, thou haft gained thy brother. But if he will not hear thee, then take with thee one or two more, that in the mouth of two or three witneffes every word may be eftablifhed. And if he fhall neglect to hear them, tell it unto the church; but if he neglect to hear the church, let him be unto thee as an heathen man and a publican." Thefe words were addreffed to the apoftles, and through them to all the minifters of Chrift to the end of the world. This is evident from the words immediately following the quotation, and which are a continuation of the fame paragraph, and could not belong to the private members of a church.

The firft ftep then which is to be taken, is to tell the offender of his fault in private without any witnefs. Here is the *fecret reproof* of the minifter himfelf. But if he will not hear and amend, the fecond ftep is, that the minifter take with him two or three witneffes. Here is the reproof of the minifter *before witneffes.* " And if he fhall neglect to hear them," fhall thefe two or three witneffes proceed to exclude him ? No : they have no fuch authority : but " tell it unto the church." This is the third ftep. Has the church then any authority to punifh him ? No : their whole authority lies in advifing and reproving him. " But if," after fuch advice and reproof, " he neglect to hear the church, *let him be* UNTO THEE *as an heathen man and a publican.* Can any one imagine that the minifter *only* is to treat the offender thus; and that the reft of the church are to give him the right hand of fellowfhip? This cannot be. The minifter is undoubtedly to exclude him from the communion of the church. This is the laſt ſtep. Then follow immediately thoſe words of our Lord, " Whatſo-ever ye ſhall bind on earth, ſhall be bound in heaven: and what-ſoever ye ſhall looſe on earth, ſhall be looſed in heaven: which words, as we before obſerved, confine the power to miniſters, whoſe church-cenſures as far as they are conſiſtent with the word of God (for we cannot ſuppoſe the authority goes further) ſhall be confirmed and ſupported in heaven: and the faithful miniſters of God, who have been more or leſs inveſted with the ſuperin-tendency of the church have found this promiſe verified. The latter words cannot be ſuppoſed to relate to an eternal excluſion from glory, for that would preclude the neceſſity of the day of judgment in reſpect to thoſe ſo excommunicated. But we repeat, Here is not a word ſaid of the church's authority either to judge or to cenſure. On the contrary, the whole authority is expreſsly delivered into the hands of the miniſter.

But we may add, that this paſſage ſpeaks of offences, which have not yet brought a public diſgrace on the church of God. The church or ſociety of which the offender is a member, is not even ſuppoſed to be generally acquainted with the fault till after the failure of the firſt and ſecond attempt for his reformation. Surely, if the offence be of a ſcandalous nature, and has already diſgraced the cauſe of God by its public notoriety, the offender ought to be *immediately* removed, after clear conviction, for the honour of God and his cauſe: much more ſo ſtill, if the offend-er has been found guilty of ſome *groſs* crime. For could any one think of having communion with a murderer, adulterer, or thief, even for a moment, though the crime was not known to any but the offender and himſelf: and ſo we may obſerve of many other crimes.

But it may be urged, that the offence muſt firſt be mentioned to the church, before the offender can be ſcripturally excluded. " Tell it to the church," ſays our Lord. And ſo we do. It is merely for the ſake of convenience, that in *large* ſocieties we tell it only to a committee or repreſentation of the ſociety, or do a-bundantly more, even make them the witneſſes of the whole tri-al. But if ſuch ſocieties were to deſire it, we would tell the whole unto the church at large. But ſtill we muſt declare, from the plain ſenſe of the word of God, that our Lord inveſts the miniſter with the whole authority both of judgment and cenſure.

2. Another ſcripture worthy of conſideration on this ſubject, is 1 Cor. v. 1—5. " It is reported commonly that there is for-nication among you, and ſuch fornication as is not ſo much as named amongſt the gentiles, that one ſhould have his father's wife. And ye are puffed up, and have not rather mourned, that he that hath done this deed, might be taken away from among you. For I verily as abſent in body, but *preſent in ſpirit, have*

JUDGED *already*, as though I were prefent, concerning him that hath fo done this deed: In the name of our Lord Jefus Chrift, when ye are gathered together, and *my Spirit*, with the power of our Lord Jefus Chrift, to deliver fuch a one unto Satan for the deftruction of the flefh, that the fpirit may be faved in the day of our Lord Jefus." It is evident, beyond the poffibility of a doubt, that the apoftle, being fully perfuaded of the truth of the fact, took upon himfelf the whole bufinefs of deciding on the guilt and punifhment of the inceftuous Corinthian. " *I, as prefent in Spirit*," fays he, " have judged *already*." He here acts as their chief minifter, and requires them to confider *his Spirit prefent with them*, as he could not be fo perfonally. They were not to meet, in order to confult whether the offender fhould be put away or not, but merely to put him from among them, becaufe the apoftle was abfent.

It may here be afked, Why did not the chief refident minifter of the church of Corinth put away the inceftuous perfon, if he poffeffed the authority? We anfwer, becaufe he was unfaithful. He connived at this enormous crime, either becaufe he did not love the caufe of holinefs which is the caufe of God, or becaufe he gave way to the evil folicitations of the people. This is evident from thofe words in the paffage before us, " Ye are puffed up, and have not rather mourned, that he that hath done this deed, *might be taken away* from among you." He does not fay, Ye have not mourned *that you did not put away* this great offender, but " *that he might be taken away* from among you." But as the perfon who had the immediate authority *did not take the offender away* from among them, St. Paul, as the apoftle of the Gentiles, fteps into the minifter's place, and cuts him off.

It might alfo be urged, that it was *an apoftle* who thus acted: and we fhould be ready to admit this as an exempt cafe, if it were not agreeable to the authority given by Chrift himfelf to his minifters—an authority, the due exercife of which by his minifters our Lord highly approves of, and the neglect of which he ftrongly condemns, as we fhall now proceed to fhew.

3. Rev. ii. 1, 2. " Unto the angel of the church of Ephefus write; Thefe things faith he that holdeth the feven ftars in his right-hand, who walketh in the midft of the feven golden candlefticks; I know thy works, and thy labour, and thy patience, and *how thou canft not bear them which are evil*." With what high approbation does our Lord here exprefs himfelf concerning the determined oppofition of the chief minifter of the church of Ephefus to all immoral profeffors. " Thou canft not bear them which are evil." But if this minifter had only a fingle vote againft immoral practices in the church, or was only chairman in the meetings of the church, to examine into the conduct of offenders or fuppofed offenders, is it likely that our Lord would have given fo high an

encomium, fo ftrong a commendation of the conduct of the minifter in this refpect? Would he not at leaft have faid fomething in
commendation of the church itfelf, without whom in this inftance,
if the power of cenfure lay in them, the minifter would be almoft
a cypher? For the minifter, in fuch cafe, would have little to do
in the bufinefs, unlefs as a complainant or informer. Befides, our
Lord adds in the 2d verfe, " And *thou* haft tried them which fay
they are apoftles, and are not; and haft found them liars." And
again, ver. 6. " But this thou haft, that thou hateft the deeds of
the Nicolaitans, which I alfo hate." From the whole of which it
appears, that the minifter was the fole judge both of the morals
and doctrines of the church which he fuperintended, the church
not being at all mentioned by our Lord as having any authority in
thefe matters.

4. Rev. ii. 12—15. " And to the angel of the church in Per-
gamos write; " Thefe things faith he which hath the fharp fword
with two edges;—I have a few things againft thee, becaufe thou
haft there them that hold the doctrine of Balaam, who taught
Balak to caft a ftumbling-block before the children of Ifrael, to
eat things facrificed unto idols, and to commit fornication. So haft
thou alfo them that hold the doctrine of the Nicolaitans, which
thing I hate." But why fhould our Lord *caft all this blame* on the
minifter *alone* without taking the leaft notice of the church, *if the
power of cenfure refted in the church*, and not in the minifter; or no
farther in the minifter, than as having a fingle vote in the church?
Is it, we muft repeat, at all probable, is it morally poffible, that
our Lord would have written thus to the angel of the church, if
that angel, or chief minifter had not poffeffed authority to cleanfe
it from the followers of the doctrine of Balaam, and of the Nicolaitans?

5. Rev. ii. 18—20. " And unto the angel of the church in
Thyatira write; " Thefe things faith the Son of God, who hath
his eyes like unto a flame of *fire*, and his feet are like fine brafs;
—I have a few things againft thee, becaufe *thou fuffereft* that woman Jezebel, which calleth herfelf a prophetefs, to teach and to
feduce my fervants to commit fornication, and to eat things facrificed unto idols." But how could he poffibly avoid *fuffering* her
to remain in the church, if the church poffeffed the power of
cenfure and excommunication, and was determined to keep her
in? Or, how could he poffibly have prevented her being turned
out, if the church had in it the power of expulfion, and had expelled her?

We may here juft obferve, that moft of the churches of Afia
Minor, mentioned in the 2d and 3d chapters of the Revelation,
if not all of them, were founded by St. Paul.

6. We fhall inftance in only two more portions of the word
of God on this fubject, (I.) Heb. xiii. 7. " Remember them

which have the rule over you, who have spoken unto you the word of God: whose faith follow, considering the end of their conversation." And (2.) ver. 17. " *Obey them that have the rule over you, and submit yourselves: for they watch for your souls,* as they that must give account: that they may do it with joy, and not with grief: for that is unprofitable for you." Observe, [1.] the persons here described as having the rule and a right to obedience and submission, were persons *who had spoken the word of God to the people,* and *watched over their souls,* and consequently were *their preachers and pastor.* But, [2.] To suppose that *they ruled in the church,* and *had a claim to obedience and submission,* and yet had not the authority *of cleansing the church from immoral and heretical persons,* would be exceedingly absurd. These last quoted texts are collateral and inferential proofs, the former are *expressly* so.

2dly. Let us consider the subject in the light of reason. 1. Is there any propriety in constituting a husband the judge of the guilt or innocence of his wife, or the wife of her husband; the parent of his child, or the child of his parent; the brother of his sister, or the sister of her brother, &c. Would not natural affection almost unavoidably move them in such cases to be partial to each other? Might not resentment move a master to be partial in his judgment against his servant? Might not fear, on the contrary, influence the servant in favour of his master? A long acquaintance also, perhaps even from childhood, has a powerful effect upon the minds of men, and would strongly tempt them to cover sin, to the destruction, not intentionally but eventually, of the work of God. The intermixture of temporal interests would also be a strong motive to induce many to make large allowances for the offender. " My income is small, and my family large: such a one is my customer, and also many of his relations; and shall I vote against him to the injury of my family? Perhaps he may repent, and be better in future. Such a one has obliged me in various respects, and shall I be so ungrateful as to condemn him wholly?" Those who are acquainted with the operations of the human mind, must be very sensible how often these reasonings would warp the minds of the judges, and produce a partiality in their decisions, which would be ruinous in the last degree to the work of God. Additionally to all this, we must recollect, that different countries, and different parts of the same country, are addicted to particular vices: and those are but little acquainted with human nature, who do not know that men are strongly tempted to cover those sins, which they themselves are inwardly inclined to, or which it is their interest to commit. For instance, in a part of the country where the maple-tree grows abundantly, and there are various manufactures of sugar, would not the church be strongly inclined to make large allowances for those who would labour in their sugar camps on the Lord's day?

Let thofe anfwer, who are acquainted with the nature of that manufacture. Again, In a part of the country, where the buying the fouls and bodies of men is a common practice, would not many in the church be tempted to favour thofe who were guilty of that practice, becaufe they themfelves might be the next to fall into the fnare? Yea, we have had proofs of this—of private members of the church, who have attempted to affume the power, not only of judging or rather clearing the offender, but *of judging the law itfelf!*

To give therefore the authority of judging and cenfuring offenders to the private members of a church, would be to form a court which in innumerable inftances would have the ftrongeft temptations to partiality. We do not mention this to fhew the leaft difrefpect to the private members of our Society: on the contrary, many of them may exceed us in piety and every grace. But it is contrary to all the rules of juftice to appoint thofe to be judges, who may in fo many inftances be ftrongly tempted to be partial. At the fame time we muft obferve, that THE WORD OF GOD is that which we principally ftand upon, knowing well that every paffage in the New-Teftament which relates to the prefent fubject, is wholly on our fide.

2. Our original defign in forming our religious Society renders the exiftence of this authority in our minifters abfolutely neceffary. But what was this defign? *To raife a holy people.* Our plan of economy fhuts us up from the influence of any other motive in refpect to our minifterial labours. It is impoffible for us to *enrich* ourfelves by Methodift-preaching. Again, We bear a conftant teftimony againft *the pleafures* of the world, and therefore fhould be efteemed, even by our own people, as the greateft of hypocrites, if *we* indulged ourfelves in them, and would foon be excluded the connection by the various means of trial to which *all of us* are fubject. And *as to honour*, we are almoft the only defpifed people in Chriftendom, as a religious body. The fecondary rank of mankind and the poor are the only perfons (with a few exceptions) who receive the Gofpel. The rich and great, in general, even thofe who have not embraced the favourite doctrines of the times, will not fubmit to the way of the crofs, but, on the contrary, look down on the Preachers of it as the greateft enthufiafts. And fhall we thus facrifice all that the world holds dear and at the fame time lofe the only aim of all our public labours, by falfe complaifance? No. *We will have a holy people, or none.* In every part of our economy, as well as doctrine, we aim at crucifixion to the world and love to God. *This muft be the price of our labours.* We require not riches, honours or pleafure, *but a holy people.* We have a right to difpofe of our labours as we pleafe, as far as they refpect our fellow-creatures: and *we will not beftow them on any other condition.* If we labour in any place a fufficient time for a

trial, and are not able raife a people devoted to God, we will leave it: we have a right fo to do, and none have juft ground of complaint. Again, If we have encouragement from any people, but they afterwards deceive us, and return to the world " like the dog to his vomit," (2 Pet. ii. 22.) they have broken the condition on which we labour among them; we have nothing more to do with them; and if we continue in that place, it is for the fake of others and not of them. But, bleffed be God, if we meet fometimes with difcouragements in this refpect, they are amply compenfated by the increafe of vital godlinefs. We love our people; and they in general amply repay our labours by their holy converfation. They are the joy of our hearts, and will, we truft, be our crown of rejoicing on the great day. But ftill we muft obferve, that our immoveable fupport, on which we reft our fentiments upon this fubject, is THE WORD OF GOD. And we may add, that the prefent point has been feldom difputed, as far as we know, by any, except thofe who have been difaffected to us, or have openly feparated from us.

An appeal is allowed in all the cafes mentioned in this fection, to the following quarterly meeting. For though the power of appeal be not mentioned in the laft claufe, which relates to the fowing of diffentions, yet it certainly is implied. Our work is at prefent in its infancy in comparifon to what, we truft, it will be through the bleffing of God. Our minifters, who have the charge of circuits may not be always fo aged and experienced as we might wifh them to be: the appeal to the quarterly meeting is therefore allowed to remedy this defect. And this no one can object to. No one, we think, can imagine, that the members of a clafs, or the members of the largeft fociety, would form fo refpectable or fo impartial a court of judicature, as the prefiding elder, the travelling and local preachers, and the leaders and ftewards of *the whole circuit*. But the point is quite out of the reach of debate in refpect to thofe who believe the facred writings and fincerely reverence them. The New-Teftament determines beyond a doubt, that judgment and cenfure in the cafes before us, fhall be in the minifter: nor could we juftify our conduct in invefting the quarterly meeting with the authority of receiving and determining appeals, if it were not almoft entirely compofed of men who are more or lefs engaged in the miniftry of the word, the ftewards being the only exceptions.

We fhall now juft add fome portions of facred writ, in relation to the immoralities which are referred to in this fection, that our minifters who have the overfight of circuits may have them under their eye. Matt. xv. 19. " Out of the heart proceed evil thoughts, murders, adulteries, fornications, thefts, falfe witneffes, blafphemies." Luke vi. 44, 45. " *Every tree is known by his own fruit.*"

A good man out of the good treafure of his heart, bringeth forth that which is good: and an evil man out of the evil treafure of his heart, bringeth forth that which is evil; for of the abundance of the heart his mouth fpeaketh." See alfo Matt. xii. 35. Mark vii. 21, 22. " From within, out of the heart of men, proceed evil thoughts, adulteries, fornications, murders, thefts, covetoufnefs, wickednefs, deceit, lafciviousfnefs, an evil eye, blafphemy, pride, foolifhnefs." Gal. v. 19—21. " Now the works of the flefh are manifeft, which are thefe, adultery, fornication, uncleannefs, lafciviousfnefs, idolatry, witchcraft, hatred, variance, emulations, wrath, ftrife, feditions, herefies, envyings, murders, drunkennefs, revellings, and fuch like : of the which I tell you before, as I have alfo told you in time paft, that they which do fuch things, fhall not inherit the kingdom of God." Eph. v. 5—8. " This ye know, that no whoremonger, nor unclean perfon, nor covetous man who is an idolater, hath any inheritance in the kingdom of Chrift and of God. Let no man deceive you with vain words; for becaufe of thefe things cometh the wrath of God upon the children of difobedience. Be not ye therefore partakers with them. For ye were fometimes darknefs, but now are ye light in the Lord: walk as children of light." Rev. xxi. 8. " The fearful and unbelieving, and the abominable, and murderers, and whoremongers, and forcerers, and idolaters, and all liars, fhall have their part in the lake which burneth with fire and brimftone: which is the fecond death." xxii. 14, 15. " Bleffed are they that do his commandments, that they may have right to the tree of life, and may enter in through the gates into the city. For without are dogs, and forcerers, and whoremongers, and murderers, and idolaters, and whofoever loveth and maketh a lie." For fcripture references againft divifions and fowing diffentions, fee the notes on the 22d article of religion.

SECTION IX.

*

Of Slavery.

Queft. WHAT regulations fhall be made for the extirpation of the crying evil of African flavery?

Anfw. 1. We declare, that we are more than ever convinced of the great evil of the African flavery which ftill exifts in thefe United States ; and do moft earneftly reccommend to the yearly conferences, quarterly meetings, and to thofe who have the overfight of diftricts and circuits, to be exceedingly cautious what perfons they admit to official stations in our church; and in the case of future admission to official stations, to require such security of those who hold slaves, for the emancipation of them, immediately or gradually, as the laws of the states respectively, and the circumstances of the case will admit: and we do fully authorise all the yearly conferences to make whatever regulations they judge proper, in the present case, respecting the admission of persons to official stations in our church.

2. No slave-holder shall be received into society, till the preacher who has the oversight of the circuit, has spoken to him freely and faithfully on the subject of slavery.

3. Every member of the society who sells a slave, shall immediately, after full proof, be excluded the society. And if any member of our society purchase a slave, the ensuing quarterly meeting shall determine on the number of years, in which the slave so purchased would work out the price of his purchase. And the person so purchasing, shall immediately after such determination, execute a legal instrument for the manumission of such slave, at the expiration of the term determined by the quarterly meeting. And in default of his executing such instrument of manumission, or on his refusal to submit his case to the judgment of the quarterly meeting, such member shall be excluded the society. *Provided also,* That in the case of a female slave, it shall be inserted in the aforesaid instrument of manumission, that all her children who shall be born during the years of her servitude, shall be free at the following times, namely—every female child at the age of twenty-one, and every male child at the age of twenty-five.—*Nevertheless,* if the member of our society, executing the said instrument of manumission, judge it proper, he may fix the times of manumission of the children of the female slaves before mentioned, at an earlier age than that which is prescribed above.

4. The preachers and other members of our society are requested to consider the subject of negro-slavery

with deep attention, till the enfuing general conference; and that they impart to the general conference,
through the medium of the yearly conferences, or
otherwife, any important thoughts upon the fubject, that
the conference may have full light, in order to take
further fteps towards the eradicating this enormous evil
from that part of the church of God to which they
are united.

SECTION X.

Of the Sale and Ufe of Spirituous Liquors.

Queft. WHAT directions fhall be given concerning the fale and ufe of fpirituous liquors?
Anfw. If any member of our fociety retail or give
fpirituous liquors, and any thing diforderly be tranfact-
ed under his roof on this account, the preacher who
has the overfight of the circuit fhall proceed againft him
as in the cafe of other immoralities; and the perfon accufed fhall be cleared, cenfured, fufpended or excluded
according to his conduct, as on other charges of immorality.

N O T E S.

Far be it from us to wifh or endeavour to intrude upon the proper religious or civil liberty of any of our people. But the retail-
ing of fpirituous liquors, and giving drams to cuftomers, when
they call at the ftores, are fuch prevalent cuftoms at prefent, and
are productive of fo many evils, that we judge it our indifpenfable
duty to form a regulation againft them.—The caufe of God, which
we prefer to every other confideration under heaven, abfolutely
requires us to ftep forth with humble boldnefs in this refpect.

C H A P. III.

S E C T I O N I.

Of building Churches, and the Order to be observed therein.

Quest. 1. IS any thing advisable in regard to building?

Answ. 1. Let all our churches be built plain and decent; but not more expensively than is absolutely unavoidable: otherwise the necessity of raising money will make rich men necessary to us. But if so, we must be dependent on them, yea, and governed by them. And then farewell to Methodist-discipline, if not doctrine too.

2. No person shall be eligible as a trustee to any of our churches or schools, who is not a regular member of our society.

3. No person who is a trustee, shall be ejected while he is in joint security for money, unless such relief be given him as is demanded, or the creditor will accept.

Quest. 2. Is there any exception to the rule, " Let the men and women sit apart ?"

Answ. There is no exception. Let them sit apart in all our churches.

Quest. 3. Is there not a great indecency sometimes practised amongst us, viz. talking in the congregation before and after service? How shall this be cured ?

Answ. Let all the ministers and preachers join as one man, and enlarge on the impropriety of talking before or after service; and strongly exhort those that are concerned, to do it no more. In three months, if we are in earnest, this vile practice will be banished out of every Methodist congregation. Let none stop till he has carried his point.

Quest. 4. What fhall be done for the fecurity of our preaching-houfes, and the premifes belonging thereto?

Anfw. Let the following plan of a deed of fettlement, be brought into effect in all poffible cafes, and as far as the laws of the ftates refpectively will admit of it, viz.

THIS INDENTURE, made this   day of
            in the year of our Lord one thoufand
            hundred, and   between
of the   in the ftate of   (if the grant-
or be married, infert the name of his wife) of the
one part, and   truftees, in truft for the ufes
and purpofes herein after-mentioned, all of the
in the ftate of   aforefaid, of the other part,
WITNESSETH, that the faid   (if married
infert the name of his wife) for and in confideration
of the fum of   pounds, fpecie, to   in hand
paid, at and upon the fealing and delivery of thefe
prefents, the receipt whereof is hereby acknowledged,
hath (or have) given, granted, bargained, fold, releaf-
ed, confirmed, and conveyed, and by thefe prefents
doth (or do) give, grant, bargain, fell, releafe, confirm, and convey unto them, the faid   and their
fucceffors (truftees, in truft for the ufes and purpofes
herein after mentioned and declared) all the eftate,
right, title, intereft, property, claim, and demand whatfoever, either in law or equity, which he the faid
            (if married, here infert the name of his wife) hath
(or have) in, to, or upon all and fingular a certain lot
or piece of ground, fituate, lying, and being in the
            and ftate aforefaid, bounded and butted as
follows, to wit, (here infert the feveral courfes and
diftances of the ground to the place of beginning) containing and laid out for   acres of ground, together with all and fingular the houfes, woods, waters,
ways, privileges, and appurtenances thereto belonging,

or in any wife appertaining: TO HAVE AND TO HOLD all and fingular the above mentioned and defcribed lot or piece of ground, fituate, lying, and being as aforefaid, together with all and fingular the houfes, woods, waters, ways, and privileges thereto belonging, or in anywife appertaining unto them the faid   and their fucceffors in office, for ever, in truft, that they fhall erect and build, or caufe to be erected and built thereon, a houfe or place of worfhip, for the ufe of the members of the Methodift epifcopal church in the United States of America, according to the rules and difcipline which from time to time may be agreed upon and adopted by the minifters and preachers of the faid church, at their general conferences in the United States of America; and in future truft and confidence that they fhall at all times, for ever hereafter, permit fuch minifters and preachers, belonging to the faid church, as fhall from time to time be duly authorifed by the general conferences of the minifters and preachers of the faid Methodift epifcopal church, or by the yearly conferences authorifed by the faid general conference, and none others, to preach and expound God's holy word therein; and in further truft and confidence, that as often as any one or more of the truftees herein before mentioned, fhall die, or ceafe to be a member or members of the faid church, according to the rules and difcipline as aforefaid, then and in fuch cafe, it fhall be the duty of the ftationed minifter or preacher (authorifed as aforefaid) who fhall have the paftoral charge of the members of the faid church, to call a meeting of the remaining truftees, as foon as conveniently may be; and when fo met, the faid minifter or preacher fhall proceed to nominate one or more perfons to fill the place or places of him or them whofe office or offices has (or have) been vacated as aforefaid. *Provided*, The perfon or perfons fo nominated, fhall have been one year a member or members of the faid church immediately preceding fuch nomination, and of at leaft twenty-one years of age; and the faid truftees, so assembled, shall proceed to elect, and by a majority of votes appoint, the person or persons so nominated to fill such vacancy or vacancies, in order to keep up the number of nine trustees for ever; and in case of an equal number of votes for and against the said nomination, the stationed minister or preacher shall have the casting vote.

Provided neverthelefs, That if the said trustees or any of them, or their successors, have advanced, or shall advance any sum or sums of money, or are or shall be responsible for any sum or sums of money, on account of the said premises, and they the said trustees, or their successors, be obliged to pay the said sum or sums of money, they, or a majority of them, shall be authorised to raise the said sum or sums of money, by a mortgage on the said premises, or by selling the said premises, after notice given to the pastor or preacher who has the oversight of the congregation attending divine service on the said premises, if the money due be not paid to the said trustees, or their successors, within one year after such notice given: And if such sale take place, the said trustees or their successors, after paying the debt and all other expences which are due, from the money arising from such sale, shall deposit the remainder of the money produced by the said sale, in the hands of the steward or stewards of the society belonging to, or attending divine service on the said premises; which surplus of the produce of such sale, so deposited in the hands of the said steward or stewards, shall be at the disposal of the next yearly conference authorised as aforesaid; which said yearly conference shall dispose of the said money, according to the best of their judgment, for the use of the said society.   And the said   doth by these presents warrant, and for ever defend, all and singular the before mentioned and described lot or piece of ground, with the appurtenances thereto belonging, unto them the said   and their successors, chosen and appointed as aforesaid, from the claim or claims of him the said his heirs and affigns, and from the claim or claims of all perfons whatever.

In teftimony whereof, the faid   (if married infert the name of his wife) have hereto fet their hands and feals, the day and year aforefaid.

Sealed and delivered in the }
    prefence of us, }
(Two witneffes.)

                    Grantor's (L. S.)
                    his wife's (L. S.)

Received, the day of the date of the above }
    written indenture, the confideration there- }
    in mentioned, in full. }

Witneffes. }   Grantor's (L. S.)

County, ſſ.

BE IT REMEMBERED, That on the day of   in the year of our Lord one thoufand   perfonally appeared before me, one of the juftice's of the peace, in and for the county of   and ftate of   the within named   the grantor (if married infert the name of his wife) and acknowledged the within deed of truft to be their act and deed, for the ufes and purpofes therein mentioned and declared; and fhe the faid   wife of the faid   being feparate and apart from her faid hufband, by me examined, declared that fhe made the fame acknowledgment, freely and with her own confent, without being induced thereto through fear or threats of her faid hufband. In teftimony whereof, I have hereto fet my hand and feal, the day and year firft above written.

Here the juftice's name.   (L. S.)

N. B. 1. It is neceffary that all our deeds fhould be recorded after execution, for prudential as well as legal reafons.

2. Let nine truſtees be appointed for preaching houſes, where proper perſons can be procured; other-wiſe ſeven, or five.

N O T E S.

1. We have already ſpoken on the duty of raiſing houſes for the worſhip of God, in our notes on the 10th ſection of the 1ſt chapter.

We however think it our duty to remark concerning the paſ-ſage which relates to *rich men*, that thoſe rich men who have join-ed us in America, have ſhewn no deſire at all to govern us: they have been neither haughty nor overbearing. The latter part there-fore of the anſwer to the firſt queſtion probably refers to ſome rich people in other parts of the world. Matt. xix. 26. " Jeſus beheld them, and ſaid unto them, With men this is impoſſible, but with God all things are poſſible." See alſo Mark x. 27. and Luke xviii. 27.

2. " The ſitting of men and women apart" was the univerſal practice in the primitive church. A general mixture of the ſexes in places of divine worſhip is obviouſly improper. 1 Cor. xiv. 40. " Let all things be done decently, and in order."

3. Sufficient advice is given in the anſwer to the third queſtion on the *indecency* there condemned. Holineſs becomes the houſe of the Lord. We go there to ſpeak to God, and hear his word, and not to converſe with each other. Eccleſ. v. 1. " Keep thy foot when thou goeſt to the houſe of God, and be more ready to hear than to give the ſacrifice of fools: for they conſider not that they do evil.

4. In reſpect to the deed of ſettlement, we would obſerve, that the union of the Methodiſt ſociety, through the ſtates, requires one general deed, for the ſettlement of our preaching houſes and the premiſes belonging thereto. In the above plan of ſettlement we have given to the truſtees an authority and ſecurity, they never poſſeſſed by virtue of our former deeds, namely, the pow-er of mortgaging or ſelling the premiſes in the caſes and manner above mentioned. By which we manifeſt to the whole world, that the property of the preaching houſes will not be inveſted in the general conference. But the preſervation of our union and the progreſs of the work of God indiſpenſibly require, that the free and full uſe of the pulpits ſhould be in the hands of the ge-neral conference, and the yearly conferences authoriſed by them. Of courſe, the travelling preachers, who are in full connection, aſſembled in their conferences, are the patrons of the pulpits of our churches. And this was abſolutely neceſſary to give a clear, legal ſpecification in the deed. If the local preachers, ſtewards,

and leaders (who have an undoubted right to preach, meet their claffes, &c. in the preaching houfes at due time, according to the form of difcipline) were fpecified, it would be neceffary to add a defcription of their orders; which would throw fuch obfcurity upon the whole, that a court of juftice would either reject the deed, or be at a lofs to determine concerning the little peculiarities of our form of difcipline. But we do hereby publicly declare, that we have no defign of limiting, in the leaft degree, the privileges of any of the public officers of our fociety, but by this deed folely intend to preferve the property of our church by fuch a clear, fimple fpecification, as fhall be fully and eafily cognizable by the laws.

SECTION II.

Of the Printing of Books, and the Application of the Profits arifing therefrom.

* *Queft.* 1. WHO is employed to manage the printing bufinefs?

Anfw. John Dickins.

Queft. 2. What allowances fhall be paid him annually for his fervices?

Anfw. 1. 200 Dollars, for a dwelling-houfe and for a book-room.

2. 80 Dollars for a boy.

3. 53 Dollars $\frac{1}{3}$, for fire-wod: and,

4. 333 Dollars, to clothe and feed himfelf, his wife, and his children. In all, 666 dollars $\frac{1}{3}$.

Queft. 3. What powers fhall be granted him?

Anfw. 1. To regulate the publications according to the ftate of the finances.

2. To complain to the yearly conference, if any preachers fhall neglect to make due payment for books.

Queft. 4. What fum of money fhall be allowed diftreffed preachers out of the book-fund, till the next general conference?

Anfw. 266 dollars and $\frac{1}{3}$ per annum.

Queft. 5. How is the money mentioned above, for the benefit of diftreffed preachers, to be drawn out of the book-fund?

Anfw. By the bifhop, according to the united judg-
-ment of himfelf and the yearly conferences.

Queft. 6. In what manner fhall the accounts of the general book-fteward be examined?

Anfw. The Philadelphia conference fhall from year to year appoint a committee, who fhall examine quarterly his receipts and difburfements and other accounts.

Queft. 7. What mode fhall be ftruck out for the recovery of bad or fufpected book-debts?

Anfw. 1. Let every yearly conference appoint a committee or committees for the examination of the accounts of the travelling book-ftewards in their refpective diftricts.

2. Let every prefiding elder, and every preacher who has the overfight of a circuit, do every thing in their power to recover all the debts in their circuit or diftrict, and alfo all books which may remain in the hands of perfons who fhall have refigned, or been withdrawn from the office of a travelling book-fteward.

Queft. 8. Shall any drafts be made on the book-fund before all its debts are difcharged?

Anfw. There fhall be none, till the debts are difcharged, except 'in the cafe of diftreffed travelling preachers.

Queft. 9. What directions fhall be given concerning the regulation of our prefs?

Anfw. The general book-fteward fhall print no books or tracts of any kind, without the confent of a bifhop and two-thirds of the Philadelphia conference.

Queft. 10. Will the conference recommend, and engage to promote the publication of a Magazine, intitled *The Methodift Magazine,* which fhall confift of, compilations from the Britifh magazines, and of original accounts of the experience of pious perfons, and fhall be publifhed in monthly numbers?

Anfw. The conference will recommend fuch a magazine, and defire that it may be printed.

NOTES

The propagation of religious knowledge by means of the prels, is next in importance to the preaching of the gofpel. To fupply the people, therefore, with the moft pious and ufeful books, in order that they may fill up their leizure hours in the moft profitable ways, is an object worthy the deepeft attention of their paftors. On this account we are determined to move in the moft cautious manner in refpect to our publications. We have a great efteem for our general book-fteward, and are much obliged to him for his fidelity and ufefulnefs in his important office: but we fhall in future fubmit our publications to the judgment of no fingle perfon. The books of infidelity and profanenefs with which the ftates at prefent abound, demand our ftrongeft exertions to counteract their pernicious influence: and every ftep fhall be taken, which is confiftent with our finances, to furnifh our friends, from time to time, with the moft ufeful treatifes on every branch of religious knowledge. And the confideration that all the profits fhall be lodged in our chartered fund for the benefit of the diftreffed preachers, both travelling and fuperannuated, will, we truft, prove a confiderable additional inducement to our brethren, to purchafe our books.

SECTION III.

The plan of Education recommended to all our Seminaries of Learning.

To the Public, and to the Members of our Society in particular.

THE firft object we recommend, is to form the minds of the youth, through Divine aid, to wifdom and holinefs; inftilling into their tender minds the principles of true religion, fpeculative, experimental, and practical, and training them in the ancient way, that they may be rational fcriptural chriftians. For this purpofe we recommend that not only the mafters, but alfo our elders, deacons, and preachers, embrace every opportunity of inftructing the ftudents in the great branches of the chriftian religion.

It is also our particular desire, that all who shall be educatad in Methodist seminaries, be kept at the utmost distance, as from vice in general, so in particular, from softness and effeminacy of manners.

The masters, therefore, should inflexibly insist on their rising early in the morning; and we are convinced by constant observation and experience, that this is of vast importance both to body and mind. It is of admirable use, either for preserving a good, or improving a bad, constitution. It is of peculiar service in all nervous complaints, both in preventing and removing them. And by thus strengthening the various organs of the body, it enables the mind to put forth its utmost exertions.

On the same principle the masters should prohibit *play* in the strongest terms; and in this we have the two greatest writers on the subject which perhaps any age has produced (Mr. Locke and Mr. Rousseau) of our sentiments; for though the latter was essentially mistaken in his religious system, yet his wisdom in other respects, and extensive genius, are indisputably acknowledged. The employments which we would recommend for the recreation of the students, are such as are of the greatest public utility, *agriculture* and *architecture;* studies more especially necessary for a new settled country; and of consequence the instructing of youth in all the practical branches of those important arts, will be an effectual method of rendering them more useful to their country. Agreeably to this idea, the greatest statesman that perhaps ever shone in the annals of history, *Peter* the Russian emperor, who was deservedly stiled *the Great,* disdained not to stoop to the employment of a *ship-carpenter.* Nor was it rare, during the purest times of the Roman republic, to see the conquerors of nations and deliverers of their country, return with all simplicity and cheerfulness to the exercise of the plough. In conformity to this sentiment, one of the completest poetic pieces of antiquity (the *Georgics* of *Virgil*) is written on the fubject of hufbandry; by the perufal of which, and fubmiffion to the above regulations, the ftudents may delightfully unite the theory and the practice together. We fay *delightfully*, for we are far from wifhing that thefe employments fhould be turned into drudgery or flavery, but into pleafing recreations for the mind and body.

In teaching the languages, care fhould be taken to read thofe authors, and thofe only, who join together the purity, the ftrength, and the elegance of their feveral tongues. And the utmoft caution fhould be ufed, that nothing immodeft fhould be found in any of their books.

But this is not all. We fhould take care that the books be not only inoffenfive, but ufeful; that they contain as much ftrong *fenfe*, and as much *genuine morality* as poffible: As far, therefore, as is confiftent with the foregoing obfervations, a choice and univerfal library fhould be provided for the ufe of the ftudents, according to their finances: and on this plan, we truft that our feminaries of learning will in time fend forth men who will be bleffings to their country in every laudable office and employment of life, thereby uniting the two greateft ornaments of intelligent beings, which are too often feparated, *deep learning* and *genuine religion.*

The rules and regulations with which you are here prefented, have been weighed and digefted in our conferences: But we alfo fubmit them to your judgment.

GENERAL RULES proposed for the Methodift Seminaries of Learning.

1. THE ftudents fhall rife at five o'clock in the morning, fummer and winter, at the ringing of a bell.

2. All the ftudents fhall affemble together at fix o'clock, for public prayer, except in cafes of ficknefs; and on any omiffion, fhall be refponfible to the mafter.

3. From morning prayer till seven, they shall be allowed to recreate themselves as is hereafter directed.

4. At seven they shall breakfast.

5. From eight till twelve, they are to be closely kept at their respective studies.

6. From twelve to three, they are to employ themselves in recreation and dining——Dinner to be ready at one o'clock.

7. From three till six, they are again to be kept closely to their studies.

8. At six they shall sup.

9. At seven there shall be public prayer.

10. From evening prayer till bed-time, they shall be allowed recreation.

11. They shall all be in bed at nine o'clock, without fail.

12. Their recreations shall be gardening, walking, riding, and bathing, without doors; and the carpenter's, joiner's, cabinet maker's, or turner's business, within doors.

13. A large plot of land shall be appropriated for a garden, and a person skilled in gardening be appointed to overlook the students when employed in that recreation.

14. A convenient bath shall be made for bathing.

15. A master, or some proper person by him appointed, shall be always present at the time of bathing. Only one shall bathe at a time; and no one shall remain in the water above a minute.

16. No student shall be allowed to bathe in the river.

17. A *Taberna Lignaria** shall be provided on the premises, with all proper instruments and materials, and a skilful person be employed to overlook the students at this recreation.

18. The students shall be indulged with nothing which the world calls PLAY. Let this rule be observed with the strictest nicety; for those who play when they are young, will play when they are old.

* A place for working in wood.

19. Each ftudent fhall have a bed to himfelf, where-ever he boards.

20. The ftudents fhall lie on mattreffes, not on fea-ther-beds, becaufe we believe the mattreffes to be more healthy.

21. The mafters fhall ftrictly examine, from time to time, whether thofe who board the ftudents (if they board out of the feminary) comply with thefe rules, as far as they concern them.

22. A fkilful phyfician fhall be engaged to attend the ftudents on every emergency, that the parents may be fully affured that proper care fhall be taken of the health of their children.

23. The bifhops fhall examine, by themfelves or their delegates, into the progrefs of all the ftudents in learn-ing, every half year, or oftener if poffible.

24. The elders, deacons, and preachers, as often as they vifit the feminaries refpectively, fhall examine the ftudents concerning their knowledge of God and religion.

25. The ftudents fhall be divided into proper claffes for that purpofe.

26. A pupil who has a total incapacity to attain learning, fhall, after fufficient trial, be returned to his parents.

27. If a ftudent be convicted of any open fin, he fhall, for the firft offence, be reproved in private; for the fecond offence, he fhall be reproved in public; and for the third offence, he fhall be punifhed at the difcre-tion of the mafter.

28. Idlenefs, or any other fault, may be punifhed with confinement, according to the difcretion of the mafter.

29. A convenient room fhall be fet apart as a place of confinement.

SECTION IV.

Of Chriftian Perfection.

LET us ftrongly and explicitly exhort all believ-ers to go on to perfection. That we may all speak the same thing, we ask once for all, Shall we defend this perfection, or give it up? We all agree to defend it, meaning thereby (as we did from the beginning) salvation from all sin, properly so called, by the love of God and man filling our heart. Some say, " This cannot be attained till we have been refined by the fire of purgatory." Others, " Nay it will be attained as soon as the soul and body part." But others say, " It may be attained before we die: A moment after is too late." Is it so, or not? We are all agreed, we may be saved from all sin before death, i. e. from all sinful tempers and desires. The substance then is settled. But as to the circumstances, is the change gradual or instantaneous? It is both the one and the other. " But should we in preaching insist both on one and the other?" Certainly we should insist on the gradual change; and that earnestly and continually. And are there not reasons why we should insist on the instantaneous change? If there be such a blessed change before death, should we not encourage all believers to expect it? And the rather, because constant experience shews, the more earnestly they expect this, the more swiftly and steadily does the gradual work of God go on in their souls; the more careful are they to grow in grace; the more zealous of good works, and the more punctual in their attendance on all the ordinances of God: (whereas just the contrary effects are observed, whenever this expectation ceases.) They are saved by hope, by this hope of a total change, with a gradually increasing salvation. Destroy this hope, and that salvation stands still, or rather decreases daily. Therefore, whoever would advance the gradual change in believers, should strongly insist on the instantaneous.

N O T E S.

In respect to the doctrine of christian perfection we must refer the reader to Mr. Wesley's excellent treatise on that subject.

SECTION V.

Against Antinomianism.

Quest. 1. WHAT can be done to guard against Antinomianism?

Answ. 1. Let all the preachers carefully read over Mr. Wesley's and Mr. Fletcher's tracts. 2. Let them frequently and explicitly preach the truth, but not in a controversial way. And let them take care to do it in love and gentleness: Not in bitterness, returning railing for railing. 3. Answer all the objections of our people as occasion offers: But take care to do it in a christian temper.

Quest. 2. Wherein lies our danger of it?

Answ. 1. With regard to man's *faithfulness*, our Lord himself hath taught us to use the expression; therefore we ought never to be ashamed of it. We ought steadily to assert upon his authority, that if a man is not faithful in the unrighteous mammon, God will not give him the true riches.

2. With regard to working for life, which our Lord expressly commands us to do. Labour, (ἐργάζεσθε) literally, *work for the meat that endureth to everlasting life.* And in fact every believer till he comes to glory, works for, as well as from, life.

3. We have received it as a maxim, that " A man is to do nothing in order to justification:" Nothing can be more false. Whoever desires to find favour with God, should cease from evil, and learn to do well. So God himself teacheth by the prophet Isaiah. Whoever repents, should do works meet for repentance: And if this is not in order to find favour, what does he do them for?

Once more review the whole affair.

1. Who of us is *now* accepted of God?

He that *now* believes in Christ with a loving, obedient heart.

2. But who among thofe that never heard of Chrift?

He that according to the light he has, feareth God and worketh righteoufnefs.

3. Is this the fame with, He that is fincere?

Nearly, if not quite.

4. Is not this falvation by works?

Not by the merit of works, but by works as a condition.

5. The grand objection to one of the preceding propofitions, is drawn from matter of fact. God does in fact juftify thofe who by their own confeffion neither feared God nor wrought righteoufnefs. Is this any exception to the general rule?

It is a doubt whether God makes any exception at all. But how are we fure that the perfon in queftion never did fear God, and work righteoufnefs?

His own thinking fo is no proof. For we know how all that are convinced of fin, undervalue themfelves in every refpect.

6. Does not talking without proper caution of a juftified or fanctified ftate, tend to miflead men? Almoft naturally leading them to truft in what was done in one moment? Whereas we are every moment pleafing or difpleafing God, according to our works; according to the whole of our prefent inward tempers, and outward behaviour.

N O T E S.

The fubject of antinomianifm has been fo fully handled by that great writer, Mr. Fletcher, that we need not enlarge upon it, when it has been fo completely confidered by him.

THE END.

CONTENTS.

CHAPTER I.

R

CONTENTS.

CHAPTER II.

CONTENTS.

CHAPTER III.

(193)

NOTES BY EDITOR

—refer to pages as marked.

Title page. Inscription to Sam'l Williams, probably Samuel W. Williams, who wrote *Pictures of Early Methodism in Ohio* (New York: Bangs and Emory, 1827). William Colbert, Methodist preacher in Baltimore Conference and elsewhere, wrote extensive unpublished journal (in Garrett-Evangelical Theological Seminary), died 1835.

Contents. Same as 1792, except: Ch. I, 9 and 10 reversed; 21, 26, 28 inserted 1796; Ch. II, 9 and 10 added 1796; doctrinal tracts and ritual omitted—reinstated in 1800.

iv.   Note ecumenical interpretation of Articles of Religion as appropriate to all Reformed churches.

5.   Specifically, in the Ordination Certificate, "superintendent." A large literature has risen in discussion of the import of Wesley's ordinations.

6.   Neat distinction between "essential" and "expedient." Here a first reference to Roman Catholic Church.

7.   Timothy and Titus "traveling bishops" of Ephesus and Crete. One of many efforts to find biblical roots for the itinerant general superintendency of Methodism.

9.   On changes made by Wesley in the Thirty-nine Articles of the Church of England as here

prepared in 24 (25) Articles of Religion, see Paul
Blankenship, "The Significance of John Wesley's Abridgement of the Thirty-Nine Articles."
Methodist History, II, 3 (Apr. 1964), 35-47. The
bishops restricted their comments to scriptural
proof texts.

19. Another chance to strike at Rome. Cf.
notes, p. 21, and elsewhere on sacraments.

27. These comments are directed especially
against James O'Kelly, who flouted the authority
of Asbury and walked out of the General Conference in 1792 when his motion for appeal of
ministerial appointment from the bishop to the
Conference was rejected.

29. The bishops omit the obvious texts which
suggest primitive Christian communism (Acts
4 and 6).

31. The principle of delegation to General
Conference was first legislated in 1808 and became effective in 1812.

32. Geographically defined annual conferences were established in 1796.

33. In effect the Western Conference was
open-ended to the West, spawning new circuits
which were then organized into new annual conferences. The term "district" was applied to
annual conferences, had not yet become a sub-
division.

34. Methodist polity frequently has been
criticized for anti-democratic tendencies, notably
by O'Kelly. This is an attempt to answer the
criticism.

35. A specific problem of the status of local
preachers, who were neither fish nor fowl,

neither traveling preachers nor laymen. A traveling preacher who ceased itineration was "located" at his own request, usually to take up farming and a family. He was licensed to preach in the place where he lived, but had no warrant to "take the world for his parish" nor to vote in annual conference.

37. John Fletcher, born Jean Guillaume de la Flechère in Switzerland, was Wesley's designated successor and leading theologian until his death in 1785, six years before Wesley's death.

37-8. Note already a tendency to limit or restrict the principle of full itineracy, which in its original form led some to liken Methodist circuit riders to Jesuits in their commitment to go where sent.

39. This provision was annulled by the Restrictive Rules enacted in 1812, by which General Conference was prohibited from taking any action which would interfere with episcopacy.

40. Mather was a British Methodist preacher who was ordained by Wesley for British ministry in 1788. He died in 1800. The trustees referred to are of the General Conference, later of the Annual Conference. Control of church property was another issue of conflict and misunderstanding. It played a large part in the rise of Negro Methodist denominations and in the various schisms in the church. The courts have maintained the principle that ownership of church property resides with the Conference, not with the local church.

41. Reformers pushed for the limitation of the appointive power of the bishops, or its elimination, by vesting authority in the Annual

Conference itself. This became a central principle in the formation of the Methodist Protestant Church.

42.   Again O'Kelly, who charged Asbury with tyranny, is in mind.

44.   Some leaders, like Joseph Pilmore and, to some extent, Thomas Coke, saw advantages in episcopal areas. Asbury was strong for *general* itinerant bishops.

46.   The opinions of Jerome, which Coke and Asbury undoubtedly obtained from Wesley, are in general accurately reported here. The college of presbyters played a special role in Alexandrian episcopal elections and consecrations, and the bishops are here calling on ancient precedent for the Methodist episcopacy. The old term "presiding elder" was later changed to "district superintendent."

50.   The issue of manner of selection of presiding elders was already open. It became one of the dominant factors in the reform movement of the 1820's.

53.   References to "society" mean the local congregation, or sometimes group of congregations. The term was inherited from Wesley in England.

73.   Quarterly tickets were given out by the preacher to active members of the societies who remained in good standing. They were a useful means of discipline and helped to distinguish regular members from visitors, especially in such services as the love feast.

80.   Wesley's term was "the United Societies of the People Called Methodists."

84. This was the first form of ministerial training—field experience under an older minister.

98. Richard Baxter (d. 1691), English Puritan, wrote *Gildas Salvianus, or The Reformed Pastor.*

108. *The Causes, Evils, and Cures of Heart and Church Divisions, Extracted from the Works of Mr. Jeremiah Burroughs and Mr. Richard Baxter* (Philadelphia, 1792), by Asbury.

113. Heresy trials have played a small role in Methodist history. Although early Methodists expressed concern about wrong doctrine, they were remiss in defining heresy and doing much about it. Note that here the whole matter is treated as an addendum to discipline for immorality.

120. These cautions on communion are parallel to the standard early question about membership: "How may we prevent improper persons from insinuating themselves into the society?" Methodists, however, rarely set formal bars to participation in the sacrament of the Lord's Supper.

125. The Chartered Fund, urged by Bishop Coke for support of retired ministers, was introduced into the Discipline in 1796. See Sec. xxviii below. It derived income from general subscription. The fund here in Sec. xxvi was contributed in addition by the preachers.

131. A principal motive for a retirement fund was preservation of the itineracy.

132. This was one of the original Wesley-derived portions in the Discipline from the beginning.

135. The importance accorded to society and class meeting is indicated by the length of these notes.

138-9. Notice how the original rules against slavery are already being compromised. Cf. p. 133, in General Rules.

148. The class meeting plan included every member of a society. The band plan provided special interest and special need groups.

152. The love feast, in part a substitute for the social aspects of the Lord's Supper, was celebrated with bread and water. The Select Society was a special group of those "going on to perfection." It was an institutional expression of the doctrine of perfect love or sanctification.

169. The Christmas Conference of 1784 maintained the strong early Methodist witness against slavery. The rules here given were introduced in 1796. The bishops have no comment.

178. Here the early form of the Methodist Publishing House, formally established in 1789.